*Your comments
& Suggestions are [...]
& welcome. please also
review this book online*

The Power & Intelligence of Karma & Reincarnation

*thank you
Dharma*

Dharma

Clink Street

London. New York.

Published by Clink Street Publishing 2015

Copyright © Dharma 2015

Second edition.

ISBN: 978-1-909477-63-6
Ebook: 978-1-909477-64-3

Foreword

The narrative of God and faith for the vast majority of people on this earth has been written, unfortunately, by weak men. With this book I hope to change that narrative.

When humans first started to think about God times were very tough, life was a bitter struggle and naturally people hoped and prayed for a super being to help them, comfort them. The dominant religions of today reflected that attitude, made God in the image of the most powerful man of those days, the king or emperor. This super being is our savior, will save us from having to face a tough, difficult life. If we pray hard, this super being will give us the easy life that we ask for.

That has been the narrative of the past and sadly, still remains the narrative of the present. It is time for a paradigm change—time for the strong to write a new narrative about faith and God. Time to stop asking God for this and that and start saying—"What can I do for God?" Time to stop being selfish, hoping to run away to a nice easy life and to grow up, face life head-on. Imagine that—God would be in for a shock—someone actually wants to help me? Instead of constantly demanding gimme this, gimme that, keep us in comfort? Someone wants to be a giver and not a taker?

It is amazing to me that Hindus of so long ago discovered this strength—it is their ideas that I put before you. These are not my ideas but the ideas of Sanatana Dharma (popularly called Hinduism). These people saw the weakness, the cowardice, the laziness taking over, people giving in to fantasy, eager to believe in charlatans, who made up delightful stories of magic lands awaiting them after death. They came up with the idea of Reincarnation—the idea that once you die, you do not get to run away but you must come back, back to the same life that you had before, basically telling them that you must face life head-on and not seek to live in fantasy "avatar" lands; yes, Heaven was the fantasy land before computers were invented.

Naturally the latter idea doesn't get converts, doesn't get followers hence some of the major religions of today have dropped that idea. They found greater success with magical stories of fantasy lands of endless milk and honey—no more pain or suffering, endless joy and happiness—quite frankly, the very first Ponzi scheme (obviously wouldn't be called after Mr. Ponzi then, his schemes would be called Heaven schemes).

Let's face it, we ALL want to live the good life—the choice is—do you want to go away and be given the good life (Heaven) OR do you want to make good things happen through sheer hard work, sacrifice and making good decisions (Reincarnation)?

Do you think that the prosperous nations of today were handed their riches or did they get there by sheer hard work, sacrifice and good decisions? How about the well-off? Did they work hard to get where they are today?

When trouble strikes, when a flood is about to hit your village, a coward who implores everyone to run away might get more to hear and follow him than a Hero who asks us to stand tall and true and fight. That is, in a nutshell, what this book is all about. With this book I give thanks to my first Teachers—my mother and this great faith.

You know what other religions offer. They constantly preach this: no more pain or suffering, joy and happiness for eternity. The Buddha went looking for a way out of pain and suffering. If we have to have a slogan for Hinduism, let it be this: We Offer Pain, We Offer Suffering, We Offer Life! For pain and suffering come along with life, they cannot be separated from it—to live is to face pain and suffering. To wish for a life without pain and suffering is to invite death.

Most religions reel in converts with the promise of an easy life, I find it funny when the followers claim to "love" God but what they really love and are after is the easy life that this sugar daddy will give them. "Look what OUR God will do for you" is the slogan of most religions. Sanatana Dharma (Hinduism) asks—what can you do for God? This book and the teachings of Hinduism will resonate with those who want to give back to society, to this world. Those who strive for a better world must realize that one life is not enough, there is still work yet to be done and God needs you down here.

God deserves better; let me say it again, God deserves better than be seen as nothing more than a sugar daddy or just a meal-ticket, who has nothing better to do than keep billions in easy comfort, free-loaders who want nothing to do with real life or make a honest living, but want to laze on the couch for eternity at His expense. Our ancestors, who faced a much harsher world, can be excused for hoping for an easy afterlife, but the hold of sugar daddy God religions in the modern world is disappointing.

There is a reason why this e-book is available for a low price—the reason is that I want the ideas in this book to spread, it is not about making money. Yes, money is import-ant and can certainly help, but by keeping the purchase price low, I can reach more people—it is my strong belief that the popular view of God must change—from a weak man's point of view of God as a master, a sugar daddy, to a strong person's view of God as a Teacher, our Parent. We can't keep living in the past, clinging to old medieval ideas of God, we have to move forward into the future.

Read this book from the viewpoint of a taker, one who hopes to get to the easy life of heaven, and I think you will hate it.

Read this book from the viewpoint of a giver, and you just might like it.

Once you think deeply about the ideas of Reincarnation and Karma, you will come to realize that there is intelligence here, wisdom here—we are not just giving you a sugar pill—pray to X God and He will give you the good life—that's basically it for some other religions—frankly, we need to have higher aspirations.

There are a few quotes in this book that I am quite proud of, let me know what you think of them and of this book. I can be reached at KarmaReincarnation@google.com.

Where there is God's work being done, there is God! God is here, God is right here!

Embrace Truth, reject God—gain both
Embrace God, reject Truth—lose both

Religion is an affiliation, not a qualification

The gift of pain and suffering

Life! REAL LIFE!

Enlightenment, not forgiveness!

God Sri Rama is Krishna is Allah is Jesus is Durga is the Buddha is....

Eyes cannot see God; prayer is not done with words;
Only the heart can see God; prayer is done with action

God is work, work is God

Karma and Reincarnation represent the future, the way forward, adulthood, self-reliance, strength and leadership

Fight (Reincarnation), not flight (Heaven)

A good unbeliever is closer to God Rama than even a good Hindu

Faith is for all; religion is for the few

Pain, suffering, life, God;
No pain, no suffering, death, no God

No Hell in Hinduism. Period.

Why choose to be utterly useless, when you can be a God?

A second chance to set things right (Reincarnation) beats being forgiven every time!

Heaven=pleasures of the flesh; Moksha=pleasures of the mind, heart and soul

Death (Heaven) OR life, REAL life (Reincarnation)?

God deserves better

KARMA and REINCARNATION

What is Karma? Why is it linked to Reincarnation? We all know what Reincarnation is—being reborn in another body, starting over in a new life.

The meaning of the word Karma, which is a Sanskrit word, is **Action** or **Work**. That's it! It's not a spiritual payback system, as it is popularly understood in the West. So, when Hindus say they are judged (wrong word to use in Hinduism—a Parent does not judge their children, but the paucity of the English language forces me to use this word) by their Karma, it means we are defined based on what we accomplished in life, our actions, our character, our conduct, our morals—religion does not matter, belief does not matter.

Funny thing, this is exactly what you hope for in real life—when you apply for a job or are up for a promotion, do you not expect to get that position based on your accomplishments or achievements? Amazingly, religions have brainwashed even the best of us to accept the idea that actions don't matter, only religious affiliation does!

It is pretty simple. When you choose Karma and Reincarnation, you choose to come back and work for a bright future for this planet, for all humanity and all the other forms of life that share this blue planet with us. You choose to participate in the future. This way is hard, which is why so many people create fantasy worlds "up there". Whether up there or down there, the key word is that it is *away* from here: a magical world where one can just sit and enjoy—that's the key.

By choosing Karma and Reincarnation, you are saying that you are an *adult*. You determine your own future, choose your own path, stand tall, stand firm and blaze your own trail. You also choose to follow in the footsteps of the greats (sadly most of them unknown) who have sacrificed their lives so that we may have a better future.

Are you one of those who looks at your life as an unfinished saga? Much, much more left for you to do, so many more worlds to conquer? Do you love life? Do you intensely feel the plight of others? Are you excited about the future and want to be a part of it? Do you still want to work, contribute? Hate the idea of being put out to pasture? Then Karma and Reincarnation is for you.

This is how Karma works: As you lead your life, you make choices, you work, and you commit to certain values, ethics and principles. These choices, these actions, of yours affect not only yourself but also others close to you. Sometimes they benefit you as well as others.

When, through your actions, your Karma, you do good things that lead to the benefit of others, you accumulate good Karma. Obviously, when you do bad things, you accumulate bad Karma; and it is this bad Karma or debt that you must repay. This is one of the reasons you come back.

Let's make the idea of Reincarnation real simple: You take a day off from work or are on a holiday—what do you want to do? Well, you could just laze on the couch, watch TV all day, the big game, enjoy yourself—Heaven!

OR

You could spend the time at a homeless or animal shelter—maybe one of the homeless tries to attack you in a drunken rage or a dog might bite you, but you don't let that deter you—you continue your work because you feel you are doing God's work—helping make this a better world—Reincarnation!

Let us go back to a time when man first started to form civilized societies, before any religions came into being. Life was particularly hard. It was tough to make a living, and naturally people wondered if their life was ever going to get any better. Then, in stepped some "religious" people to give the people what they wanted: a nice easy life after death.

Some right-thinking people realized that these ideas fostered a climate of cowardice and weakness. Hoping things would be better elsewhere meant a life of constantly being on the run, chasing the elusive pot of gold at the end of the rainbow.

As Shakespeare wrote, "Cowards die many times before their deaths; the valiant never taste of death but once." The weak will forever be on the run seeking that elusive easy land and the easy life.

One of the great stories of Hinduism is about a man who leaves unpaid debts upon his death. He has to come back and repay. Hinduism says: You gave your promise, you promised to repay; please keep your promise. These are your debts, and your obligations. You *may not* beg and ask for forgiveness nor try to backdoor your way out of your obligations and responsibilities. In Hinduism, you are an adult and treated as such.

You are also asked to be strong. Do not ask nor beg for pity. Pity is an ugly four-letter word. Only the weak beg for pity and forgiveness. The strong will work to repay their debts and fulfill their obligations.

I don't get it—it is an insult to get a job without earning it—it is an insult that you got a position or a promotion because you know or were cozy with the person making the decision and here are religions convincing people that begging for pity is the way to go? That knowing the "right" God will be rewarded?

The emphasis here is on ethics, morals, and cherished

principles. One would think that all religions would teach that, or all the good, moral people would demand that; but unfortunately for the majority of the people on this planet, this does not seem to be the case.

Karma cannot be viewed in isolation. We have to realize that Hinduism is a Teacher faith. Our goal, or to be more exact, our path is Moksha: enlightenment, knowledge, to be touched by the hand of God, to be one with God, to become a Buddha. This has to be earned! Each life is like taking a class. Our goal is the PhD of PhDs: Moksha. Karma can be viewed as the accumulation of our "grades".

The goal is to constantly improve and become a better person. The better person you become, the closer you move to becoming a Gandhiji, or a Buddha, and the closer you move toward Moksha.

One of the disappointing things about Hindus is that they have failed to realize the beauty of Karma and Reincarnation. Ruled for centuries by a foreign power and religions that took each and every opportunity to denigrate the natives, their culture and religion, some Hindus have been caught up in this hate, couched in nice, "reasonable" language. The fact is that if you have high academic standards, set high goals in life, wish to become a surgeon, scientist, or obtain a PhD, it will be difficult and will take time. Endless hours, days, weeks and years will be spent in pursuing this greatest of goals, and what goal could be higher than Moksha? It will take time, it will take several lifetimes, but the effort will be worth it—to earn praise from God.

In developed countries, the citizens make the right choices. Crime rates are lower, and there is law and order, not because there are effective laws and police around every corner enforcing them, but because the citizens have realized that following the law benefits everyone.

That's the teaching of Karma. You won't get punished

for not following the rules of the road. Sometimes some are punished by getting into accidents, but the majority of the rule-breakers will sail through. However, they are then saddled with an ineffective transport system. Every problem contains its own solution.

Better citizens make better decisions and vice versa. The good citizen develops good habits, educates him or herself and accumulates good Karma and is rewarded for it. The criminal trashes his neighborhood and breaks windows. Bad actions equal bad

Karma. Thus he pulls down his society along with him.

Hinduism has been called a way of life. You get to see that here.

The Hindu God is neither king nor queen, She is our Parent, our Teacher. The very word *punish* does not befit a Teacher/Parent faith. In an adult world, no Teacher will punish you if you do not attend class or attend to their teachings or finish your projects. In the end, if you do not attend to your studies, the only one to be hurt is yourself. Every problem contains its own solution. You will learn your lesson soon enough.

It is a poor Parent that simply punishes a child for a wrong action. The child must learn, must be educated on what he or she has done wrong. The goal is to improve, become a better child—on the path to Moksha!

No one is punished. Instead, you are gently reminded of your past debts or obligations. Think back about your own life. Have you ever encountered a situation where you have been given the opportunity to make a difference? We all have.

That is your Karma calling.

This is why we are born over and over. To me, it is an opportunity to give thanks to God. It is a chance to be with God, to become God! To reach for the stars, to reach down for the hand of God! Hindus have been given the chance to taste and drink from the fountain of life again and again. We Hindus have been given the gift of life over and over. What a wonderful gift!

Let us make use of this gift. Let us move on the path towards Moksha. Let us learn from our mistakes and move forward as better people. Ultimately isn't this what faith is all about—to make us better people?

We are reborn so that we may correct our mistakes. This is the only way we are ever going to learn anything. If every mistake is forgiven, how can we ever improve, how can we ever learn?

Begging your way out is the easy thing to do, the easy back door; but it also prevents you from becoming better. The easy thing to do or say is to forget a loss; but we can learn from losses—and we must.

Hinduism is a Teacher faith. You have just received failing marks—an F. Begging your way to a D or C is not only shameful, it does not help you at all. The next time you get the same question, you are going to fail again, because you never learned to correct your mistakes. You never improved.

The gift of life, the gift of learning, the path towards God, is self-denied.

Ultimately Karma and Reincarnation is about gaining your dignity and freedom. You no longer will have to be down on your knees begging for mercy. You are given a second chance to do the right thing.

Just as the good things in life are EARNED after a long, hard struggle, so is Moksha. It must be EARNED! It will not come easily, which is why we must be born again and again; but like King Bruce, we keep trying, keep working hard, because the place beside God is worth it—Moksha is worth it.

This will be painful. It will be difficult. But, as you will read over and over in this book, Hinduism is tougher, it is harder.

This is also precisely why Karma and Reincarnation has been mocked and misunderstood by even Hindus, who see the harshness and the difficulties of life and look around for an easy way out. Religions have come up with the concept of a nice, easy, comfortable Heaven. Some Hindus see Moksha not as enlightenment, but a release from birth and death.

Sadly they throw away the gift from God! The gift of life! They throw away the chance to be with God, for God is here, God is right here. *Where there is God's work being done, there is God.* Ergo, God is right here! Idolaters equate God with a life of ease. Let us take any holy man or woman in history: Gandhiji, Kabir, Schindler, or Mirabai. They were all with God, and none of them had an easy life.

Pray tell me, why would God be amongst the dead? Roam amongst the dead OR be with those who are alive? I would bet my bottom rupee on the latter—God is here, God is right here!

This question applies to you too, dear reader—why would you want to spend an eternity amongst the dead? Like living in a cemetery, live in the land of the dead?—Who in his or her right mind would do such a thing? Do not be a fool, choose to be reincarnated, choose life, yes, warts and all.

Ultimately life is the eternal struggle between the weak coward and the strong warrior. When the going gets tough, the coward will create fantasylands (Heaven) and seek to run away to them. When the going gets tough, the tough get going. The strong warrior will stand his ground and will fight his way out and work to make life better right where he is (Karma and Reincarnation).

Onward, soldier! (Reincarnation) OR quit, turn tail, cut and run (Heaven)?

Cowards for Heaven; Warriors for Reincarnation.

Some have expressed the concern that Reincarnation

would entail being reborn as an animal or a bug. Let me assure you that would not be the case. Hinduism teaches us that human life is the highest form of life. Once we gain it, we do not go back, unless one wants to, that is. It is like being in the 10th grade. If you fail 10th grade, do they make you go back to the 8th? You stay here until you pass. There are a few, the Hitlers and the Stalins who throw away their human life and throw away their opportunity and go back to a primitive life, but the vast majority of us will come back as a human.

What did I mean by wanting to be reborn as a bug? Human life is unique, we are subject to much pain and suffering and those who give up, quit on human life and seek the easy pleasures of the flesh may find themselves back in a lower form of life, where pain and suffering is non-existent.

There are those who wish for other guarantees, to be born in the same country or ethnicity. To them I say that life does not come with guarantees. We know those who were voted most likely to succeed who ended up in the gutter and those who we did not even notice, went on to make their mark.

As Joseph Campbell, the noted philosopher, once said, "Life has no meaning. YOU give it meaning."

Only death comes with guarantees. The guarantee of being forever free from pain and suffering (which is why it has been mistaken for a Heaven), forever free from having dreams, hopes and desires.

Choose Karma and Reincarnation if you feel that you have something to contribute and that you are needed here—that you can make a difference and help shape the future of humanity.

The King and the Teacher

A Chinese proverb: "Teachers open the door. You enter yourself."

Before we get started, we need to define some issues. A coward doesn't see things the same way as a warrior or a hero. The lazy person has a different view of life from the strong go-getter. Religions have shaped our views of God, and it amazes me that millions of highly educated people keep falling for outdated, primitive views of God.

Most religions see God more like a king to be obeyed unconditionally. Unfortunately people sometimes end up obeying the edicts of their religions, and these religions end up infantilizing their followers.

These religions originated in ancient or medieval times when kings ruled. Have they simply elevated their local king to a God level, God made in the image of a king? It certainly seems so.

The king demands absolute loyalty, and there is no place for disloyal people (atheists, people of other faiths) in his kingdom. Followers in the presence of their king get down on their knees, shaking with fear, and begging for mercy. Non-followers get threatened with dire consequences and must obey or else.

When you view God as a king, a master, you hear and use words like *fear, beg, obey, submit, judge, mercy, punishment, one-man rule*. When you view God as a Parent or a Teacher, the terminology changes: ethics, values, principles, dreams, hopes, achievements, responsibility, pride, and disappointment.

Hinduism is a Teacher/Parent faith.

What does this mean? It means we are the children of God and that we belong in God's lap, not on the ground. Students sit in front of their Teacher. They do not go down on their knees. It means that there are certain rules and obligations that we devotees as students and children of God must follow.

It is unseemly to kneel to a Parent or to a Teacher. You can greet and show your respect in other ways than to kneel down and lower yourself to a slave/servant level. It is the servant who hangs his head down. It is the slave who gets down on his knees. Today we have terrorism and the stupid insistence that evolution is wrong, based on this blind-obedience mentality.

In a king religion when God says the sky is green, all the servants and slaves will hurry to agree. In a Teacher faith, every follower must disagree.

In a king religion it does not matter what you think and it does not matter what you do with your life, only the king's opinion matters. In a Teacher faith, it's all about you. You take responsibility for your actions, your conduct, and you decide whether you want to be with God (Truth) or not.

In a king religion one is judged by their allegiance, loyalty (religion). In a Teacher faith, one is defined by their Karma— actions, conduct.

The goal of the follower of a Teacher faith is not a place (heaven), but a state of mind (Moksha). Moksha is the awakening of the mind, heart and soul. Moksha is to be touched by the hand of God.

Not much is expected of a slave/servant: keep your head down, await orders and complete them pronto. If the master says, "Stay, don't move," the slave/servant blindly obeys. If your ultimate goal in life is to sit on your behind and do nothing for eternity, enjoying the pleasures of the flesh, this doesn't say much about you.

Much is expected of a child/student of God. Parents and the Teachers wait eagerly and expect their child/student to do great things and to surprise them, to make them proud, to reach for the stars! The child/student is encouraged to be the next Einstein, the next Mozart, the next Gandhiji, or the next Lincoln.

It won't be easy. Let us recall King Bruce. He continually failed, but he never stopped trying.

When the going gets tough, it is easy to quit, to pack up and leave; but this is where the hero separates herself and shows her true grit!

This faith is not very complicated. It is just like being in class. Your goal is the PhD of PhDs. It will take some time and effort, patience, sacrifice and hard work.

This is not to the liking of some religions. They prefer to drop out like a kid who drops out of school and goes to work in a restaurant, only to regret his choice much later. They prefer to check out of life.

Heaven is like choosing to drop out of school after 1st Grade; Reincarnation, the pursuit of Moksha is akin to pursuing a PHD

It pays to stay in school, just as it pays to embrace Karma and Reincarnation.

Just like getting an F in school, your conduct in life may get you an F from God. You got that F because you deserved it. If you want that A, you will have to earn that too! This faith is harder, but it will make you tougher and stronger.

This faith will give you your dignity. You get to stand tall in front of God, with your head held high. You simply go back and you get another chance to try again. Like King Bruce, you will try, try again and make God proud of you.

Anybody can sit and praise God, but how many will get to earn praise from God? That is the goal of every child: Moksha, to earn praise from God.

How do we do that? By showing our character, by showing what we are made of. Speak the Truth, be honest, help others, be compassionate, make a difference in the lives of others, and educate yourself, as well as others.

Let me make this clear. Moksha is earned. You cannot ask for it, nor can it be simply given. It must be earned. This is why we are reborn and why the teaching of Karma and Reincarnation has to be the most important concept ever!

Karma and Reincarnation allow us to stand tall before God. We don't have to live in fear. We don't have to beg and grovel on our knees. We stand tall, acknowledge our mistakes and then are given another chance to put things right, to pay back our debts. That is the right way, the Godly way.

Speaking of fear, let it be known that if you are in the presence of a being and you are in fear, that being is certainly not God.

In the presence of God, there is no room for fear.

Tell me, if you happen to meet for the first time a long lost loved one, what is the first thing you do? You go hug her! You go hug! Go hug God! Go hug God the first time you see her!

We choose to come back. We choose life, REAL LIFE, warts and all, and we choose to be with God. It is these people that will one day find the cure for cancer. It will be these people that will one day travel to the stars! It will be up to us to banish poverty and hunger! It will be us who get to battle terrorists, nuclear-armed dictators and global warming.

It is the Hindus who will decide the future of humanity. Come on, can't we make better use of our time rather than to dream of sitting on our butt in some magic land doing nothing day after day?

This is the right faith to do battle, for this is the warrior faith.

Every other religion is encouraging their followers to up and run away! To them, the earth is a horrible place and a place of sin. Out there is a nice Hawaii waiting for us! We get to sit on our butts (pardon the language) and enjoy!

Who would be foolish enough to want to come back? To stay with God and work for a better earth? The one who realizes that running away won't solve our problems and that running away from problems is for cowards, the weak and the lazy. It is not for the strong.

A child of God does not run away. The student of God

will not quit. We will run towards the problems, not away from them.

Hinduism is for the strong.

In this faith, pity is an ugly four-letter word.

What does it mean when we say this faith is for the strong? We have to fight our own battles. There is no magic man coming to our rescue. You are struggling with a math problem and you go to the Teacher for help. Does she simply hand you the answer? If she did, what kind of a Teacher would she be? You will have to solve this problem by yourself. All the Teacher is going to do is to point you in the right direction. She will give you suggestions and hints, but it is up to you to follow through.

For much of human history kings ruled the general populace. One-man rule was common. The king was the answer to life's problems, and this king is with us today in the form of God who is seen as the answer to all our problems. God will either beam down a Heaven to us or beam us up to one.

The Teacher God will not do that.

The Hindu God does not interfere. This explains so many questions that people frequently keep asking: Why do bad things happen? Why doesn't God stop bad things from happening? Why doesn't She help? When good things happen you see many people pointing to the sky and telling everyone that a miracle happened, but they keep quiet when bad things happen. Did God not cause that also? God gets the credit but none of the blame?

This is the part that frustrates most people. When people are facing adversity they hope for a quick solution in the form of magic or a miracle, and bingo! There is the answer to their problems. This is not Hinduism. There are no easy answers. You will have to dig your way out and this way will be hard!

When your little child falls and starts to cry, you rush to help and soothe his hurt feelings. As the child grows up, the same thing happens, but your behavior changes. It is not that you love your child any less. The child is now an adult who is older and stronger. He will now have to face life's problems on his own.

This is what Reincarnation is all about. God says we are adults now. It is the child and the weak who create fantasy Heavens, wanting to go back home and run away from the problems of life.

There will be struggle and lots of hard work, but God will be with us all the way.

You won't find easy platitudes in this book. Hinduism is not going to tell you what you want to hear, that the nice easy life is waiting for you. If that is what you want to hear, then this faith is not for you.

Hinduism is a Teacher faith. Like every classroom, it can only be called a classroom if it is open to all! No exceptions. We see the contrast with a king religion here. A king cannot harbor a disloyal person in his kingdom—no man may serve two kings. That's a threat to his crown. That is why his Heavens are heavily segregated. That is why the followers of such religions are conspicuous by their body language: they are down on their knees, with their head held down, and shaking with fear.

When I see Hindus prostrate themselves in temples, I shake my head in disapproval. They see God as a king. Hinduism has never taught fear of God. Even Durga, the black fearsome-looking Goddess is referred to as Ma or Mother. Who would fear their own mother?

Now we see why the followers of king religions use threats. Why their Heavens are heavily segregated. You are with the king or else! Just as a king might limit his kingdom to loyal subjects, these religions limit entrance to their Heavens to members only!

A king can do that, but not a Teacher. The classroom must be open to all, or it ceases to be a classroom.

The Teacher faith is more welcoming, or it stops being a Teacher faith. All good souls are dear to God Rama: Hindu, Christian, Muslim, Buddhist, atheist, agnostic, gay, lesbian, animal, Klingon. All souls are welcome. Rama has a big heart, and there is room here for everyone.

If you choose this faith, please follow the rules. Do not insult God by making her a king or queen.

Don't you ever get down on your knees!
Don't you ever beg for mercy!
Don't you ever ask for pity!

In a Teacher faith, when a student encounters trouble, all a student will ask his Teacher is for advice. How do I (emphasis on the "I") handle this? How do we resolve this? The student does not expect the Teacher to go out and solve the problem for him. All the student wants is guidance. The real grunt work is up to him.

This faith is not for the spineless, the weak, or the coward looking for an easy way out.

This faith is for those who will set their goals higher: to earn praise from God!

This way is tougher and harder. This way towards pain and suffering. This way towards danger.

Life's problems won't go away by themselves. They have to be faced by a strong will. They have to be fought and they have to be won.

This is the essential teaching of Karma and Reincarnation.

I ask the reader to make his or her first decision right here.

Choose where you want to be: in God's lap or down on the ground. A child of God sits in God's lap. A student sits in front of his Teacher, whereas a slave is down on his knees on the ground. No qualifications are needed to be just a servant, a slave, but you must qualify to get the honor of sitting in God's lap. God doesn't expect much from a servant—that is why the servant is one-and-done, but as a child of God, much is expected of you. Tell me, have you made God proud?

Warren Buffet, the famous multi-billionaire, says he will leave none of his wealth for his children, everything will go to charity. Will he leave something for his staff? His maid, his butler, or driver? Maybe. One day all his money may be lost, all his servants will be gone then, that is what servants do—they are only there as long as times are good. Mr Buffet may fall sick—who will be around to take care of him? Only his children. Children will stick with God thru thick and thin (Reincarnation), whereas Servants are there only as long as the good times last (Heaven)

Decide where you want to be. As you know by now, more is expected of a child of God and a student of God. Decide whether you want the responsibility and are up to accepting the challenge.

I think the king religions are the religions of the past, teaching primitive and backward ideas, geared towards the weak. The Teacher faiths are the faiths of the future, these are for the strong.

This is a bit early, but once the reader has gotten through the book a bit or even after finishing it, I ask the reader to make a choice—do you want God to be a king or a Teacher? I have laid out the various scenarios, the advantages and disadvantages of each view, so please make a choice.

Be a God-loving child of God, not a God-fearing slave/servant.

I ask the reader to read my book though the lens of a child of God or a student of God, to be strong and not give in to weakness. Only then will this book resonate and make sense.

Stuck in the Past

We seem to have progressed so much on most other fronts, but when it comes to religion we seem to be stuck with old, outdated ideas – stuck in the past. Back in the day people did not have many opportunities to make something out of themselves, the rich and powerful stayed rich and powerful, the new generation of the rich and powerful came from within their ranks. But today things have changed – nobody's and even the very young can dream big and have made such dreams come true. Women, especially have benefitted the most in the modern age. It is no longer a case of who-you-know but what-you-know and we are thankful for the change. But not religions, they still preach the old who-you-know, the old X knight in shining armor will come riding to our rescue, they keep us weak and worthless. Reincarnation frees us from such old ideas, our life, our world is what we want it to be, what we make it to be, responsibility falls on our shoulders. The question is – are we Strong enough for Reincarnation? For Hinduism?

1. Karma and Reincarnation Mean Taking Responsibility

Embrace Truth, Reject God—Gain Both
Embrace God, Reject Truth—Lose Both

There is an old story told in Hinduism. A person dies leaving debts. He comes back as his creditor's son and tries to repay his previous life's debts. The message is clear. Do not think you can beg your way out. Pay your debts.

Let's be clear that not all debts are monetary. Debts can take several forms: making a promise and not keeping it, cheating, stealing, killing, causing harm, abusing, mocking, discriminating, etc. These are all various forms of debt, or bad Karma as it is called in Hinduism.

Imagine that you made a bad investment with money borrowed on credit and now are burdened with a lot of debt. Do you declare bankruptcy? Do you seek mercy from the judge? (Heaven and forgiveness)

OR

Pay back the debt, even if it takes all your adult life? (Karma and Reincarnation)

Will you step up and shoulder the responsibility and meet your obligations?

OR

Get down on your knees, make yourself smaller, and sneak away?

When something bad happens because of you, will you stand tall and face the music? Will you look people in the eye and accept total responsibility?

Let us take an example. Your child is playing with a neighbor's child and in a fit of anger breaks the other child's toy. What would you have him do? Come to you, stand tall in front of you and accept that he made a mistake? Or would you rather he comes to you crying and begging for sympathy?

Which is the right thing to do? Which action will make you proud?

Your child has stood before you and accepted his mistake; so are we done? No. There are apologies to deliver and a new toy has to be bought. The price of that new toy comes out of your child's allowance.

The right thing to do is also the tougher thing to do.

Or can you imagine something even more astounding? While one kid cries and tries to get sympathy and pity (as if he is the one who has been wronged!), another kid brings his piggy bank with him. He wants you to take him to the toy store so that he can buy his friend a replacement toy using his own savings! Wow! Will the latter action not make you jump up with joy and hug that child? Yes, it will! Make God hug you with joy! WOW!

What are you waiting for? Make God jump with joy with tears in Her eyes! Take responsibility for your actions, DO NOT ask for pity, DO NOT cry, DO NOT beg, stand proud, your head held high and ask for a second chance to make things right.

That is what a Parent is for and what a religion should be for—to teach the right values and the proper ethics. This is the difference between Hinduism and most religions. This faith is about doing the right thing, about ethics, values and principles.

The message that Hinduism teaches us is about taking responsibility for your actions, never trying to dodge your way out, and never trying to sneak away. Sadly, most religions teach us how to evade our responsibilities. Once we are dead, our past actions do not matter. What does matter is how we can get to that glorious Heaven, the victim be damned. Does anyone care about the victim? Suppose a person has died after taking money from his elderly Parents who are now forced to struggle. Imagine having to decide between eating dinner and taking much-needed medicine or going without both because of a lack of money! Such pain and suffering is no longer your responsibility? You no longer care? Is your goal now how you can get to Heaven? Off you go to that happy land? Any thoughts about how your loved ones are getting along?

Are we that unfeeling, that selfish, that we do not care? Hinduism thinks otherwise. We must care, we do care, and we must do the right thing. Let us come back and take care of our responsibilities. If we took on a debt and we made a promise to pay it back, let us keep our promises. If we have hurt someone, let us apologize to *that* person. Our feeling bad about what we have done and apologizing to God is like unburdening ourselves in front of our psychiatrist. It helps *us* but let us ask ourselves, how does this help the victim? It does not. The only person that we need to apologize to is the victim. But guess what? He or she could not care less that we feel bad. We have to make amends. That is the only way.

Even if this God says you are forgiven, does that mean that the debt has gone away? Has your creditor gotten his money back? Imagine that you have been taken to court over unpaid debts and the judge takes a liking to your begging and groveling and says you don't have to repay. How nice for you! But how nice is it to cheat your creditors?

You made this mess! Isn't it your responsibility to clean it up?

The great thing about Karma and Reincarnation is that you get to keep your dignity. If you are in debt when you die, you will get a chance to come back and repay the debt. In most religions you don't have that choice—you are left down on your knees, humiliated, asking for pity. You are scared that your "loving" God will send you down to Hell to be tortured for eternity!

Begging is dehumanizing—it is the worst situation anyone can ever be in. If you are willing to beg for an easy life, what else are you willing to do for it? Lie, cheat, abuse others, or worse? Are these the values that are being taught by your religion?

Even if you are ashamed of your actions, please do not beg your way out. Stand tall, hold your head high, and take whatever punishment God gives you. These are the same lessons that your Parents taught you: Don't lie, don't cry, and don't make excuses.

Instead of asking for forgiveness, ask for Enlightenment.

Ask that you may see the wrongs you have done, the crimes you have committed, and the people you have hurt. Then you will have the chance to correct those mistakes and make things right. Wouldn't that make the world a better place?

That is what Karma and Reincarnation are all about.

It is a matter of perspective: The strong see setbacks, mistakes in life as an opportunity—a welcome fact of life, a chance to shine. But the weak see such things as a burden. Religions have rushed in to cater to these people. They encourage people to toss that burden aside and run away as quickly as they can.

Not Hinduism.

Is God a cheater? Descartes says God does not deceive.

Hinduism agrees. God is not a cheater nor does She coddle cheaters. But religion does cheat. Religious leaders do coddle cheaters. These religions cheat the victims and reward the criminals and the perpetrators because that is where the converts are.

Is that what you have reduced your God to in your hurry to escape your debts, your responsibilities, and your obligations?

Does God exist to make us happy?

Such are the machinations of the weak, the cowardly.

Whatever horrible thing you have done, the last thing you should be doing is trying to get out of doing the right and honorable thing. Recall your values and principles. What would you have done if you had caused a horrible accident? Would you run away or would you stop and help the injured and dying? Later, when an investigation is made, would you step forward and take responsibility for what happened? Is this what you expect of yourself? Is this what you would do if put in such a situation?

Then there is only one option left for you. As a Hindu, you stand tall before God with your head held high, and accept what you have done, accept responsibility and be eager to come back and make amends. You have an opportunity to set things right and to put a smile on the faces of those who you have wronged.

I am sorry if this sounds harsh. *Hinduism is harder and tougher.* It expects better from you. Are you up to it?

The mind-boggling thing to me is that people think they can abandon their cherished values, principles and ethics **in front** of God! Forget about earning your way in. Forget about your responsibilities. Forget about your loved ones back on earth and agree with everything he says even if they contradict your cherished values.

For Hindus, God means Truth and God means principles

and values. One cannot exist without the other. For others God is a magic genie ready to make their dreams come true if they can just please Him.

Does your religion seem to be stuck in the past or behind the times? These religions came into being when times were different. Slavery was common, women were second-class citizens, and the concept of evolution was totally unknown. Of course their teachings are primitive and backward. Life was harsh, it was tough to make a living, and people were not as strong as they are today. These religions catered to a weak populace.

Their pitch is incredibly seductive: run away and dump all your problems on the next generation. Leave your work unfinished. After all, what is here? There is hard work, sacrifices to be made, and the myriad problems of the world to deal with. Instead it is off to the easy life you go! Leave your loved ones behind to deal with the problems.

It is amazing to me that Hinduism, a much older faith, is teaching stronger, better values that make more sense today!

It is sad that we seem to be living in a topsy-turvy world where begging is seen as the way to go. The person who says one must earn one's way to God is mocked as arrogant and self-righteous. When I ask people, "Is that what you teach your children—to beg their way in life? Or do you teach them to earn, work and pay for everything?" they fall silent.

Trying to fit outdated, primitive values to the modern world will not work.

This responsibility is not forced in Hinduism. Few things are. You must come to this realization by yourself and do the right thing because you want to. Come to God because you want to, not because you are under a threat. In life, all of us are given chances to make amends. Opportunities open up. Whether we take them or not is up to us.

Hinduism will put strength into you. It will make you strong. This is a faith for the strong adult, the brave and the good. It is definitely not for the weak or cowardly.

God asks if you would like to go back and pay back your debts. Would you like to keep your promises? Would you like to stay with your loved one and share in their joys and pain? Would you like to go back and help people and animals in need? Would you like to do the right thing?

What will be your answer? Say yes to God. Then join us Hindus. Make God proud of you.

Did you notice that I did not confine Karma and Reincarnation to Hinduism? It does not matter what religion you belong to or even if you do not belong to one, everyone gets the same opportunity: life or death. You can do the right thing and fulfill your responsibilities or quit and run away.

Let me clue you in. There is nothing "up there" except death. There is no Heaven and there is no easy life. It's either life or death. That's it! Fools chasing after mythical Heavens and the easy, carefree life, get death.

Are you ready to be an adult? Are you ready to assume responsibility for your life, your decisions, and your conduct?

Then arise! Stop begging. Stop looking for pity. Get off your knees. Arise and take your dignity back!

God Sri Rama thinks that you are strong. She demands strength from you. Be strong and do the right thing. The strong ask for a second chance to fulfill their obligations, and they are given this gift! Please stand tall before God, your eyes clear, your head held high.

Strength is a beautiful thing!

Hindu Pride—The Buddha

For hundreds of years in many parts of the world, the religion you belonged to meant the difference between life and death. Sadly, even today, thousands are being killed around the world because of their religion.

This is much better compared to what went on in the past. Mass killings were justified in the name of religion along with abuse and bigotry to make people convert to the dominant religion.

These religions used a *scorched-earth* policy to kill, rape, torture and terrorize anyone who is of any other religion. To burn their holy books and scriptures, bulldoze and tear down their places of worship, making sure to take attendance at their worship places, so those that are not attending and may still be secretly holding on to their previous religion can be found. Find them and brand them as heretics and evil and kill them off.

So many Buddhas were lost in this way, so many religions never saw the light of the day. It is scary to think that we might have lost two more religions of today that we are quite familiar with—the Jewish religion and the Native American religions—their people hunted almost to the point of extinction!

As they say, dead men tell no tales. Turkey is under fire today for the genocide against Armenians. Their "mistake" was that they left some Armenians alive. So did Hitler. The survivors are here today to light the fire of conscience; but sadly, for these older religions that did not survive the brutality, there is no one to tell their stories.

In this depressing and disappointing landscape, Hinduism shone like a beacon of light, a democratic faith that gave room to more than one voice. This tolerance and acceptance is built in to Hinduism, like the great aphorism, "**Truth (God) is one, but the wise call it by many names.**" Please note the word Truth rather than the word God in this great aphorism.

Many writers define religions with one word—for Christianity it is love, for Buddhism it is compassion—for Hinduism let this one word be Truth. Let Truth define Sanatana Dharma (Hinduism). This one word is not limited to just telling the Truth, but walking the Truth, doing the right thing, reaching down for the hand of God!

Hindu pride—you will never find a Hindu who will condemn people of other faiths to Hell. Ask yourself—why is that? Maybe what I write below will give you a clue and you will join us Hindus in not condemning others.

If the Buddha had been born in any other place except Hindu India, he would have been summarily dragged into the streets, beaten, bloodied and finally hacked and tortured to death!

The Buddha's teachings would have been consigned to the fire and his teachings forbidden to be spoken or rewritten, and finally, his followers also would have been put to death.

That did not happen. The Buddha was lucky to be born in Hindu India. Here, he was allowed to freely wander around the country, proselytizing, teaching his knowledge to everyone, converting people to his faith. He was not threatened with dire consequences, nor was he beaten or abused. He went around the country preaching his faith and for a time, India became Buddhist, until Hindu leaders used the same tactic and went around preaching Hindu values to the lay public and won them back.

It was not just the Buddha, but also the other religious founders who discovered the same freedoms to preach their respective faiths. The Sikh religion has 10 Gurus. Over the centuries, all of them traveled around Hindu India, freely proselytizing. So did the Jain Gurus! Jewish leaders have acknowledged that Hindu India was the one place where their fleeing tribes found safety and comfort.

Zoroastrianism is an interesting case. Popularly called Parsees (Persians), these people originated in Iran. It was once a very popular religion boasting some thirty million adherents. Slowly over time the religion eroded and the small faith was set upon by Islamic fundamentalists. The few remaining Zoroastrians had to flee and found safe refuge in Hindu India where they remain to this day.

Bohra Islam is another interesting case. Deemed not Muslim enough by their brethren, they too had to flee and find refuge amongst Hindus. Imagine that, Muslims fleeing Muslim persecution finding safe refuge amongst Hindus.

Most recently, we have the case of Tibetan Buddhists fleeing Chinese persecution and finding safe haven in India. India is a poor country and while we could certainly use Chinese help to modernize our country and escape poverty, we chose to do the right thing as defined by our faith.

Swami Vivekananda writes that Charvakas, who are atheists, went around preaching their atheist ideas in Hindu Temples. Imagine that!

I swell with pride whenever I go to a website and they list stories and discussions by religion and almost half the religions listed therein were born in just one country—India!

Most scholars agree that polytheistic religions are more tolerant and accepting. We have many Gods (actually, many names for God), so why not one more? It is not uncommon to find Hindus praying at Muslim shrines or have a locket with a picture of Jesus along with other Hindu Gods.

Technically though, Hinduism is not a polytheistic religion. One can call it a mono-polytheistic religion. Yes, there are many Gods, but they are all one and the same. So many names but it is the same person that all humanity prays to.

God Sri Rama is Krishna is Durga is Allah is Jesus is Buddha is Ganesha is....

A Hindu may go to a Krishna temple and pray to Goddess Durga or Ganesha. There is nothing wrong in that. All prayers are going to one and the same place. A favorite

Hindu quote is that all religions are like rivers, all flowing to the same ocean, God!

No wonder the Buddha felt free and unthreatened to talk about his faith and his revelations.

Even more amazing, Hinduism welcomed the Buddha into its pantheon of Gods. The Buddha became one of God Vishnu's incarnations. Imagine that, a man who goes around converting people away from Hinduism, and Hinduism is saying this man is God! Can you imagine that, in these days of preaching religious hate against anyone not sharing your beliefs?

Imagine that—in one country, a man who preached against the dominant religion is welcomed by the same as a God—in any other country the same man would have been branded as evil, a Satan, giving the license to a mob to beat him to death!

Any Teacher who teaches the Truth is God, for Truth is God. The Buddha, according to Hinduism, was teaching the Truth and so deserved the status of God. As I keep saying in this book, be with Truth and you are with God. Be a good person, be honest, treat others well, tell the Truth, help others and you are with God. It does not matter even if you call yourself an atheist, an unbeliever of God.

One Christian writer lamented that we are one people Monday through Saturday but on Sunday we go our separate ways—10 Christians get together and they may head to 10 different churches. One hundred thousand Hindus get together and decide to go to a temple. They can all go to the same temple, and most times they do.

No Hate in Hinduism

So many innocents have been mass murdered in history for the "crime" of their belief! Amazingly, in the 21st century with all our education, intelligence, patting ourselves on the back for our progress, those hateful ideas are still with us. I find it appalling that people still go around preaching "our way or else!" This is the evil that starts the hate, the separation that has led to so much killing. Today we hear about one religion ganging up and killing the members of another, and we shake our collective heads and say that this shouldn't happen, and yet the vast majority of humanity has no problem with their chosen "God" doing the same: separating people by religion. Go to any YouTube Hindu video and read the hate pouring in from members of other religions. You will never find a Hindu doing the same. There are no Hindu priests preaching hatred against other religions. Ask yourself, why is that?

Hinduism says all God cares about is character, nothing else matters. Once we die, only our soul goes to meet God. The soul has no gender, no body, no religion, no baggage and no earthly belongings. All it has is the total of your karmic (works) deeds.

The unique teachings of Hinduism stand in stark contrast to the rest of the world even today. Can you name one non-Christian leader amongst all the nations of Europe and America? The U.S., Germany, England, Spain, Australia, Brazil, Mexico, etc.—are any one of these countries' leaders an unbeliever or non-Christian? Any member of any sports team? Can you name a non-Christian star from Hollywood? How about television? How about in Muslim countries? Any non-Muslims? There is not one leader that is not of the majority!

I have been in the US for more than 25 years now, and any time anything related to Hinduism comes up either on TV or a Hollywood movie, I have learned to cringe, because I now know what is coming: something mocking, something abusive, something derogatory. At this point I am glad that Hinduism doesn't come up that much in the American media.

Try India. You will find plenty of positive examples of other faiths in movies and on television. Atheists are shown in a positive light. It makes me proud to be a Hindu, but it doesn't have to be this way. I shouldn't feel proud to be doing the right thing, but I do because the rest of the world seemingly makes it so hard to see others as basic human beings.

In India, a few years ago, all the top posts in government were occupied by non-Hindus including the presidency, the prime minister, the leader of the nation. In the so-called greatest and most powerful nation in the world, the sitting president felt the need to strenuously declare his religion. Apparently, it was a crime to not belong to the majority religion in the so-called land of the free and home of the brave.

Even a woman of Indian heritage running for governor felt it necessary to lock up her Sikh heritage and project to the outside world that she was a member of the majority religion. Freedom comes cheap—down on one's knees apparently.

One of the richest men of India is a Muslim. All of our sports teams are a study in religious diversity. Muslims have led Indian sports teams. The top heroes of Indian cinema today are Muslims.

If there is one faith that is teaching us to put people first and to put character above religion, it is Hinduism.

One last point about the Buddha. Buddhists have resented Hindus making the Buddha a God. The Buddha never believed in God or Gods. It is said that he was against that whole concept, so making him a God was an insult to him. Here they make a mistake in assuming that the Hindu concept of God is the same as what most religions teach. God here is not someone who sits in the Heavens and has magical powers. God, in the Hindu tradition, is anyone who comes to your rescue or helps you become a better person. The Buddha gave the world enlightenment, he rescued the world from ignorance, he was a Teacher; hence he deserves our respect as a God. Hindus also revere their Parents as Gods. This is not to be taken literally or that this is the popular notion of God. People who help you, come to your aid in times of need, and who make you a better person are all referred to as Gods. This is common in India.

Hinduism humanizes God, brings Her down to our level. There is no need for magic or miracles here, just a plain old human being doing extraordinary things.

2. Karma and Reincarnation Mean We Are at a Higher Level—We Are Children/ Students of God

Slave/Servant: "What can God do for me?"
Child/Student: "What can I do for God?"

This is the flip side of the segment that I wrote earlier about God seen as a Teacher or a king. *Without exception we are ALL God's children. God Sri Rama's heart is vast and there is room here for everyone.*

In the modern world that we live in, we are constantly told that the world has gotten smaller. We don't live on islands like we used to in the past, when some of these religions were born, when foreigners and outsiders were viewed with suspicion and the religions reflected that attitude.

In today's world, the physician trying to save the life of your child may be a Hindu or an atheist. Your company's fortunes and the fate of your job may depend on the Chinese or the Japanese consumer and vice versa. The stranger reaching out a helping hand when everyone else had looked away might be from the other side of the globe. The fact is that the world is getting smaller with people from totally different backgrounds being thrown together. Yet the world is dominated by religions that insist on keeping people apart, teaching an us vs. them attitude. Our God vs. their God. A slave/servant attitude fits nicely into this context.

French mathematician Blaise Pascal felt that if we do not believe in God, we will be punished. That reminds me of the North Korean athletes who, upon winning their medals in the Olympics, made groveling statements about their dear leader who had inspired them, saying he was the real reason for their success.

Fear! A slave talking in fear!

A servant will not allow anyone to talk against or speak ill of his master. The slave's well-being depends on the well-being of his master. To save his master, the slave will not only be ready to sacrifice himself, he will be even willing to kill his own people at the behest of his master.

And why not? After death, the good slave/servant will be taken care of. He will be off to a lovely paradise where he will get to live it up and enjoy forever and ever! He just has to show his undying loyalty to his master, down on his knees. What a good slave I am.

Slave/servant religions' pamphlets are filled with promises of how their God will make you so happy. That's the carrot being dangled in front of you.

Sadly this slave-like attitude has led to intense hate for anyone not agreeing with their view of God. Many millions of good people have paid the price for this mentality. Even today, we see suicide bombers blindly obeying. Do they not realize the harm they are causing to innocents? Once you realize that these are slaves/servants and that they *must* obey the orders of the master, or what they perceive as the orders of the master, once you grasp the idea, it is easy to see why these religions nor their followers do not believe in Reincarnation—come back, do the right thing and set things right by the victim. Because when a servant makes a mistake, his first thought is not for the victim, but how his master will react. For example, let us say a servant takes out his master's car for a drive and injures someone. All the servant can think of is, "What will my master say? Will he be upset?" As long as the master says, "It's okay, you can go about your duties,"—the servant is happy. Hence the teaching of begging for forgiveness, not from the victim, mind you, but from the master.

It is easier to be a slave, to follow blindly, to be a child and be told what to do. It is harder to lead, to be the adult, to take on responsibilities, and to make bold decisions and stand by them. If those decisions turn out to be wrong, it is harder to stand tall and own up to them, to be held responsible.

No wonder people find it easy to lower themselves to a slave level.

Hindus are at a higher level. We are the children/students of God. Our goal is higher: Moksha. To be touched by the hand of God. To earn praise from God! What goal could be higher?

Serving God is a part-time job: spend some time volunteering, helping others, raising funds, chanting, praying, and the rest of the time you can do other fun things.

Earning praise from God or being a child of God is a full-time endeavor, a lifetime endeavor, and not just one life, but many, many lives!

Instead of thinking of serving God, imagine walking in the footsteps of God Sri Rama, Jesus and the Buddha! Which is harder? Tougher? Can you walk away from all the riches in the world like the Buddha did? Can you be true to your word like God Sri Rama was?

This will be tough and well-earned. Make no mistake about it. That is the real difference. We have all seen beggars on the street. What do they achieve? Begging will only get you meaningless things. When you earn what you desire, when you work hard and achieve your heart's desires, what you gain is so much sweeter.

You are a child/student of God! Start acting like one! A

child of God belongs in God's lap, not on the ground on his knees! That position is reserved for the slave/servant. Remember who you are. Do not demean yourself.

It is incumbent upon us to behave in the proper manner.

The first thing that we must change is to never, ever fear God. If this fear of God has been taught to you by your religion, please discard it NOW! No child should ever fear her own Parents. No student should ever fear her Teacher. Respect, yes, love, yes, but fear? That's a no-no. It is an insult to God by which you then lower God to the level of a master and yourself to the level of a slave/servant.

Why lower yourself when we are already born at a higher level?

As I keep saying time and again, this way is harder, this way is tougher.

Even if you are down to your last rupee and haven't eaten for days, if you see a soup kitchen on your left and a job to your right, you will head to your right. Earning your way, no matter how long or how difficult it becomes, gives you your dignity.

Hinduism is asking you to stand tall before God, your head held high.

You never learn the value of anything if it is just handed to you. If you are simply given something, it loses its value. An unearned gift turns into a curse. When you earn whatever you take, nothing can go wrong and not even God can cheat you, as King Midas was cheated. He got cheated because, instead of earning gold, instead of working for what he desired, he simply wished for it! When wishes come true, beware! If you wish for luck, beware. You also invite bad luck to follow.

We know nothing worthwhile is easy. King Bruce: How many times did he try? Nothing was guaranteed to him. He could have tried a hundred times and failed all one hundred times! How many of us doubt that he would have kept going and would be getting ready to try for the 101st time?

This is the future. The person with the brains, the educated person, will be the one who will dominate the future world. This is why you see terrorism today. The world that the terrorist wants, a brawn-dominated, women-confined-to-the-kitchen world, is slowly slipping away and they can't handle it! They fiercely cling to an ancient religion of yesteryear, a religion more attuned to primitive times.

Life is too tough—the good things in life only come when one makes a clear goal, works hard and makes good decisions and so the terrorist gives up on life, falls easy prey to religions promising him the easy life.

Reincarnation says don't give up on life! There are only two options here: death OR life! Giving up won't make things better, it only gets worse! What's the old saying? When the going gets tough, the tough get going? Are you tough enough for life?

Hinduism is the religion of the future. The "king religions" are religions of the past. They talk about a primitive time. Their values are set in medieval times.

It is here you see the marked difference between being a servant of God vs. being a student of God. The servant is all about the reward he is about to be given: *What can God do for me?*

For the student the question is reversed: *What can I do for God? How can I make God proud of me?* Every child wants his Parents to be proud of him. Every student wants her Teacher to be proud of her.

Being a servant is easy. You simply obey orders. You are only a follower. A student is more than that. We are the leaders. Leaders don't look around for orders, but take to heart the lessons that have been imparted to them by their Parents and their Teachers.

The servant's job is easy. His life on earth is brief. He checks into work, puts in his few hours and then checks out forever! The rest of eternity is to be spent elsewhere, i.e., death. The memory of his life on earth will fade away.

The student has a higher responsibility: earth. We are responsible for its well-being, our well-being, and the well-being of other life forms that share this planet with us.

When a religion says actions don't matter, in a way they are right, to be a servant qualifications (actions) do not matter, what qualifications does a servant need? Just an able body, able to take and obey orders, is enough. To be a child of God, to have the honor of sitting in God's lap—now THAT takes qualifications! Any human with a feeble beating heart can be a servant, but to make God beam with pride that takes a lot of amazing accomplishments, a pure heart.

How are we doing?

A lot of rich people have servants – Butlers, Drivers etc. In India, people are so poor that even ordinary people have servants. During festival times, or a religious celebration, or a happy occasion like a wedding, it is quite common for the master to reward his servants with gifts, monetary or otherwise. But times may change, one day misfortune might strike and the rich person might lose all his money. Sick and bedridden, one finds only the children by the side of their father, taking him to the hospital, tending to his sickness. *And the servant? Long gone! This is the clear difference between a Child and a Servant – the servant sticks around as long as times are good, the Child is there for God thru thick and thin, we are there for the long haul.*

In my conversations with people of other religions, this is the mind block that I face. They are looking at things from the servant perspective, whereas I am trying to make them see it from a child of God's perspective, from the perspective of a student of God. They just can't see it: life is too difficult;

the temptation of a nice, easy life awaiting them in Heaven is too hard to resist.

Let us say you are a young person starting out in life. You have to move out of your Parent's home and start a life of your own—how do you do that? Well, you can go get a job—that involves getting a skill, an education, looking for jobs, interviews, letting the company know what value you will bring to the firm. You are not getting paid for free, you bring value to the firm, which appreciates your work by paying you.

OR

Find a rich guy or woman, make sure your back is properly bent or better yet, get down on your knees, let him, or her know that you are weak, worthless person unable to stand on your own two feet and so require his or her help in getting something to eat. You then become his or her lackey, yes-man or woman, shine his shoes, do her bidding and "live" the life of a servant.

Is it better to work hard, earn money the right way and be happy and content with eating just stale bread as long as it is earned?

OR

Is it better to go find a sugar daddy, get down on your knees, beg and grovel, use empty praises, and brown-nose your way to an easy life?

The former is a child of God, the latter is a slave. I can't say God has any use for her children lowering themselves to being slaves or servants. I don't see God humoring these worthless people as they eagerly chase after these fantasy Heavens. I see them embracing death—eternal useless death.

It's either that or they come back as bugs, say dust mites, no worries, no responsibilities, happily munching away on your dead skin cells—Heaven!

All efforts to make them think like a child of God and to focus more on conduct, character, and making God proud of us fail miserably. A master will beat his servant, a master will run a Hell; but will a Parent ever torture her own child? Never! Again, when I say there is no Hell in Hinduism, that God Sri Rama is no torturer, these people go crazy.

Here once more, I ask the reader to make a choice—do you want to be a child of God or His servant/slave?

Want Versus Need

Does God need you in Heaven? She already has billions to cater to, millions more showing up every day, begging for a hand-out, so obviously, the answer is a big NO, NO.

So, the fact is that you *want* to be in Heaven, right? Who doesn't? Everything will be taken care of, and you won't have a care! Of course you want to be in Heaven.

But where is the *need*? Where are you needed? Not in Heaven, but right here on earth. One of my favorite authors is Alf Wight, known as James Herriot to thousands of his fans. James was a veterinarian who started his practice back in the 40s in Yorkshire (rural England). His books about his animal practice sold well and made him a rich man. He writes about the time he was offered a chance to work in the city in a small animal practice. This practice would have meant no more getting up in the middle of the night or working in cold, dreary barns in winter. He could have avoided getting kicked by cows and being charged by bulls. The job would have enabled him to get a good night's sleep, arrive at work at the same time every day, and work with small dogs and cats in clean and warm working conditions. A dream job!

However, James turned the job down. Why? Because the small animal practice did not need him—the small farmer did! The farm animals needed him, and so he stayed where he was needed.

There are many famous people in history who chose their line of work not because it was the easiest option but instead because they wanted to be where they were needed.

Heaven is supposed to be a happy place—a place without pain or suffering. If so, it was already a happy place *before* you were born and it will continue to be a happy place after you get there. *Whether you are there or not does not matter. Your presence or absence will not change the place. You don't matter there; no one cares whether you are there or not.* If there are already trillions of people in Heaven, you will be just another number, a statistic. And down on earth, everyone will forget you except those who truly loved you. But even they must die someday, and at that point your death will be truly eternal—you will be neither wanted nor remembered, neither in Heaven nor on earth.

God doesn't need another scrounger in Heaven. However, She does need you down here. Your loved ones need you down here. People are counting on you to be here with them; society needs good people here.

Even a dog can teach us. During the recent tsunami in Japan, a video of a dog that refused to abandon his friend became famous. Millions were riveted to this video of this dog who rejected shelter, warmth, food and comfort, loving people hugging it and other dogs to play with (Heaven), to stay with his stricken friend, a friend who was sick and ill and could not move. His friend needed him and dog stayed to comfort his friend. The dog chose to stay and endure cold, hunger, loneliness, thirst and fear! He knew that his injured friend needed him, so he chose to stay! The dog chose Karma and rebirth, the dog chose God over pleasures of the flesh, the dog chose to do the right thing!

That dog was with God, and God was with that dog.

If there were ever a mascot for Hinduism, that dog would be it! What a wonderful animal.

If you were in that dog's situation, what would be your response? Each one of us *will be* put in that situation when we face death in our final days. What will be your choice?

As I have said over and over in this book, the pain is here. The need is here, and God is here. Why would you choose to be anywhere else?

What will be your choice, satisfying your wants in Heaven or responding to needs on earth?

3. Karma and Reincarnation Mean the Gift of Life

Where There is Life, There is God.
Where There is Death, There is no God.
Choose life, Real Life. Choose to be With God.

As I have pointed out before, why would God be with the dead? The dead do not need nor want God, it is us, those who are alive, who need and want God. God is here, God is here with us!

Life is a gift. Life is priceless. Life is a great gift from God. Most religions teach that life is a sin, ergo we are all sinners. But Hinduism does not view life in this manner. The total opposite—in fact, this gift is to be savored over and over again! Like visiting our favorite hangout and enjoying our favorite food or drink over and over again. Hinduism gives us the gift of life, to be enjoyed again and once more!

Life may not be much. It is hard, it is unforgiving, but it beats giving up, it beats running away to fantasylands; and finally, it definitely, certainly beats death!

By the way, if life is a sin, then how can suicide, an escape from sin, also be a sin? That's something to think about. What is Hinduism's opinion on suicide? No one will say it is a good thing, obviously, but a sin? No. Let us first think of the person who thinks of committing suicide. Obviously, this is a soul who is in terrible pain and to whom life has dealt a bad hand, day after day, living in pain. A person who has been abused as a child, a young man who has lost his job and has run out of his savings, a young woman who has lost her only true love, a Parent who watched her young child die in her own arms... unable to bear the unending pain, their thoughts turn toward suicide. To say to these people that God will torture them further for doing so is terrible! These people are turning to God in their moment of crisis and God will punish them further? Nothing could be further from the Truth.

The fact is religions catering to the weak and cowardly have built a fantasyland waiting "up there". Here's the problem: people do not want to wait, they want to run away to that fantasyland! This could be seen as promoting suicide! Now, that will never do. It will give the religion a bad name! Thus, we have the injunction against suicide.

Here is the religion promoting death. By promising a wonderful fantasyland that awaits one after death, it looks foolish if people kill themselves in an effort to get to that nice and easy life.

I do have a complaint with God. The people who consider this earth a place of sin, a horrible place, why put them through this? Why even give them life? We will be asked if we want to continue further in another life. Those who choose Heaven get eternal death. Those who choose life are the Hindus!

These are a few of my favorite things about life:
1. Falling in love
2. Holding a newborn baby
3. Wedding day
4. Opening day
5. The smell of the earth while and after it rains

6. A child's shriek of delight
7. A pet overjoyed to see you
8. A great book or a play or a movie
9. An accomplishment
10. Beautiful music
11. The chatter of nature
12. Vacation
13. Hobbies
14. Playing with your grandchild
15. Good food and drink
16. God's paintings: sunset, sunrise...
17. Summer
18. Childhood
19. Blue skies
20. Friends
21. Ice cream!
22. Goooooooooal!
23. The end of a war
24. Healing a sick child
25. Baby's first steps, her first words
26. Camping, campfire, snuggling together
27. The beach
28. Fall
29. Spring
30. Creativity
31. Making treats for grandkids
32. We won!

And I could go on and on, and I am sure you can think of many more. In fact, try listing the things that you are thankful for, and you will come to appreciate the gift of life and why all life is priceless.

Have you ever wondered about the path not taken?

The what-ifs? The unknown calling in life that you cannot explain? Thanks to Reincarnation, there is yet time. If not in this life, then the next. What a great gift!

These are merely the selfish joys. Try the joys of the truly gifted and enlightened. The joy of bringing a smile to a complete stranger's face, the joy of helping others, making a difference in their lives. Not just great souls but even ordinary people can also join in such joys.

Remember, all the above can only be done here and nowhere else! Only life will give us this opportunity.

And finally dreams—we all have dreams when we were young, not to say that older folks cannot have dreams. Dreams of achievement—becoming a movie or sports star, a dream job, travelling the world, the next Einstein, writing the next great novel… the list is endless!

Again, remember, you can dream only down here! Only while on earth! In Heaven dreams go to die. Nothing to do in Heaven, nothing to achieve—no more dreams.

What has history taught us? Has life gotten better by itself? Did Hitler decide to voluntarily kill himself? Was the new Jewish nation protected by an invisible hand? Did diseases that ravaged millions vanish into thin air? Famines used to ravage the earth in history, but that is now history.

How did all this happen? It happened because of good hardworking people getting down to work. Tilling the land, working in the factory, in the laboratory, ignoring the pains of the wounds of war—sheer hard work, sacrifice, blood, sweat, toil and tears by untold millions.

Would you let their sacrifice go in vain?

Everyone gets a taste of life. The question is do you want more? The fort is being attacked, the village is being raided. Do you want to stand your ground and fight? If not, there is always the back door (Heaven). Going to school is hard;

many drop out. They go work in a popular restaurant, but years later they regret their actions. Choosing Heaven is like choosing to drop out of school. Life teaches you that nothing worthwhile is going to come easy.

To me, this is like the wish that came true for King Midas that turned into a curse. What will a slave/servant do all day in Heaven? Eat, drink, poop and sleep? That's it? That's your big goal in life?

We all hear about God's grand plan. That's God's plan? Sleep, eat, drink, poop, watch some TV, sleep and repeat over and over? Is that the grand plan?

What about a drug addict who spends his day drugged out of his mind? Is he in Heaven? He is very happy enjoying himself. Does anyone think that is a life? It is nothing but death!

What will be your choice? Life or death? Remember, death is eternal. Do the right thing or run away? Be strong and brave or be weak and a coward?

Hinduism does not offer you an easy life. We offer work. Life, as we saw before, is not *all* bad. It can be wonderful, but you will have to work at it. Some people are born lucky, but most of us are not. Sadly, most do not want to work at it, and these are the people who make easy prey for easy-breezy religions.

Those that find God in work will prosper. The Vedas talks about four ways to reach God, and one of the ways is Karma (work) Yoga.

Through work may you find God.

In the end, if life is too tough for you and you wish to check out, God is not going to force you to be reborn. Sadly, many people miss out on the joys of life and instead they choose eternal death.

Paradise can exist here, but it is not going to build itself. It has to be worked on. As a Hindu, you say, "I am ready, whatever it takes, however long it takes." One day, it will all come to fruition. One day, man will reach the stars. Let us make it happen.

William Faulkner said, "Between grief and nothing, I will take grief."

I feel sad for those people who fall for the easy promises of some religions, chasing after the easy life, they reject God's gift of life and settle for death! Please do not settle for death, for nothing. Hinduism offers you a chance to live! A chance to steer the destiny of your country and the world and to embark on a brand new future!

You have to be here to make it happen. Say yes to life! Say yes to God!

Hinduism offers us life. The alternative is an eternal, permanent, useless death.

Hindu Pride—God is Female

Hinduism remains the only major religion to pray to God in a female form. Just like the male trinity consisting of Brahma, Vishnu and Siva, there exists the female trinity of Saraswati, Laxmi and Parvati—female Gods equaling the men. Hinduism is unique in this regard.

Saraswati is popularly known as the Goddess or dispenser of learning. Laxmi is the giver of wealth. And Goddess Parvati or Durga is the Goddess of power. Shakti!

One may also come across the image of Ardhanariswara, half-man, half-woman or half Siva and half Parvati, his consort. These images tell us that men and women are equal partners in life.

Things changed as time went on. People changed. They became weaker. Weak people usually look for scapegoats for their problems, such as women in a male-dominated world.

Later religions reflected this misogyny against women. Women came to be seen as the source of all evil. Women were also labeled as weak, troubled, needing help from "strong" men. They quickly slipped into second-class status in many later religions.

Man was the head of the family and would be making all the decisions. It is the woman's duty to honor and obey the man.

Such beliefs are absent in Hinduism.

Ironically, the more "modern" religions quickly relegated women to second-class status whereas the much older Hinduism gave them equality!

As always, whenever I refer to these teachings of Hinduism the question that is always asked is, "What about the plight of women in India?" They are quick to lump anything bad into the lap of Hinduism. Notice that when it comes to other countries their majority religions are not blamed for the ills within their societies. There is racism in America. Is that the fault of Christianity? How about slavery? Can we blame that on religion?

There is no country in the world today where it can be said that women are equal to men, not one! Women still earn less than men. They still shoulder the majority of household work. Countries like Japan or Mexico are male-dominated, but do we then assign blame to Shintoism, Buddhism or the Catholic religions?

One can blame a religion when the teachings of that religion reflect the happenings in a country. For example there is extreme homophobia in several countries. We need to ask what does their majority religion say about homosexuals? Does it welcome them or does it censure them? Then, and only then, can we assign blame to an individual religion.

Otherwise it is like blaming the Teacher for the bad

choices of a student. All a Teacher or a Parent can do is teach the child the value of an education, the value of staying in school; but does every child listen and follow through?

Hinduism is teaching the right values. That's all anyone can ask for. People change, societies change. It is unrealistic to expect to have the same society that we had 2,000 or 10,000 years ago. And in another 500 years the society that will come into existence then will be much, much different from the one we have today.

At one time, Jews fleeing from the persecution of Christians found safe refuge among Muslims! Imagine that. Today they seem to be at each other's throats. At one time the Islamic world was at the forefront of knowledge, science and new ideas. Sadly those times are long gone.

It is as if they were different people then—and they were! We are different people from the ones that existed 2 or 10,000 years ago, and our progeny will also be different from us, with different values and ideas of what is right and what is wrong.

Hopefully Hindus will rediscover the glorious teachings of Hinduism and re-embrace the values that are being taught by this great faith.

4. Karma and Reincarnation Mean There Is No Place for a Hell, No Sadistic God Running a Torture Chamber

Absolutely the number one worst idea that religions have ever invented is the concept of Hell—a brutish, sick, vile, disgusting place of torture, pain and suffering.

Who comes to mind when you think of places of torture where people are beaten, abused and made to undergo brutal punishment? Do you not think of Hitler? Saddam Hussein? Stalin?

Now, imagine the opposite of such a person—a kind, loving person who would not hurt a fly. Mahatma Gandhiji? The Buddha?

Now tell me, what is your conception of God? Whom do you see as God? Is God brutal, like Saddam or kind like Gandhiji?

A God who could turn a Hitler or a Stalin into a peaceful Gandhiji with one thought—does that God need to use brutal and abusive methods? How can this be right? I struggled with this question for a long time—before my own epiphany, when I realized that there is no need for Hell.

The moment I realized that there is no place for Hell in Hinduism was a moment of revelation for me, a eureka moment. I felt as if a great burden had been lifted off of my shoulders. The more I studied the Ramayana, the epic story of my God Sri Rama, the more I dwelt on his personality, the more I felt uncomfortable with a person who would use torture to make a point. I simply could not envision my Rama torturing anyone, no matter what their crimes. A loving, kind God does not torture. Let me repeat, God Sri Rama does not torture. Period.

I believe that we are all children and students of God! All of us. There are no exceptions. But some people have lowered themselves to become slaves of God. They fall down on their knees, shaking with fear, groveling for mercy from a vengeful, violent God. They turn God from a loving, caring Parent/Teacher to a wrathful master who must be obeyed unconditionally. The concept of Hell came from the mind of such a slave, down on his knees, shaking, cowering with fear, his head down, unable to lift his eyes, wondering what kind of punishment awaits him.

Let us start thinking like children of God. Would a mother torture her own child for eternity? The very thought of this sickens me. Respect your Teacher, love your Parents, but never fear your Parent or Teacher. No father wants his children to be afraid of him. No Teacher wants her students to be afraid of her.

Wouldn't it be hard enough to watch your son or daughter being tortured, let alone being the torturer? No mother would whip her own son, no father would rape his own daughter.

The domino effect of Hell:

And then it hits you: of course, this is not a Parent, this is a master. Only a master could be so heartless as to torture his slaves. No wonder these people live in fear. Imagine being so heartless as to torture someone for eternity! No Parent could be so heartless; but a king might, a master would. Anyone familiar with the history of slavery in America knows the brutal life that slaves were forced to lead under their masters.

Yes, a master will whip his slave until blood flowed like water; masters have gladly raped even underage slaves.

Please come to the realization what this concept of Hell has done to God—it has turned God from a loving Parent to a brutal sadistic master and the follower in turn has fallen from the lap of God down to the ground, now just a slave/servant—yes, we have truly fallen.

I urge all Hindus and those who view themselves as children of God to let go of this hateful concept of Hell. You lower yourselves down to the level of slaves living in fear of a wrathful master, you lower God down to the level of a heartless monster. None of us knows what happens to us after death. Those who say they do know are merely speculating. It is called a *belief system* for a reason. Let God decide what She wants to do with evil people. Let us not speculate, but even as a speculation is this the best we can do? God, a heartless master? Think, reader—why would any religion preach such a view?

Let us make one thing clear—there are no evil babies, there are no evil children. All babies are born seeking love and affection. The saying is true: "It takes a village to raise a child." As adults, we reflect our upbringing. We are an amalgam of our Parents, our family, our neighborhood, our schools, our friends and our society at large. As we grow up, we form opinions by watching the example of our elders.

One of the most beloved books of all time, at least personally for me, is the series of veterinarian practice books by James Herriot. In one book he writes about a young boy, unloved by his Parents, who turns into a troublemaker. But then he takes in a dog. The little dog falls sick, and to pay for his treatment, the young boy takes on odd jobs, a shilling here, another there—all to save the life of the one creature that gave him love!

If, as a child, a person is exposed to hate and revenge masquerading as justice, then he will most likely turn out to be a hateful person. If, as a child, all he sees is gang violence, drugs, drive-by shootings, uneducated elders with little or no values, it will be very difficult for that child to grow up to be a productive citizen.

We can clearly see that we cannot walk away from evil that permeates our societies. Simply saying, "I am a good person, I bear no responsibility," will not do. We are *all* responsible for the condition of our societies. Not only are we held responsible for our actions, we are also held responsible for the condition of our society.

As Gandhiji so eloquently put it, "An eye for an eye makes the whole world blind." In a nutshell, this describes Hell. A person has been bad. He has committed evil acts, and so God's "justice" would do the same? Torture for torture? Pain exchanged for pain? A gang member sees one of his members killed by another gang. He gets his group together, and kills a member of the rival gang. What would you call this act? Vengeance or justice? Who in his right mind would call this justice?

The image of someone who goes to Hell never changes. It is always the bad guy—the guy who rapes, murders and steals. What about an ordinary person? What is your opinion on gays? What is your opinion on abortion? What if your view does not reflect the view of God? Is torture the answer? As you are beaten and tortured, will you then realize your folly? *That* is how one is enlightened? Will you then think, "Ah, I was wrong to think gays were nice/bad people"?

A torturer can make you do or say anything the torturer wants. A theist can be made to abuse and mock God, while an atheist can be made to say he fervently believes in God.

To think that a being who has created this marvelous universe with millions of galaxies and billions of life forms would stoop to imitate a common brutal despot is, frankly, primitive. Let us remind ourselves that concepts like Hell came about in primitive times, when man thought that the Heavens rotated around the earth. We were the all-important ingredient in this limited cosmic vision.

These religions teach a primitive, backward view of God—a caveman view, I dare say. When the caveman first heard thunder and saw lightning followed by fire and destruction, he naturally assumed that God "up there" was in an angry mood. So, it was natural for him to get down on his knees and beg this angry God for mercy.

That's the violent, angry God of primitive, caveman times that exists today! In the 21st century!

The concept of Hell is a human invention. It came from the mind of a person who may have been abused by one stronger and could do nothing about it. And so he invented Hell as a place where God would exact revenge for his suffering. Later, some proselytizers used it and are using it today to frighten the innocent into converting.

Such methods have no place in Hinduism. Karma and Reincarnation is God's non-violent way of justice. No one is punished for evil acts; instead they get another chance to undo the bad Karma of their previous life.

Frankly, religions that do not teach the concept of Karma and Reincarnation may be stuck with the brutal concept of Hell. Where would evil people go? Certainly not Heaven! But thank God for Hinduism. The rest of us can discard this disgusting concept that lowers God to the level of a Saddam!

For the Hindu, God is a Teacher. A Teacher instructs, a Teacher encourages, a Teacher does not punish. The goal of a Hindu is Moksha—enlightenment, knowledge. There is no knowledge to be gained at the end of a whip, by brutal punishment.

Let us Hindus make it perfectly clear: God Sri Rama does

not torture. Period. God Sri Rama does not break legs, rape, sodomize, water-board, whip, beat, humiliate, cage, brutalize, pull fingernails, use the electric prod, burn skin with cigarette butts, scare, threaten or abuse. Repeat: God Rama does not torture. Period.

The very concept of Hell invites hate into your heart. When you wish Hell upon another person, no matter how evil he or she might be, even a Hitler, you invite hate into your heart—a hate that will burn you. It makes "good" people kill in the name of religion. Let God deal with evil people the way She sees fit; but let us, as humans, not condemn anyone to such a horrible fate.

To me, it is not a surprise that the apostle of non-violence is Mahatma Gandhiji, a Hindu. Only a Hindu could have come up with such a peaceful method of resolving issues, of getting across his point in such a profound way.

Hinduism has had this tendency of absorbing ideas and images from other religions and the non-religious. Sadly, this has resulted in this concept of Heaven and Hell slithering its way into Hinduism.

Doesn't Hinduism say the atma, the soul, is undying—that it is the body that is left here on earth after death? The atma cannot be burned by fire, water cannot wet it, the wind cannot move it? And yet, how is this indestructible atma supposed to be punished in Hell?

Hindus have made a mess of this concept. Some believe that we are responsible for our actions from a previous life, and will be punished in this life. But then how to explain a Hell? Would it not be double-counting? Would it not be being punished for the same crimes twice?

Let us be clear that one is not punished for the evil acts of a previous life—for then it would be no better than a Hell. All you get is a chance to correct your mistakes, like a student who fails a test gets to retake the test or sit for another year and redo the class. Lack of knowledge, falling behind his peers, is its own punishment.

Imagine life in ancient times. We think we have it pretty bad, but today is like a paradise; life is so easy when compared to ancient times. If they were not battling diseases and famines, they were desperately trying to earn a living. There was no social security nor a pension to help them in old age, they were at the mercy of their king or relatives. There were no banks to keep your money safe; instead your money was kept in a safe in your home, and one bad night meant going from being rich and well-off to instant poverty! This explains the constant wars over land: land was one asset that could not be easily stolen.

In such harsh times, justice meant instant violence. With the king and ruler being far away, it meant that local society had to deal with any transgressions. With no money to expend on jails and the keeping of prisoners, anyone breaking the law could expect swift and brutal punishment. Read about true-life incidents in books like *Mutiny on the Bounty*, where unruly sailors received whippings for their trouble.

From such harsh times came the concept of Hell—a cruel and barbaric place that fit the ideas of those times.

Well, I hope we have moved forward from those barbaric days; at least we don't whip unruly sailors anymore, thank goodness.

Time was that when a child misbehaved in public—crying for a treat and not letting up—the poor Parent had but two options:

1. Give in, give the child his treat (Heaven), or
2. Punish the child, give the child a beating (Hell)

But today's Parents know better. They choose a third option:

3. Teach the child right from wrong (Karma and Reincarnation)

If you educate the child on why he is not getting a treat, the
child learns, you raise a better child and you become a better
Parent for it. Everyone benefits.

Using fear as a tool does not make the child a better
person. You may make your child do what you want by
using threats, but you know that he is going through the
motions. He has not learned anything.

But teaching the child to learn right from wrong is harder,
isn't it? Much, much harder! It is so much easier to yell at
the child: "Do it! Or else!", "Do it, because I said so!" It is
much, much tougher to see the child's view of things, to
get down to his or her level and gently guide them onto the
proper path.

Karma and Reincarnation is God's non-violent, loving
way of educating her children.

This is what Hinduism teaches, that God wants you to
become a better person, but not by using physical and emotional violence. Come to God because you want to, not
because of threats of punishment.

Imagine a 7,000-year-old faith that speaks the language
and laws of today, one that reflects present-day values and
principles.

No Hell in Hinduism. Period.

4 Major Religions—2 Divisions

The four major religions can be put in 2 categories—on
one side are religions where which religion one belongs to
is all-important. Work—Karma—doesn't matter, actions
do not matter (all this talk of God's grand plan then
becomes sheer nonsense)—what is important is that you

pray to the "right" God, use the "right" name and belong to the "right" religion.

At the other end are Buddhism and Hinduism—here action—Karma—is all that matters. Once we die, who we were no longer matters—we no longer are male or female, democrat or republican, rich or poor, religious or non-religious, believer or non-believer, achiever or underachiever, young or old—none of these matter—the only thing that matters is what you have done with the life that God has given you—have you made your Parent proud?

I ask the followers of Hinduism and Buddhism and others who think likewise to separate themselves from the other two major religions—let us make it clear to everyone that this is what we stand for—the values and principles that we hold dear on earth remain the same in the after-world. It is an insult here on earth to be judged based on one's religious qualification—apparently for the other religions the rules change, they do not for us.

In the 21st century it is sad to see millions thinking that they can get Heaven simply by knowing the name for God supplied by their religion (can people not see that the religion has a vested interest in making you think this way?)—God is that gullible, or is it that people are that gullible? I vote for the latter—the lure of an easy life in heaven apparently dims the thinking brain.

Whether you are up for a promotion or applying for a job, what would you want to be defined by? Your qualifications (Karma) or your religion? Your kid has just applied to a prestigious university—what should the selection criteria be? Her accomplishments, her hard work, her sacrifices or her religion? How is it that even the highly-educated have let themselves be brainwashed that religion is all-important? Ask yourself which is the harder way? To be defined based on your accomplishments or your religious affiliation? Obviously the former, but would any sane, intelligent, moral, ethical person have it any other way? As I keep asking, are we still weak? Do we still look the easy way out?

How do you please your boss? Flattery? Or plain good, old, hard work? Clearly, most people would say the latter. Then why is it that when it comes to religion some people are so easily brainwashed? Yes, flattery is quicker, faster—the weak and the morally bankrupt would choose that route—are you one of them?

You have a choice—is it who-you-know OR what-you-know? You got a job because the boss is your uncle or because you have the necessary qualifications? Was the position given to you or did you earn it?

Hinduism is the what-you-know faith—a place in God's heart must be earned!

Do you believe in finding success from the sweat of your brow, sacrifice and hard work or some guy who will give you the happiness that you want? Certainly, the latter is far easier, but beware of easy promises, that is how Ponzi schemes are born.

If one's actions do not matter and religion is all-important then we realize that individual accomplishments do not matter—you are now judged as part of a group, you are but a statistic—amazing that the leading religions of the day are Communist, socialist religions! We have had a horrific example of this type of thinking—under Hitler, Jews were not judged based who they were as individuals, young or old, male or female; an accomplished leader of the people, who had worked hard to uplift German society, suddenly found himself wearing an arm band one day to being pushed into a rail car destined for the gas chambers the next! His crime was his religion. Babies, children, grandmothers—their innocence did not matter, all that matters was which religion they belonged to.

Is this the kind of company that a "God" would keep?

Hinduism says that you are to be "judged" as the person that you are—an individual different from every other person on earth! Here we go again—this way is harder, tougher! Okay, let's make it a bit harder—you are not to beg your way out, you are not to beg for forgiveness. You have made your share of mistakes, now own up to them, learn from them, become a better person and if there are victims that are hurting, creditors to repay, promises to keep, Stand proud before God and ask for a second chance. Do the right thing.

Who is a follower of God Rama? Is it a person who wears saffron robes, goes to the temple daily and offers his prayers, but lies to society, his wife, and carries on criminal activities by night? Not at all, though he may declare himself a Hindu and a follower of Rama.

The true follower of Rama is a person maybe living in say Siberia, an unbeliever, a person who has never heard of Rama or the Hindu religion, yet tells the Truth, is true to his wife, his kids, his community. This person is truly a devotee of God Rama and Rama has a place in his heart for such people.

I ask Hindus and Buddhists and other religions who feel the same way and teach the same morals to declare themselves as such—let us break from those who preach that religion is some sort of qualification.

Actions, not religion, matter.

This may be easier to understand if we discuss the end-result a bit, the goal. Is it Heaven—a place to indulge in pleasures of the flesh? Such things can be given as we shall see, but for Hindus and Buddhists, Moksha is the goal—Moksha cannot be given, it can only be earned! To be reborn as a bug and indulge in pleasures of the flesh is easy, to become a God takes sacrifice and hard work. To vegetate and lie on the couch is easy, to become the next Einstein, the next Gandhiji will not be easy and it should not be.

If your goal in life is to beg for something, finding someone who will give you a handout, then following a teaching that assures you of such a person makes sense. Your goal is the easy life and religions are happy to exploit that want and greed and are happy to make all the promises that you hope for—then they have you. Now you work for them, not God.

But if you believe in paying for what you take, earning whatever you obtain—whether it is food, a job or entrance to a college—then realize that principles and morals do not change once you die—morals and ethics do not die at God's door and if they do, then you know you are not in the presence of God.

Believer or Follower?

As we have noted, the terminology is important – a believer is more likely to be a King religion member, whereas a Follower is a member of a Teacher faith. One must believe (swear allegiance) in the King, then one is rewarded. It is pitiful to see these people talk endlessly about getting to heaven, it seems that is all they think about and all God is good for – the good life – and religions take advantage by promising them the King like God who will deliver it to them

A Follower is one who aspires to be like his or her Teacher or Parent. As we noted, a follower of Rama must tell the Truth, be honest, and do the right thing. From the Buddha we learn to be compassionate, from Jesus we learn to love – simply going to the Temple and throwing some namaste's at God won't do – Hinduism demands more from you, has higher expectations of you

Instead of seeing God as a giver of the easy life, we must see God as the giver of Knowledge and right conduct – the King God is about "life" elsewhere, and the Teacher God is about Life right *here and now*

5. Karma and Reincarnation Because Heaven Is a Myth, Fantasy.

Heaven is a Fantasy; Life is Not a Fantasy, Life is Real Heaven is for the Dead; Earth is for the Living; God is With the Living

"Rather would I be a serf on some poor man's farm than Lord over all the spirits of the dead"
—Achilles, the Odyssey

"The function of man is to live, not to exist (forever)"
—Jack London

Ever notice how every fairy story ends with the words, "and they lived happily ever after"? What do certain religions promise? A life of joy and happiness for ever and ever? Live happily ever after? Frankly I can't see a God who would just let millions and billions of people just sit and vegetate for eternity.

The concept of Heaven makes absolutely no sense. Are we really to believe that a sentient being has nothing better to do than to play nursemaid for billions of people who show up at His door? Does he have nothing better to do than to be their (horrors!) *servant*? For *eternity*?

Reminds me of the genie in the bottle story and yes, let

me emphasize, a children's story. The genie has all these wonderful and powerful magical powers, but apparently prefers to live in a little bottle and yes just loves to be the servant of anyone who rubs the bottle! What happens if a dog or someone like Hitler rubs the bottle? The all-powerful genie is serving a dog? He is killing millions at the behest of Hitler? Of course, you will immediately say "this is a children's story"! Exactly! And you are an adult, for God's sake, and you think God has nothing better to do than be a sugar daddy, a nanny to billions? Just like the genie killing millions at the behest of Hitler, God will torture billions of innocents at the behest of a sick religion?

People fantasizing about the easy way to an easy life, and quite a few religions happy to feed their fantasies.

What does it mean if your ultimate goal in life is to sit and do nothing for eternity? It is a preference for fantasy over reality. Is this the best we can hope for?

At some point we let our kids know that Santa does not exist, but we are happy to believe in a Santa for adults. Even worse, we can't be happy with our good fortune—our neighbor must get coal in his stocking. But wait, it gets worse: the neighbor must suffer because he did not share in our delusions.

Think about this for a second: Heaven came first, God came later; God was an addendum to the concept of Heaven. People wanted to get away from the harshness of life and run to a dreamland, but someone was needed to run the place. Enter God!

These people couldn't care less if God were in this Heaven or not, as long as they get their cushy life of joy and happiness. Why would they want to live the rest of eternity doing nothing—being totally useless? They talk about serving God, but how? By sitting in Heaven? By being a parasite, a freeloader, and mooching off of God? Who is serving whom?

Instead we should work with the poor and the unfortunate. We should help save lives by raising funds for research. How about looking for a lost child, or saving animals from a terrible fate? This is how you serve God! It is a lot of work, and such work can only be found here on earth.

One of the main arguments of this book is that Heaven is the product of a weak mind—running away from a harsh life, running away from responsibilities. Instead of working hard and making a better life, one creates a dream-land and run away. Let us not forget that this dream-land comes ready-made, God has created this wonderland, nothing to do for us but to sit back and enjoy! The perfect dream-land of the weak.

Successful people and countries are those that stop complaining and get to work. They do not let difficulties stand in the way. Failures always complain and point fingers at others: This is not good, that is bad, foreign countries don't want to see us succeed, etc. They don't for one moment think that it is their problem—that it is up to them to fix it. Instead they think that someone else will come and fix things. God will come down any day now and fix everything with a wave of His magic wand!

Heaven is the lifesaver for the weak, those who are unable to work hard and make the necessary sacrifices. The weak run away to a comic-book world.

In the end the weak end up cheating themselves—in fact, they cheat themselves of life itself, the gift that God has given us. Tell me, reader: what does a being who is trying to take your soul have to offer? Does he not offer the easy life—food, sex, and drink? And in return does he not ask for your soul? Some souls come cheap——just make some nice Ponzi promises of the easy life and watch them line up!

We can do better. Something given for free is worthless. There is no such thing as a free lunch. We know that. The only thing of any value is that which is earned!

But the Hindu concept of Karma and Reincarnation simply cannot compete with the offerings of many religions. What does true Karma and Reincarnation have to offer? More pain and suffering?

All I can do is ask you to take a good look at your values— the values that you were taught as a child and the values that you are teaching your children. There is no free lunch. If something sounds too good to be true, it probably—no, it definitely—is!

Heaven is for the retired, the defeated. You sit in a corner in a rocking chair, day after day, night after night. Can we not aspire for something better? Yes, we can.

Heaven is nothing but a projection—a way to assuage our fear of death. Who is not afraid of death? We *all* fear death. When a dear one dies, we don't really know what has happened. Young people ask questions, and we try to come up with something comforting. Imagine a father who has just lost his wife and his children come crying to him for comfort, asking, "Why isn't mommy answering?" So he says that she is in a better place. She is happy "up there", looking down on us. This story has probably been repeated throughout human history all the way back to the Stone Age.

People came up with a concept of Heaven to make themselves feel better. Way back in the past, life was pretty bad; it was tough to make a living. There were no labor laws, which meant that you could be hired and fired at will. If you missed a day's work, you did not get paid. Even today millions of laborers drag themselves out of their sickbeds so that their families will not go hungry. This situation was even more common in the past, in all countries and on all continents. The practice of medicine was primitive, unable to counter the illnesses and diseases that ravaged the land.

Life was especially hard for older people—no pension, no social security, no Medicare, no generous government to take care of them. Forget retirement—if you had no kids to depend on, you worked until you dropped. Imagine doing not just office labor but hard manual labor out in the elements!

Older people relied on the kindness of their children, their relatives, and society at large. An accident most probably meant a slow death due to starvation. Older people battled the physical deterioration of their bodies, suffering the mental anguish of loneliness, depression, anxiety, and despair.

Even today the press proclaims the ideal senior as one who is fiercely independent—one who does not want to impose on her kids. God forbid the younger set should devote some time to take care of their aged loved ones as they were once taken care of! The aging Parent gets the message: your children do not need you anymore. Your job is done; it is time for you to leave.

Do you know why elderly people talk to themselves? Not because they have gone senile, but so they can hear a voice, to feel that someone is talking to them, that they are not alone. Some of them leave the TV on even when they are not watching, just to get the feeling that someone else is there with them, talking, a glimpse of their former life.

In some cases, death might come as a relief! A dead person is no longer in pain. In fact, the person often looks serene and peaceful. No more pain, at last. Ah, Heaven, where there is no pain or suffering!

So is it all just waiting for us—only death stands between us and all that happiness? Does God await our death? How macabre! What started out as a nice story to tell your grieving child has turned into something that bright, educated adults have fallen for!

Heaven is a myth. It is no different from the genie in a bottle, the tooth fairy, or the pot of gold at the end of the rainbow. These are all children's stories!

Heaven is a concept that was born in our minds. It is a reflection of our hopes and desires, and a result of our fear of death. We have even invented the idea of 72 virgins waiting for men who want to satisfy carnal desires. Surely we do not think that God runs a brothel?

Heaven is that faraway mountain that looks smooth. But we know that this smoothness is a mirage. So why do the weak continue to paint a rosy picture of a fantasy place? The answer is simple—it gets them away from here. Here is bad. Here, good things don't fall from the sky. If you want good things here, you have to work for them.

Say a flood is about to strike a town. There is much work to do—prepare sandbags, move people and animals to safer areas, construct shelters, give people food and water, etc. It is a lot of work, effort, and worry. The selfish and weak want nothing to do with this situation—they just get in their trucks and drive till they reach safety. They run away to safe areas and wait till the flood subsides and everything gets repaired.

Let someone else handle it.

Just get in your truck and just gun it! Get on the highway and flee! Leave your troubles behind you! Instantly you will feel better! Or maybe you may not, but the coward definitely will—no more anxiety, no more worry—Heaven!

Do you see where you are headed, what you have chosen to do? You are far away from trouble. You find a nice hotel, spend a restful night, wake up the next day, and go down for some hot breakfast. As you sip your coffee and watch TV, you see the devastation that the flood has caused. And then you see them: your spouse, your little child, your neighbors—all wading in knee-deep water fighting to save your home and your town! They are disheveled but are determined not to let the flood win.

If you don't feel that you have shrunk to the size of an ant as you see these scenes, you have no heart.

Heaven is the ultimate selfish act.

Once you choose heaven you are basically saying problems on earth are no longer your problem—let the next generation deal with them. You turn your back on your loved ones, your kids, your friends—off you go to enjoy yourself and if misfortune befalls your loved ones or your country, well, "Good luck dealing with them, hope you guys will overcome them, I am a bit too busy having fun."

Hinduism asks us to please stay. Help. You may be fighting to find a cure for a disease, a breakthrough is at hand! Stay and finish the job. Madame Curie gave her life for science. Think she is sitting on her butt doing nothing in heaven? I think not.

Those who stay and work are choosing Karma and Reincarnation. Those who run after fantasy Heavens are like kids who drop out of school—they cheat themselves in the end.

It is amazing that these cowards are running away and yet they expect God to reward them for it!

Will you be one of the people who beg and grovel their way to a nice, easy life? Can you really stoop that low? Will you have to beg each and every day, three times a day, for your daily bread in Heaven? "Please, sir, may I have some more?" If you are willing to do that, why wait? Why not do it here? Just go find a sugar daddy—a rich man or woman—and brownnose your way into his inner circle. Laugh loudly at his jokes, praise him sky-high, run his errands, and maybe he will throw you a bone! Plenty of people do that in today's world—do you see yourself being one of them? Have you sunk that low?

Do you see what your religion has reduced you to?

Heaven is the lottery that we all hope to hit. We love to think of how we would enjoy all those riches. We make grand plans—all the vacations that we are going to take and the houses and big cars that we are going to buy—but then we come back to reality. No one quits his or her job for the hope of hitting it big.

Heaven is a back door. It is a way to run away from the pressures of life—a hiding place, a bed to dive under when trouble strikes. But then a child sees the coward running away through the back door. The child laughs and threatens to tell everyone. She is not allowed to do this, and so she is threatened for not sharing the belief in a pleasant afterlife!

The threats of Hell are the threats of a coward.

No beggar has ever gotten rich by simply begging. If you think you can cry your way to a nice retirement home, you are sadly mistaken. If you want Heaven, work for it! Make God proud of you.

Let's look at other examples that show why the concept of Heaven is so illogical:

1. Can you imagine God addressing a group of people and saying, "Okay, Jack, you go down to earth and live there for eighty years. Sadhana, you live for three months. After death, you come right back here to me and enjoy Heaven for eternity!" Jack must be wondering why he is being sent off to earth for eighty years. He sees that Sadhana is also being sent off, but she gets to live for only three months! How come Jack has to spend eighty years working hard to make a living, whereas Sadhana hardly spends any time at all? And then God says, "Make sure you don't do bad

things while you're down there, or else!" Poor Jack—
and only Jack, not Sadhana, as we shall see in a little
bit—might be sent to Hell! Life is scary!

2. Let us suppose a child dies at the tender age of three
months. Obviously this child goes straight to Heaven,
right? But what if she had lived, and as an adult had
committed a horrible mistake? Imagine that, driving
under the influence or mindlessly talking on her cell
phone, she causes a serious accident that causes the
deaths of several innocent people. She risks going to
Hell by living! Are these religions seriously saying
that it is better not to live? Better to die early and go
straight to Heaven? All children go to Heaven, don't
they? What is the point of life if all you are doing is
risking Hell? Is all of life meaningless?

Once when I posed this question, a member of
a religion that believes in Hell countered by saying,
"How do you know that a child will go straight to
Heaven?" It is amazing how much brainwashing a
religion can do: Here is person who would send an
innocent child to Hell! Here I am, a Hindu, hoping
that the child will find a place near God. Apparently,
I am wrong.

3. Think of two people born in totally different environ-
ments. One may have been, say, born a prince—with
the proverbial silver spoon in his mouth, taken care
of since childhood, and living the easy and casual life
as an adult. He thinks, "Should I go golfing or play
tennis? Should I take Kate to the party tonight, or
Anita? Decisions, decisions!" He participates in several projects for charity and lives a good, clean, and
comfortable life. He goes to Heaven, right?

The other person is not so lucky. He's born to Parents who neglect him. He loses them early in life and

is brought up by uncaring relatives. He runs away from home, lives on the streets, and turns into a hard, bitter person. He commits several crimes in his short life. So he gets Hell?

Pick up the newspaper or look on the Internet: we see these sad stories every day. Good people die in drug wars, and what happens to their kids? Some get sold into sex slavery. Or get chained to machines, made to work night and day!

The only people that some kids see are alcoholics or drug addicts with little or no education, or vicious gangs controlling their neighborhood. There is no one to show these kids love and affection. Gangs become their surrogate family. Do these kids deserve Hell? Isn't this concept wrong? The family environment that one is born into can dictate one's future—not in all cases, but in many. Some are born luckier than others. Should a person be punished for bad luck?

Even if God has mercy on the unlucky ones, does that make things equal? Why do the lucky ones get to live a rich and happy life while the unlucky ones have to endure a horrible life? Perhaps they both end up in the same place; but I am sure that if you were one of the unlucky ones, you would wonder why you had to endure such a terrible life.

Speaking for myself, I am a very lucky person. I count my blessings every day. My Parents were loving people. We were not rich; but believe me, no child cares about being rich—all he cares about is love and affection. However, as children grow to be adults, a good education is essential. I had that opportunity.

In contrast, I recall a servant girl back in India whom I knew. She was married at an early age and burdened with two kids and a husband who drank too much. Her life was not a bed of roses. But the worst misfortune was that her intelligence was wasted. A few times I was shocked to see how bright she was. She could quickly solve problems that stumped the rest of us. I have often wondered, what if we had switched places? What if she had been given my opportunities? Now she leads a hand-to-mouth existence while I live in relative comfort.

Consider a horrific chapter in America's history: the time of slavery. Human beings were treated like animals, flogged until blood ran like water off of their backs. They worked inhuman hours, were raped at will, and were bought and sold like common cattle. What happened to the owner who committed these horrible crimes? Is he in Heaven now because he begged for mercy?

How can such a situation be fair? Why does one person get to lead a life of comfort and happiness while another is forced to live in unimaginable pain (and then is sent to Hell for making a mistake)?

4. The average life expectancy of a person is, say, 70 or 80 years. Some religions tell us that the rest of eternity is spent in either Hell or Heaven. What is 80-odd years divided by eternity? A minuscule amount of time! It is an insult to common sense that such an infinitesimally small amount of time would make such a huge difference in the way a person will spend eternity. Based on such odds, would you even choose to be born?

5. Imagine that the very same people who tell you about Heaven go to the doctor and get bad news. You would think they'd be happy because they no longer have to live in a sinful world and work for a living. Finally, they have a chance to be with God and enjoy

the bounties of Heaven! But no—they want to stay! Why is there not even one person who is happy to die—even among those who expect to go to a wonderful place that awaits them? Could it be that when it actually comes to going to this wondrous place that they keep telling everyone about, they have doubts? They beg the doctor to help them stay here. They fight tooth and nail to stay! Why would they keep God and Heaven waiting? It doesn't make any sense.

Kicking and screaming! Grabbing the doctor fiercely, crying, begging, pleading, "Please doc, SAVE me!" They are asking the doctor to save them from God! From Heaven! From paradise! What?

People are ready to spend thousands of dollars in order to stay alive. They are ready to go into deep debt... for what? So that they can stay away from all that Heavenly glory? The so-called "eternal life" is calling and they don't want to answer! They do everything in their power to avoid "eternal life" and instead grasp desperately at this so-called "life of sin".

Hmmm, maybe living in sin is not so bad after all! LOL.

We are all born atheists. When we face death, we go back to being atheists, no longer wanting Heaven. It is only in between birth and death that we appear to be theists?

Every year, medical science makes more progress. People are healthier and are living longer thanks to modern medicine. One day we may conquer death! Imagine that!

Why aren't religious fundamentalists worried? Why aren't they putting a stop to medical progress? If we conquered death, the gateway to Heaven would be closed. The horror! God could finally retire—close the entrance to Heaven—because no more souls would be showing up. How come no one is protesting this vision of the future?

God, Heaven—oh how glorious! Want to go there? NO!

No?

The reality is that Heaven is just a fantasy.

That's why people are reluctant to die: They know that Heaven is just a pleasant dream, not to be taken seriously. It is nice to dream, but one can't live on dreams. When the moment comes to actually move on—when people are on their deathbed—they realize the Truth that was there all along: God is here! God is right here with us. Their consciences are speaking up: "Don't go! Do not leave God! Do not fall for the promises of charlatans!"

Then and only then, now that they see death arriving, they realize the true value of life. life is a great gift from God. Savor it and enjoy it. Make yourself useful; make your mark on the world. Let the world cry for you in your absence.

6. Someone once told me that his people do not fear death. But why would he need to say that? Why would you fear going to Heaven to be with God? Would anyone say, "I don't fear going to Hawaii," or, "I don't fear winning the lottery"? His statement seems to be ridiculous, unless you realize that in the end "his people" think of death like everyone else does: the end of everything, the end of life.

One thing we should realize is that to be with God is to be without fear. When we are with God there is no room for fear. Hinduism has never taught fear of

God and never will. When we are with God Rama, nothing can defeat us or harm us. So where is there room for fear?

If you live in fear, then you are not with God. You are experiencing something other than God. A true God does not use threats like a common despot—"Vote for me or I will break your legs!" That is not God.

I have thought of what I would do if a being showed up before me and said, "I am your God Rama. I have come down today to bring happiness to all Hindus and to kill and torture all non-Hindus." I would say, "Kill me first! You are not my God Rama. My God Rama is ever-loving and has room in his heart for all good souls."

7. People promise you that Heaven is a wonderful place, with no more pain or suffering. It is a joyful place full of wonder. It has nice weather and nice people, and everything is taken care of for you. Great! But does that mean we lose our memories? Don't we remember who we were on earth? Don't we remember our life and see the loved ones that we left behind? If so, what if we see terrible things happening to them, such a disease, job loss, or accidents? Can we ask God to intervene? If the ancestors of the Jewish people were living in Heaven when Hitler rose to power, why didn't they ask God to intervene? When mass starvation or terrible diseases struck the unfortunate—in the Ukraine under Stalin, for example, or in India under Churchill—why didn't their ancestors beg God to do something? Innocent people continue to die to this day—in terrorist attacks such as the ones on September 11, for example, or in massacres car-

ried out by drug lords in Mexico. Surely the ancestors of these victims prayed to God to intervene.

Did God refuse?

A God who is simply awaiting your death may not be totally invested in what is going on in this world.

Take another example: A person dies and leaves his family heartbroken and grieving. In the same accident that took his life, his young child was critically injured and is now fighting for her life in the hospital. Some religions tell us that this man is now with God, on his way to Heaven. Does he care how his child is doing, or is he too busy trying to get into Heaven? Let us assume that God grants his wish: now he gets to be happy, and no more rain will fall. Does that mean he forgets about his family? Does he forget his little child who is fighting for her life? What about his wife and other family members who are worrying about the child while at the same time grieving for him?

What if things get worse for this family? The child recovers, but because of the loss of income and the huge hospital bills, the family is forced out on to the streets, take shelter in a homeless shelter. The little children forced to go to bed, hungry, without food.

And this person in heaven is enjoying himself, eating cake? Enjoying a 7-course meal while his kids go hungry?

Does one stop caring in Heaven?

And what about the joys? A Parent who has died will miss the birthdays, the graduations, the weddings, and the births of grandchildren. She will be unable to share these joys with her loved ones. Heaven, then, is a terrible place to be.

The only answer is that one goes back in time and becomes a child once again. Heaven, then, is a metaphor for the womb, the past, a happy childhood. Heaven represents going backward and living in the past. Karma and Reincarnation represent going forward and building a great future!

Remember that little child who was forced to go to bed hungry? Who will take care of that little child? Who will feed her and comfort her?

You will! You will when you choose Reincarnation and come back in another life.

It is those who choose Karma and Reincarnation who will get to feed that hungry little child. They will be feeding God Herself! What an opportunity! It is much better than any silly Heaven.

8. Let us imagine that a person choking to death is saved by a good Samaritan. Another person is saved from death by a physician who diagnosed his condition in time. But aren't we using the wrong word here— *saved*? Saved from what—being with God? Enjoying all that Heavenly glory? In that case, the two people who were "saved" were prevented from having a happier existence! The people who saved them were not good Samaritans—they robbed the very people they saved. But the people they saved can't thank them enough! This story does not make sense.

I think most people, if given the choice, would prefer to live life's ups and downs united with their families instead of running away. Obviously, we would all like to be there for the joys, but I think most people would also choose to be there fighting alongside their families when life takes a turn for the worse.

Imagine this scenario: Your great-great-great-granddaughter is lying in her crib, asleep. A fire breaks out and threatens to engulf her! You are up in Heaven enjoying yourself—or worse yet, crying helplessly and wringing your hands in frustration!

And then, there is hope! You see a man climbing up to the window, risking his life to save your child! That man could be you. Instead it is the Hindu who has chosen to go back to earth!

This is precisely what Karma and Reincarnation promise: You will be with your loved ones instead of being far away. You will stand and work for a better life, make a difference, and take an active role instead of wringing your hands from afar.

In the Mahabharata, Arjuna was faced with this choice. (Let me caution you: These stories are allegorical, teaching us a moral.) Arjuna dies and meets his father Indra in Heaven. But he does not see any of his brothers, his wife, or his mother. He is surprised and asks about their whereabouts. Indra then takes him to Hell, where Arjuna—to his great consternation—hears the voices of his loved ones calling for him. Right then and there, Arjuna decides to stay in Hell—he is suffering, but he is with his loved ones. Of course, at the end of the story it becomes clear that all of this was a test, which Arjuna has passed with flying colors.

Will you pass the test? When you are asked to choose between enjoying Heaven and being with your loved ones down here on earth, what will be your choice?

A better definition of Heaven is finding a place in God's heart. However, one must be invited. One must walk right in or not go in at all! Either you go in standing tall, earning your way, or you don't go in at all!

The coward will always paint a rosy picture of taking the "back door". He says, "Let's regroup, get stronger, avoid unnecessary war, get more allies..." What he is really saying is, "Let's save our own hides first!"

A warrior nails that back door shut—no one will be able to

run away! No Hindu will run away! We stand tall alongside God and we will fight our way out through the front door.

There is a right way and a wrong way to do things. Ask yourself, is your religion teaching the right values, or is it telling you what you want to hear?

The Gift of Pain and Suffering

"They had their hearts ripped out. They should hurt. That'll make them better"—Kansas City Football Coach Andy Reid, after his team blew a 38-10 lead and lost to the Colts on Jan 4th, 2014.

"Bad things will happen, if not to humans, to rocks?" an Old Indian aphorism.

I am not saying pain is good but as you can see from the quote above, pain has its uses.

As you know by now I have been hammering the point that concepts like Heaven and Hell arose out of having to face a harsh, difficult life and most philosophers' ideas were shaped by the times they lived in, as will be ours. The Buddha's ideas too were shaped by the times that he lived in—he saw pain, suffering and hoped to find a way out of these difficult times. When it comes right down to it, a way out is not that difficult, a way out of pain and suffering is quite easy.

As the saying goes, "It is the nail that sticks out that gets hit"—well, getting hit is not pleasant, is it? So, here's the solution—don't stick out! Don't stand out of the crowd, don't speak up, don't dream, don't aspire, don't take chances or risks and you will have no pain or suffering—as you can see, this describes Heaven. Learn to be weak, helpless and then no one will call on you, no one will ask you to do anything, you will be free of all obligations and responsibilities—again, you realize that this describes Heaven perfectly.

Most of us have gone through school—some of us have

set high goals for ourselves—top marks or grades were our goal—but guess what happens when you set that high goal? Well, now you have to work for it, slave for it, worry constantly. I myself went through this—one year my marks did not meet the high standards that I set for myself—I remember sitting down and staring at the mark sheet, crying, hitting the bed that I was sitting on—but why? Why go through all that? You can stop all this pain and suffering in an instant! Just set your goals low—a pass grade is good enough, boom—all your troubles are over—now you are free to go out and enjoy yourself. Even better, drop out of school! Now, you have all the free time in the world to play, watch TV, enjoy yourself, at someone else's expense, of course! Just a moocher, living off his Parents and then society. Hmm, does that sound like Heaven? Carefree, enjoyable days spent while someone else picks up the tab?

In your adult life also you can do the same—stop dreaming of becoming something big—because with that dream will come pain and suffering—dreams have to be worked for, goals must be achieved! By simply being just a cog-in-the-wheel you are free from all pain and suffering—Heaven!

But we realize that it is the pain that propels us forward—it is the desire to excel, the desire to achieve our goals, our dreams that creates this pain. When we fail and yes it is needed, it is the GOOD PAIN! This was what the Buddha missed, but then his world was much different then.

Are you a Parent of young kids? Happy? You get to enjoy the joys of being a Parent—kids are so precious, aren't they? But you also worry, don't you? Worry about your little kids getting sick, evil men, something bad happening to them? Yes sir, THIS is life! With the joys come pain and suffering—in real life you get both, only death or fantasy lands can promise to give you just the one.

Some guys harassing a young girl? Look away, pretend

you didn't see it—no worries! You read or watch a disturbing event in your neighborhood or country? Quick—turn the paper or change the channel—just tell yourself it is none of your business—turn to something that makes you laugh— enjoy! Heaven!

Most of us have lost someone near and dear, maybe to a disease and some people are doing something about it— either researching, funding or raising funds for a cure— using the pain to do something good—we ALL should have such pain in our lives, then we can work to make the world a better place.

Whether you read or watch on TV about people or animals in suffering, in pain, needing help, let that be your fuel to go out and do something. *Those who don't feel empathy do nothing and that is basically what the seekers of Heaven are doing. Those who do, choose Reincarnation.* But the key here is that we need to stop seeing ourselves as weak, the damsel in distress waiting for the knight in shining armor (God) to come save the day. We must realize that those were the days of the past; *the future will belong to the strong, one who hopes not for God's shelter, but one who thirsts for greatness, for God's praise as her child!*

It is pain that propels us to great heights—losing MUST hurt, if it does not, you will remain a loser for life. There are many who will see poverty, discrimination, rape, suffering, evil and look the other way and walk away, they feel no pain, there is no empathy—choose Heaven and you choose to be that way for eternity. And so Heaven is the ultimate cop-out, the give-up—no more pain or suffering, but no life either.

And then there are the Schindlers, the Gandhijis—those who willingly walk through fire so that the pain of others is lessened—Reincarnation is for such people.

What the Buddha did not realize was that life comes

pre-packaged with pain and suffering, it's a package deal, trying to find a way out of pain and suffering means a negation of life, moving away from having a life. When babies first come out of their mothers' wombs they start crying—they were in a nice warm place of comfort and now they have been brutally yanked out into a cold, hard world—but the cold hard world is what we call life. You can escape pain and suffering while in a coma but no one would want that. You can escape pain and suffering, responsibilities, worries by simply staying put on your couch and never moving—again, you then choose to not have a life.

You see this in sports all the time, in the big game, the team that sees the game as an opportunity to win, to make a name for themselves, always wins! For too long life has been looked down upon as a sin, something that we are forced to do, get it over with and then get to the easy city! I ask for a paradigm change, see life as an opportunity, an opportunity to be great, to be God!

In the animal world we see elephants caring for their young, grieving over their dead family members, but other animals don't seem to display these emotions. A deer doesn't fuss over her young that much and will move on quickly if her young get killed by a predator. It's not that the deer is born heartless but it cannot afford to love; elephants have few predators, they can afford to love, whereas the vast majority of deer young fall prey to predators. The deer would die of heartbreak if it behaved like an elephant or a human. And as we go down the chain to bugs and smaller creatures, these animals act more like computers or zombies, love and affection never enter the equation. Plants and trees don't get to have families, loved ones—there's plenty of free food, no need to work, no worries, but would anyone of us trade our lives for the life of a tree? Mother tortoises lay their eggs in the sand near the beach and then leave—their

Parental obligations end right there! Baby tortoises never get to see their Parents or play with their siblings. Most animals live a lonely life, the smaller you get, the easier the life, all the pleasures of the flesh available easily but not much else. And for us humans it is the reverse, and that is why we need to be careful with our choices, what we ask God for. Human life is special, priceless—we have been given this gift to give love and affection and pain and suffering is the other side of the coin of this love and affection—one can't have one without the other.

Also in the animal world, no mother dog is going to ask its young pup what he wants to become once an adult—there are no such dreams for the millions of life forms on earth—except for one—US! *We get to dream, but this was not always so—go back a few thousand years, simply making a living was harsh and difficult enough, people didn't live very long—back in those days kids were not asked what they wanted to be when they grew up. And it is in this context we need to understand the religions that were born in those times—a life of ease, with no work to do, endless days of doing nothing, no worries—sounded wonderful to people of those days.*

We need to realize that the context has changed—now our kids get to dream, to aspire and that is the idea of Moksha—to be God, to reach for the stars and when we do that we have fully separated ourselves from the other life forms on this planet. But once we dream, we also let in pain, first just a thought then a reality. Think of your first crush, was it reciprocated? Maybe, probably not and the thrill of liking someone, the happiness, joy is replaced with disappointment, pain.

If Reincarnation applies to everyone regardless of religion, I see those who seek heaven being reborn as bugs—say the common dust mite that lives in your bed and carpet—happily munching away on your dead skin cells, no concerns or worries, no feelings, no ambition, goals, desires nor any passions—it is born without the brain for these things. All the pleasures of the flesh, but not much else.

As I keep saying human life is a gift, a gift from God that we get to savor over and over again, a gift that comes with feelings, passions and desires—all that are denied to the lower forms of life.

Most Hindus are familiar with the teaching of a steady progression of rebirths—being born as a bug and slowly moving up the chain and finally reaching the top—being born as a human. What people do not realize is that the pain quotient also steadily goes up. Let us discuss this.

Let us classify pain into two types—mental and physical—well, to be accurate all pain is mental but humor me about this—when we stub our toe or hit our head against a hard object let us classify that as physical pain. The loss of a loved one then is mental pain. So, we humans endure pain in two different ways.

Let us go down a bit—to the animal level—we certainly know that they feel physical pain—if we are talking evolution—pain was developed so that if we fell asleep and an animal started gnawing at our leg or arm, we would feel the pain and run away or fight. But do animals feel mental pain? I think they can but they simply cannot afford to—as we discussed a deer would die of heartbreak if it felt the same way as a human mother would about its babies—imagine your young baby being ripped apart right in front of your eyes by hungry lions. For most animals life is so harsh that they can't allow too many feelings of love for their young. Let us now go lower—down to the bug level—say the ordinary dust mite that lives in your carpet and bed. Does it feel mental pain? Obviously not. How about physical pain? The bug is so small that it cannot even run away from anything—so to develop physical pain would not make evolutionary sense.

This is what the ancient Hindus were trying to tell us—we

humans are at the highest level—the highest pain level, that is. Go down a few notches to an animal level, they mainly deal with physical, a little mental (elephants may be the exception, amongst others). Go down even further, to the microscopic animal level and pain completely disappears.

And so the smaller you get, the less physical or mental pain. Imagine! No more pain or suffering! Wait! Where have we ended up? In Heaven! Did we not? Isn't that what most religions promise us? Heaven—a place where there will be no more pain or suffering?

Beware what you wish for—some wishes might just come true!

That is why I urge people not to give up on human life, realize that this human life is a gift from God, savor it, enjoy it, make proper use of it, make God proud and please ask for second helpings—God is more than ready to oblige. Run away from pain, run away from human life, all you get is the bug's life. What a waste—a child of God trading away this gift for the life of a common bug!

Maybe this is what some Hindus say when they talk about spending just a little time in Heaven (not this author)—maybe they come back as a bug, spend some time without any pain or suffering and die a quick death.

The ideas are not very complicated, they are quite simple—those who choose Heaven are saying no to life, no more pain or suffering, but no more dreams, goals, aspirations, achievements either.

And another thing—no more struggling with morals, ethics or principles either—in Heaven no such situations will arise where you will have to struggle with your conscience. You are set for eternity living in a coma.

More than one person from these religions has stated to me that good works won't get one into heaven, only if you believe in X God, well, that makes sense because what these people want is not life, where good works matter, morals ethics matter, all they want is a life of ease, a life with no responsibilities, no pressures, no demands, just an idyllic, retired life is what they want and well, no need to struggle with morals or ethics for a bug, is there?

When you as an adult first step out into the world as an adult, leave your home, we realize that, for the first time, your Parents won't be there to keep you safe, in comfort, protected from pain and suffering? So then, why do we do that? Why not stay home and stay in that bubble as a child? Never growing up? That is what again the concept of Heaven is all about—being a child for eternity, never growing up, stay in a bubble, protected world of the womb, the egg.

When the chick is in the egg, it is in a safe, comfortable environment, with food nearby. But at some point, the chick has to come out and face pain and suffering, begin life!

Heaven is a dull, dead-end, endless existence.

We too step out because we want to begin life! The idea of Reincarnation is just that—be bold, be the adult, you can dream now, aspire, get ready to taste life in all its flavors—some sweet, some bitter. We realize that sweet won't taste as good without the bitter—the bitter s part of life as is pain, as is suffering.

Fight (Reincarnation) not flight (heaven)

The ideas of the past—run away from pain and suffering! The religions of the day created sugar daddy gods who will give us refuge, keep us away from pain and suffering.

The idea of today—let us stand our ground, face our problems, fight! Let us defeat and overcome pain and suffering! So, here's the conundrum—the closer you get to God, pain and suffering will only increase! The farther away you get from God, the less of these pains and sufferings!

Our goal is to minimize that pain and suffering, not run away to fantasy Heavens. We do that in two ways, the

Buddha taught one way, the other is obvious—get involved, if you see pain and suffering, do your best to fight it. Raise funds for diseases, fight discrimination, poverty, injustice, help those in need, pay your taxes, do not cheat your customers nor your employer.

Pain and suffering are what makes us human, let's remember that. Just as good and evil are two sides of the same coin, pain, suffering and joy, happiness are also two sides of the same coin. If there is joy on one side, pain is on the other, and happiness is on one side, suffering is on the other. One can't have one without the other.

6. Karma and Reincarnation Mean that Hindus Earn Praise *from* God! Make God Proud!

Anyone can sit and praise God, but blessed are the Hindus who aim to earn praise from God!

You have a choice to make: You can sit in a temple, church, mosque, or any other place of worship and sing God's praises, or you can go out and help others less fortunate than you are. You can give your time, your money, and yourself for a cause that you hold dear in order to make a difference in your community. By your conduct, you influence the society around you.

Here's a question to ask yourself: of the two choices above, which one do you think would earn you praise *from God?* Clearly, the latter.

This is the thing that frustrates me: So many books talk about how to please God, how to pray to God, how much He loves you, etc. All of them end in the same manner: you will be rewarded—Heaven or some other wonderful place is waiting, offering joy and peace forever and ever.

This mentality comes from the mind of a servant, down on his knees and hoping for a reward from his master. But that is the sad part: We are NOT born servants. We are the CHILDREN of God! We are the students of God! Our place is higher, and our thoughts must be higher. We MUST have higher goals.

Stop looking for a handout from God. Instead, ask yourself, how can I make God proud of me? Have you not asked yourself the same question when it comes to your Parents and Teachers? This is the higher goal, the noble goal!

It is a million times harder to earn praise from God than to praise God. Any fool can sit and sing praises, but it takes someone special to reach for the stars. The one who reaches for the stars is the child of God!

Many religions promise a Heaven where you sit idle for eternity. How do you propose to make God proud of you when you choose to do that? You cannot. Choosing to sit in Heaven is like choosing to be a coward who hides under the bed. How can God be proud of such a person?

It is amazing to see the number of intelligent, highly educated people who fall for this idea of a pot of gold at the end of the rainbow. If you don't see the pot of gold, supposedly it is because you don't believe! If you believe, all that gold will be yours. And those who don't believe? They must be made to suffer!

Let me see if I get this God idea right—so a super being created this huge universe with billions of stars and life forms including ourselves. He watches over us and looks to see if we are praying to him and more important, did we get his name right? And those who got it wrong will be tortured forever and those who did will be rewarded? Is that it? Seriously? In the 21st century? Pedophiles and mass murderers of the religion have a better chance of being rewarded than soldiers who died fighting for their country? Where is the moral compass?

We can do better than that. Let's start acting like the adults that we are. Let's be strong and show our character—let's show God how strong we are and make Her proud of us.

This is why bigotry and hatred against atheists makes no sense. All God cares about is your character. It is not how much time you spend in a given house of worship or how much time you spend thinking of God. The key is, will people miss you when you are gone? Beyond your immediate family, do strangers think well of you?

Would you rather sit in a temple or go out into the world and help? Most people would rather stick to the former. It is easier to do, and it is more enjoyable as well. You can sit in a cozy place and take in the sights and sounds of the worshippers. The temple calms you and fills you with good feelings. For many people, a visit to the temple is a happy experience; in fact, for people my age, it can mean a significant drop in blood pressure. However, those good feelings are often directed only toward God, not toward other human beings. Many people's feelings are as nasty as ever when it comes to other human beings.

Contrast that with helping others. You visit a rundown area—a dirty, smelly neighborhood—and make a concerted effort to help some of the people, even if they resent your help. You might not come away feeling exhilarated, but God is with you. God is not in a place of worship; God is with those who are helping others.

Let me be clear—God is not with the former, but with the latter. God is not in a place of worship (let's stop calling singing praises as worship, let's call it what it is, heaping praises on a benefactor hoping for a reward), God is with those who are helping others.

Sometimes the price of helping others is even higher. Recently a newspaper reporter who was writing about the connection between Pakistan's Intelligence Agency and terrorism paid for his actions with his life.

In Egypt, millions of young people took to the streets and forced a brutal dictator out of power. But victory had its cost: many young people died for the cause.

Hitler did not willingly kill himself. Diseases that once

ravaged the earth have been eradicated. Mass starvation has been eradicated (although millions of people still go to bed hungry today). Many natural disasters have struck the earth over the years, killing millions and displacing millions more. But people have always bounced back.

Each time something bad has happened, good people have stood up. They have led the way. They have taken on burdens beyond the call of duty. They have worked and sacrificed, and because of their leadership, others have been inspired to pull through. They have defeated the evils that faced them.

The world is a safer, better place today because of the sacrifices that good people have made. But are we finished? Have all the problems facing humankind been eradicated? Certainly not. It is exactly at this point where Hinduism, with its teaching of Karma and Reincarnation, diverges from most religions. In most religious thought, the end of life is the end of your struggle to make a difference. *But Hinduism invites you to stay and carry on.* Hinduism invites you to earn praise from God. Einstein earned it. Gandhiji earned it. Martin Luther King, Jr. earned it, and Oskar Schindler earned it as well. And so did scores of other good people—the religious as well as the non-religious.

To make a king or a boss happy is easy: You get down on your knees, praise him sky-high, and get ready to say, "Yes sir, you are absolutely right, sir!" If he says the sky is green, you say he is absolutely right. Is this what God wants—a brainless servant? Have religions brainwashed us into believing that *this* is what God wants?

Now imagine what it would take to make your Parents or your Teachers proud of you—to make them say, "That's my boy!" or "That's my girl!" You can make them proud by doing something extraordinary, something great. That is the quest for Moksha.

Imagine that a war has been declared. You have the option to run away. The back door is wide open. Would you run out, or would you put on your armor, take your weapon, and go to the front lines? Would you risk injury and death? Who would do that?

There is much to do here on earth. God's work is incomplete. God will put us to work, and we will work alongside God. It is not going to be easy, but earning praise *from* God has never been easy.

You can both praise God and, at the same time, earn praise from Her! What could be better? A person who walks in the footsteps of Gandhiji or Rama, devoting his life to making a difference for the betterment of this world—who always strives to do the right thing, tell the Truth, be kind and compassionate, and practice ahimsa—is the true devotee of God. He is the one who is praising God and at the same time being praised by God.

Think of God as a Teacher rather than a king. How do you praise your Teacher and at the same time make her proud of you? By becoming a person of good character.

The day we associate God with the fulfillment of our ideals is the day we earn praise from God. When we idealize God as a being who will magically make us happy, we reduce ourselves to idolatry.

The key word is **EARN**. You must earn God's praise. You cannot just ask for it; it is always earned. The place in God's lap is reserved for those who are willing to earn it.

It is easy to quit, ruin your health, or drop out of school. It is easy to tear things down and run away. It is much harder to stick with something—to exercise, eat right, stay in school, build things, stand your ground, and face your problems.

Something that is given for free is always worthless. When you see a box labeled "FREE" at a yard sale, don't expect to find anything of worth in that box. It is just junk.

Being with God is not easy. When religions tell you that there is an easy way to God, they are lying. They are leading you on the wrong path. Adults tell kids that there is no Santa, but they themselves are quite happy to believe in one!

The price of greatness is high. The price of making God beam with pride is higher still!

Consider the wonderful story of the Hindu king Harischandra. King Harischandra vowed to tell the Truth always, and never to refuse anyone anything as long as it was within his power. God wished to test him, so She sent a sage to see if he could break the king. When trouble struck, would the king abandon his cherished principles and values—in other words, would he abandon God?

The good king proved that he was up to the task. First the sage asked the king for his kingdom. The king willingly gave up his kingdom and, taking only the clothes on his back, walked out with his wife and young child.

However, the old sage was not yet done testing Harischandra. He insisted on a monetary payment. But the king had nothing left, so he sold his wife and young son into bondage so that he could raise some money (an idea which his own wife suggested). The king was not alone in his strength and devotion to God: his principles were matched by those of his wife.

Later, after enduring more hardships, the king took a job in a cremation ground burning dead bodies. Even in such sadness and personal misfortune, the king did not forget his duties. He stayed true to God. It was then that God realized that this man would not break, that he would stay true till the end.

Praise God? That's easy; anyone can do it. Earn praise *from* God? Now that takes some daring. It will be the toughest test you have ever taken in your life.

During the recent tsunami in Japan, some nuclear facilities were damaged, which threatened the lives of millions. Engineers went to the facilities, at great risk to themselves, and put out the fires to stop the disaster. Some retired engineers volunteered—yes, *volunteered*—to go. They were willing to risk dying in excruciating pain if it meant saving the lives of millions of their fellow citizens.

These engineers were with God. If you weren't like them, your natural reaction would be to flee for safety. You would be abandoning God!

Hang on to your principles—your ethics, your values. You are with God. Be honest, be Truthful, be compassionate, and do good. Reach for the stars, as great people have done. You are with God. But it is not possible to be great in Heaven—only here on this earth, this blessed earth!

Do not confuse eternal death with eternal life. Do not confuse time spent in a coma with time spent living. Eternal life is for those who reach for the stars. It requires tremendous sacrifices to be called great; but along the way, you meet up with God.

Would you choose to sit and praise God or earn praise from God?

Atheism and Hinduism

"A good atheist is closer to God Rama than even a good Hindu," so says this Hindu.

Hinduism is known as a very tolerant faith, so it is no surprise that Hindus condemn neither atheism nor atheists.

An atheist is a person who does not believe in God. I say, so what? Why does one need to believe in a supreme being? The Hindu God is not an insecure person. She does not have an ego. She is not a king who demands loyalty, or a despot who says, "Vote for me or else!"

What is most important to God is your character. What

are your values in life? Have you always tried to tell the Truth and walk the right path? Have you helped people and animals along the way? Then you are with God! You are with God when you tell the Truth. You are with God when you do the right thing. You are with God when you make a difference—when you help make your community, society, and country better.

The diatribe against atheists and atheism is being led by certain religions. Atheists and atheism are a threat to their power and wealth. They want you to depend on them—to believe that the road to God goes only through them. Confess to the priest and get saved from Hell? Such arrogance!

God is not interested in high praises. She knows there is selfishness behind them. God is not interested in promises of loyalty or in people who kowtow like servants.

What does it take to be called a theist, anyway? You simply join a religion, read the scripture, and believe in a supreme being. It is easy to do. With a little cheap talk, you are a theist!

The real question is: are you with God? Mass murderers and pedophiles have called themselves theists, but they are not with God.

Being with God depends on action. It depends on your character and your conduct. Let your conduct speak for you. If you regain the trusting, innocent heart that you used to have as a child, you are with God.

One story that comes out of the Mahabharata involves the Bheeshma, the venerable elder of the Pandavas. God challenges Bheeshma to a battle and is unable to defeat him. It is not that God cannot defeat a puny human. There is moral here: If you side with Truth and with God, you can't be beaten. How could God defeat Herself? Bheeshma had Truth on his side, so he couldn't be beaten.

An atheist who makes this world better is always with

God. There is no need to pray or go to a place of worship to sing God's praises. So often we are caught up with the nice things that God can do for us. We mistakenly think that going to a temple and praising God, or offering puja, is showing our devotion. Nothing could be further from the Truth.

Stop looking to God as some kind of a Santa or sugar daddy who will shower you with goodies. The atheist doesn't do that. He does good because he wants to—he is not expecting any reward. A theist, whatever his intentions are, may be harboring a hope (deep within his heart) of being rewarded by God for being good. Because the atheist is not doing that, in my opinion he is dearer to God. He is closer to God!

All good souls are dear to God Sri Rama. It doesn't matter if you believe or not. Character matters, not religion.

I find it funny that religions mock atheists—there are no atheists in fox holes—they say. Well, I say—

There are no theists when death comes calling.

We have seen the example of the guy who talks glowingly about Heaven, but when the doctor gives him bad news, he no longer wants to go! An amazing U-turn takes place: "Okay, let's keep God waiting for now," the guy says. All that Heavenly glory, that so-called eternal life, can wait. *Some people say that death is like a door: open that door and you will find God and Heaven. However, these same people would love to see that door nailed shut!*

Most religions agree that little children are with God. But what does a child know about God or religion? Parents make her put her hands together and point her toward an image or an altar. Does the child understand what she is doing? No. Parents make that little child sing a prayer. Does she understand the words? Not at all.

So we can say that a child is like an atheist. We are all born atheists! Unless and until our Parents turn us toward a chosen religion, we remain atheists. So how can an atheist child be considered close to God? Because the child has a pure heart, with malice toward none! When people talk about an evil man they say that he has no soul, which means that God has been driven out of his heart because of his evil deeds. God resides in the hearts of children. God resides within those who have pure hearts and minds.

Let us change the paradigm:

An atheist is anyone who takes the evil path, one who drops morals, values and principles in his greed for the easy life.

A theist is anyone who walks the path of Truth, one who sticks to his principles and values, one who works to create a better world.

Let us finally define people by their character, conduct and not by what or which religion they choose to affiliate themselves with.

7. Karma and Rebirth Mean that I Am an *Adult*. I Am Not a Child, I Stand on My Own Two Feet

"There's a boo-boo inside you. This nice doctor will help us make it go away." The nice doctor might start with a treat, making the child happy and forget her ailment for a while. It will be up to the Parent to lie awake at night worrying about the boo-boo. Few want this job.

Everyone wants to be a kid. A child has no worries—everything is taken care of for her. She can go out and play all day! She doesn't have to worry about unemployment, global warming, politics, racism, sexism, poverty, hunger, nuclear meltdowns, or terrorist threats. She is not responsible for the health and well-being of her kids or her aging Parents. An adult has to think about all of those things. Who would want to be an adult?

Heaven says you can be that child; Reincarnation says choose to be that adult.

As a Hindu, you step up to the challenge. You choose to be the adult.

Before crossing a street with a child, a Parent instinctively reaches for the child's hand and the child eagerly takes it. An older child does not reach for his Parent's hand, and the Parent does not offer it. Which one are you? A little child in need of constant care or are you a growing person who can take care of himself?

Once children become adults and move out of the house, they rarely go back to live with their Parents. So why would they want to go sit in Heaven and be dependent on God? It is the aging Parents who need to be taken care of by their adult children.

Heaven represents going back to a time when things were wonderful. Who among us does not reminisce about the "good old days"? (Well, some people will tell you that the good old days were really not that good. However, if we were children at that time, of course they were the good old days!)

When we are in our 50s and beyond, we do tend to look at our childhood with rose-colored glasses; and we wouldn't be far off the mark. Everything was done for us, and we didn't have a care in the world! What a wonderful time!

Heaven represents the womb, the past—our care-free childhood days.

In childhood you were sheltered, kept away from bad news, away from harm, protected, coddled, fed and housed, nurtured, no worries, happy, played all day, you lived in a bubble. And in Heaven you will be sheltered, kept away from bad news, away from harm, protected, coddled, fed and housed, nurtured, happy, enjoy all day, kept in a bubble.

Is ignorance really bliss? You choose ignorance and weakness, so that no one will call on you for anything. If you choose to be an adult, you will be called on when the going gets rough.

Yes, in Heaven no one will call on you for anything.

However, we know that as adults we can't just keep going back. It was fun to be children, but perhaps not so fun for our Parents and other adults. Now that we are adults, we have kids. But at some point we want them to grow up too, right? We don't want them to remain kids forever. We don't want them to remain dependent on us as adults.

What would we call a person who is totally dependent on

her Parents even after childhood? An adult child? A loser? Would Parents be proud of such a child, or ashamed?

When someone dies and children ask what happened, we tell them that grandma is in a better place, that She is with God. However, when older children ask, we tell them the harsh Truth. Why the difference? Because the young child is not yet strong enough to handle the Truths of life. We let her live in a bubble, in a protected space. With an older child, the Truth must be told. She needs to grow up, face life, and learn to deal with its ups and downs.

Heaven is that bubble, that shield from the harshness of real life. To know difficult Truths—to be an adult—is to invite pain and suffering into our lives.

Let us consider the story of the Buddha: his father did everything in his power to shield him from the pain of life. The Buddha lived in a bubble, in Heaven, protected from real life. He started on his journey toward enlightenment when he opened his eyes to the pain and suffering of this world.

Are you the little child who needs to be protected from the harshness of life? Is perpetual childhood your goal? Is that what you see stretching before you for eternity?

So here comes big bad Reincarnation asking you to grow up. For a brief while we are children, but then life comes at us too fast. We grow up, and for the rest of our lives we are forced to earn a living, to sink or swim.

Think about it—does God really need another freeloader? Is a Parent happy when a penniless adult son or daughter comes back to live with him? That situation by itself is not wrong. In many traditional societies, adult children do stay with their Parents; but they contribute to the household. They do not live off of their Parents. Would you force God to cater to your needs as if you were a child? Would you go back to the womb?

Why would anyone choose to vegetate in a corner of Heaven, even if Heaven existed? When the things that we desire so desperately come true, we may not like the results. Be careful what you wish for. Is a dead-end retired existence what you really want? You will no longer be needed or wanted.

If you tell your kid about Santa and she does not believe you, will you torture her for eternity? On the flip side, if your kid believes in Santa, do you want her to continue believing even as an adult? It seems that millions of people believe in a Santa-like God; and if don't believe in their fantasies, you must suffer it!

Running away from adulthood, belief in magic, miracles—oh my! These things indicate that you are still a child, a weak person. Children believe in magic because they have not yet grasped the concept of working and making a living. They see their father and mother going off to work, but they are not exactly sure what work is or how it translates to the money that pays for things.

Ask a child how a car is able to move or your TV can bring him games and he will obviously say the genie does it. There is a hidden genie or magic man inside your car or TV that is making them do these things.

Are our ideas about Heaven and God stuck at the child level?

When I see adults talking about magic, miracles, and prophecies, I feel sad for them. They are adults according to their age; but according to their beliefs, they are still little children in need of care and comfort.

The TV watchers in the US can easily understand this question: Samantha the Witch or Archie Bunker? Basically do you want to solve life's problems with a twitch of a nose or struggle with real life as was portrayed in the sitcom "All in the Family"?

Robert Sopolsky in his book—The Trouble with Testosterone—quotes Lawrence Kohlberg, a psychologist, as saying that a child thinks of good and bad in terms of punishment and reward. Only as an adult will he understand the effects on others, the victim then comes into the picture. Goes to show that the dominant religions of today preach ideas fit for children, not adults.

Life as an adult means that we don't have the choice to live in a cocoon and avoid the problems of the world. We can try, but I don't think many of us will succeed. Yes, becoming an adult is scary: We spend so many years being taken care of, and suddenly that safety net is gone! We are on our own. It is very tempting to run back, isn't it? That is the concept of Heaven. It is a metaphor for childhood.

Going back to childhood means no more decisions to make, no more worlds to conquer, no more mountains to climb, no more work, no more achievements. It means *no more life!*

It is here on earth, with God, that one reaches for greatness. It is here on earth that one can become a Mozart or a Michelangelo. It is here that one can dream of singing like Subbulakshmi or writing poetry like Tyagaraja. It is here that heroes are found. Here on earth is where the next great person will be born—the next Einstein, or the next Buddha!

You could be the next great one! Reach down and touch the hand of God!

That could be YOU! Yes, YOU! The great one!

To be with God means to reach for greatness! Yes, reach down and touch the hand of God!

It is here that one can create great music, write great books, inspire people, accomplish great things—it is all here down on earth.

What awaits you in heaven but death?

Decide who you want to be: an adult, a grown-up person, or a child?

There is nothing wrong with turning to God for help, but what kind of help? A child will one day say to his Parents, "No! Let me do it." That child is on his way to becoming an adult.

Say no to a welfare Heaven. Say yes to an adult earth!

As an adult, we have to deal with personal problems: earning a living, paying rent, buying groceries, cooking, living and dying with our favorite sports teams, falling in love, getting rejected sometimes, dealing with heartbreaks, going to school at night while working during the day, health problems, accidents, troubles that strike our loved ones—the list is endless.

Everything falls on our shoulders. Once we have become an adult, one of the very first decisions we make is to decide on our academic major, what we want to be when we grow up. No one can tell us. We must make the decision. To some, it is thrilling; to others, it is frightening.

That's the problem with being an adult: there are no guarantees. As a child there is comfort, there are guarantees; mom and dad are always there. As an adult there's only you; it's time to cut the apron strings.

It takes an adult to deal with all the problems that the world will throw at us. Most of us are so consumed by our personal problems, we have little time to spare to deal with the problems of the world.

But some great souls have stepped forward. They have decided to walk with God! Gandhiji takes on an empire! A young man stands firm in front of a lumbering tank that could have crushed him like a fly; and yes, it did happen to a brave young American woman in Israel! Brave policemen stand up to drug dealers and gangs. A young man sits in jail unwilling to pay a bribe that would set him free. A young woman leaves her home and country, travels to a strange land to help the poor and unfortunate. Firefighters the world over rush into burning buildings and pay for it with their lives. So many do-gooders throw themselves into troubled waters to save the lives of total strangers, unfortunately accomplishing the task at the cost of their own lives. So many stories of heroism to tell.

And it is because of such brave souls this earth stands on its axis, our society flourishes, and the rest of us are lucky and lead a good life.

Movies for children are full of fantasy, magic, miracles, genies and prophecies. Adult movies are different. They are about real life, real-life problems being faced by adults who deal with them in an adult manner. No miracles, no magic, just plain hard work and plenty of sacrifices. Well, at least until recently that is; nowadays it seems most blockbusters are fantasy movies with one caped crusader after another coming to save the day with his magic pixie dust. Over in India, movies have gotten a hard edge to them. Movies of a while ago, while not fantasy movies, were more light-hearted in nature with little realism to speak of. But today's movies are much more realistic, dealing with real-life problems a lot more often. Are movies foretelling a weaker America and a stronger Asia? Only time will tell.

It may be foolish to link movies and the fate of a nation, but it is disturbing to see the plethora of fantasy-based movies coming out nowadays.

All nations, at one time or another, have faced tough, difficult times. In those days, visionary men and women were faced with tough choices. They prayed, yes, to keep the weak and cowardly happy and content, but they knew that what lay before them were tough choices and a lot of hard work to make those choices pay off.

We have had two world wars, the world was almost at the brink of an all-out nuclear war, several nations' economies are falling apart; but just as our forefathers did, we need to buckle up, make the tough decisions and follow through with them. There's no need to pray for a magic man to come through with his miracles.

Hindus are children of God like everyone else. We are all children of God. But Hindus are a bit different: we are the ones choosing to grow up, stand on our own two feet, take responsibility for our lives, our actions, our societies, our countries, our planet. When bad things happen, we are the ones looking within, not for some magic man to come to save us.

Call us the adult children of God, ready to take on responsibilities, ready to share the burdens of God, not willing to quit, to run back to the safety of mommy's skirts, ready to take on what life on this earth will throw at us and emerge victorious!

It is here that Hinduism reveals itself as a faith for adults. For a Hindu may not pray to God to come to save him from his troubles. A Hindu may only pray to God for inner strength and guidance, to ask God to give him strength to get through these troubled times, to ask God for guidance, ask God for advice on how to face his troubles and defeat them—for face them he must and face them he will.

The coward closes his eyes tight and asks for a miracle; then he hopes that when he opens his eyes again, the trouble will be gone! God will make magic, God will make a miracle and make his troubles go away!

You find these people gathering, talking about the miracle men of their chosen religion. "This guy did this or that, he made magic, he cured the ill, he did wonderful things, and the people watching it were amazed!" The people lapped it up, they loved it! Why? The crucial thing to note is the lack of any hard work, the lack of uncertainty, the lack of having to make sacrifices, having to sweat, having to stand up to problems, the lack of having to make tough decisions.

The total lack of guts.

Such tales the weak and the cowardly tell each other!

One of the things that most people wonder about is why God does not come to help when we need Her? Terrible things keep happening all over the world. Where, oh where is this loving God? Why does She not help us?

Again we must decide whether we are adults or whether we remain children. Do we need our mommy and daddy to rush to our aid, or can we handle things? It is clear that God regards us as adults. We are strong. If there is a problem, we must handle it: this is Hinduism at its finest! Stop looking for the knight in shining armor, the savior to come and save the day. We are strong. We are adults. This is our moment.

Let us choose to stay and work for a better future, create a better future with our bare hands. Let us not shame God by running away. It is here that I ask you to make your choice. Choose Heaven and you choose to remain a child forever, to live in a bubble, shielded, with bad news sugar coated. (This is the best-case scenario; the worst-case is death, eternal death.)

Here again you get to make a choice—a child, a dependant forever or an adult, one that will make God proud?

Choose Karma and Reincarnation and you choose to be the adult—the one that God can count on, the one that will lead humanity into a great future.

Hindu Pride—Karma (Action, Work)

It is appalling to me to hear some religions preach that works don't matter, what you do in life does not matter, all that matters is what religion you belong to. Even more disappointing is that millions of highly educated people believe that these words are true! Yet these very same people would be offended if they were discriminated on the basis of religion! Movies have been made about how offensive it is to judge people because of their religion—in one movie, a highly-educated Muslim man is targeted because of his religion. In Egypt Coptic Christians attacked because of their religion, Muslims in Myanmar! All wrong? Yes of course! But the very same people have no problem happily praising a being who would set people apart for their religious affiliation or lack of it and torture them for it?

Does religion kill brain cells? And morals too, apparently.

Religion is an affiliation, not a qualification. Hinduism teaches us that what is not important is which religion we belong to, what name to call God, what scripture we read— what is important is what we have done with our lives. Have we walked with God Rama? Have we applied ourselves to Truth? Have we made a difference in the lives of others around us? Have we made our family, our Parents, our Teachers, our country proud? Have we made God proud?

This is my pride, my Hindu pride—I am so proud to call myself Hindu, a faith that tells me that my God will assess me based on what I have done with my life, will not judge me but will accept me for who I am. My life matters, what I do in life matters. If you want to call yourself a Hindu, please realize that you will be defined by your conduct, your character, that there is no easy back door way to the good, easy life. Earning praise from God will not be easy nor should we expect it to be. Most people seem to seek the easy life and there are plenty of religions happy to promise them that, not Hinduism. You will be held to a higher standard, much more will be expected of you.

God deserves better. Will you measure up?

8. Karma and Reincarnation Mean Making Amends Is the Right Thing to Do

Confession is good. Making amends, atoning for our mistakes, is better and the right thing to do.

Repayment is better than repentance.

A simple scenario: You owe a huge debt. Here are your options: 1) Ask for forgiveness from the debt (Heaven), or 2) Pay it back, no matter how long it takes (Karma and Reincarnation). Which is your choice?

Doing the right thing is one of the hardest things to do. Many of us fall far short. In many religions God becomes something like an enabler, the one who will take care of our problems and then off we go to that nice Heaven awaiting us. God will take care of our troubles. Let Him deal with the problems. We get to enjoy.

Hinduism begs to differ—God is our moral guide. Nothing more, nothing less. Do the right thing, She implores. Almost all Hindus know the story: you leave debts on earth after you die, you must come back to repay! We all do. These debts are not just monetary. Some are psychological. The unsaid regret, the promises that were made and not kept, the wishes, the would-haves, could-haves, the paths not taken, the opportunities lost and yes, the monetary debts that remained unpaid.

God is not going to do your job for you. It is your word, your promise. You must keep it. Are you a person of honor? Do you always keep your word? Do you pay for what you take? Can people rely on your word?

YOU made the mistake. YOU gave your word. It is YOUR responsibility! Keep your word, atone for your mistake, take responsibility for what you have done and set things right.

Then you will find respect. Such people are looked up to, given a place of honor in history. Keep that respect, keep that honor. It is a hard thing to acquire; do not dishonor it in your haste to enjoy yourself. Just because you are now at the gates of Heaven, is it any reason to abandon your values and principles? Now, more than ever, in fact, you are in front of God! Where is your honor? Where are your values? Now, more than ever, you must hold onto your values, your principles. God is testing you. The lure of a Heaven is in front of you, and you have forgotten your promises, your word. What a horrible time to disappoint God, to disappoint yourself.

Yes, keeping your word is harder, tougher. (There are those words again!)

Your creditors are waiting: "This person has never disappointed us, he has always kept his word." You are not going to disappoint them, are you? *Why then, are you asking for forgiveness from your debts? Why are you not asking for a chance to repay your debts?* Is that not possible? Anything is possible for God. In Hinduism, this is the only way. We come back. We repay our debts.

This also explains why most other religions have mocked Karma and Reincarnation endlessly, why this concept has been reviled so much. They want the easy way out, a nice obliging judge who lets them cheat their victims. Hinduism won't let you do that. Hinduism won't let you off the hook that easily. Hinduism won't let you cheat your creditors nor your victims. The mention of asking for forgiveness doesn't even arise in Hinduism—it is a non-starter. Does that describe you? You owe a huge debt, does the thought of asking for the debt to be forgiven ever cross your mind? Get out of the debt without paying it back? If it does not, then the moral of Karma and Reincarnation will appeal to you.

A Hindu should never ask for forgiveness from his debts; a Hindu must always choose to do the right thing. Asking for forgiveness is for the weak, not for the strong. It is for the cowardly, not for the brave. The weakling and the coward always take the easy path, the less demanding path. If they can make money cheating others, they will. If they can get away with cheating their creditors, they will. Legions of people have become rich the ill-gotten way; they have left a path of pain and suffering in their wake.

They run up credit card debts then look to the courts to bail them out. They buy a house they cannot afford then abandon it. They take your help when they need it, and once they have no need of you, you become a stranger to them. Are you one of these people? Then, yes, by all means, go ahead and ask for forgiveness from your debts.

Forgiveness cheats your creditors, the victims.

Making amends is harder, tougher, more difficult. Sneaking your way out the back door is far, far easier. The path that you choose defines you. It defines who you are. It defines your principles, morals and values.

Hinduism teaches us the Truth *is* God. Morals, ethics and values are what will bring us close to God.

Ultimately, you owe an apology to your victim, but more important, you need to make amends.

Let us take an example here: let us suppose you were distracted or too tired while driving and caused a serious car crash. You see cars, now unrecognizable masses, twisted, hot, steaming metal, broken glass, and you hear the cries of the injured and dying, with streaks of blood all over their bodies. But you, miraculously, are unharmed. Your car is a bit damaged, but still operational. It is late at night; no one has yet to take serious notice of who had caused this mishap.

You can drive away! You know that you would be in a jam if you stopped, but you can take off, repair your car at a safe, trusted place, no one needs to know. But the vast majority of people do stop, they tend to the dying and injured. Later, when the investigation is made, they calmly step forward and take responsibility for what happened. They may be mocked and cursed, called evil, maybe even sent to jail for their mistake that has led to this tragedy. Their life may be essentially ruined.

Imagine doing the right thing. Imagine standing tall before the prosecutors, before the court, the judge and all those people who have lost their loved ones or have seen their loved ones seriously hurt. Imagine taking full responsibility, taking the justice handed down by the judge, and even after that, doing whatever you can to mitigate the suffering caused by you by paying for the losses.

So STAND TALL before God! Accept the mistakes that you have made! None of this business of kneeling, head hanging down, groveling for forgiveness!

But wait, let us suppose the same situation is being faced by a lesser man, a weak man. He is faced with the prospect of coming forward and accepting responsibility. The shame he has to face, the people who he respects now looking down on him, strangers mocking, making fun of him, peers and friends walking away when he comes around, not looking him in the eye. Then yes, the jail term, the loss of income, respect and freedom. He thinks about all this. Is there another way? The easy way? Yes, say the religions, there is a kindly, old gentleman who will listen to your regrets and will forgive you! Wow! All done in private, in the dark, no need to go public with what you have done, no need to face the victim, no need to face the consequences!

Honestly, religions have stopped teaching ethics and morals so long ago, I am shocked that they still find willing believers to this day—ready to dump their responsibilities by the wayside and leave by the back door.

A true-life example is in order: two teenage young men went out driving after downing a few drinks. Like most people their age (or even older people), they did not think of the consequences of driving while drunk. Well, the worst thing happened: they crashed their car and one of the two died—no, not the drunk driver, but his friend, the passenger, was the one who was killed!

When the Parents of the dead teenager heard the news, they did something remarkable: they rushed to the hospital to comfort the injured driver! This young man was responsible for killing their young son, but these great and wonderful people thought only of how the young man must have been feeling.

In the words of one of the Parents, "We already lost one child. We did not want to lose another."

What a wonderful story, what wonderful people. This is also a story of love, not hating. The Parents could have easily given into hate. The terrible pain could have given them the excuse to hurl abuses and hate the person who took their beloved son away from them. They refused to do that. Remember my asking you not to believe in Hell, not to let hate enter your heart? Let us learn from this great couple.

But this story is not about these Parents—this story is about the young man who survived the crash. This young man did not run away and hide. The Parents of the dead teenager and this young man got together and went around the country telling their story, warning other teenagers not to make the same mistake that they did.

What courage! How brave was this young man to stand right beside the Parents of his friend, the friend whose death he had caused, and to own up to his mistake! The young man stood tall and unflinchingly told his story, how wrong he was, how much he regretted his actions.

This is how you make amends. This is how you set things right. Not by shrinking in the corner and sobbing on your psychiatrist's shoulder; sure, this will make your feel better, but this is not what Hinduism recommends.

We are not going to sugarcoat this. Being with God is going to be hard. We've heard stories that tell us this: the stories of Raja Harishchandra, Mirabai, Kabir—none of them had it easy! Hindus call this *Bhakti Pariksha*, a test of your devotion. They went through some tough, tough times before God came before them! The way to God is strewn with hardship; it is dark, awful, frightening. Many will choose to turn away; they choose the easy life, the magic man, the miracle man.

But this idea that staying with God is difficult should not come as a surprise to anyone; we know that the best things in life have to be *earned*! They are not going to drop on top of your head; you will have to work hard for them, make tremendous sacrifices, time and effort need to be spent, risks taken, setbacks dealt with. So why do we think we get to go to God and enjoy Heaven for eternity just because we are dead? That is but a fantasy.

Let us take another example: A woman is brutally raped. Her mouth is taped over so that she cannot scream while she is being raped, her voice silenced. In the Hindu way, the criminal must own up. He must *first* apologize to the *victim*, then go to the authorities, admit to the crime, stand before a judge and receive his just sentence. After the criminal serves his sentence, we all know that society may not yet forgive him. He is branded as a criminal, a rapist, and society will shrink away from him. Now he is perpetually branded for life. He accepts his punishment, lives his life a changed man.

In the Hindu way, THIS is how you repent—not by feeling sorry for yourself, not by crying croc tears, not by asking for forgiveness but by realizing the mistakes that you have made have hurt others and by trying to make things right by them. The truly repentant person is not wasting time with self-pity, nor does he ask for pity, but hastens to comfort the victim, pay back his creditor. This is the right way, the way of God Rama.

The Hindu way is of the strong. It is the way of the leader, the hero. Making amends benefits everyone—it restores to the victim the loss, it gives you back your pride and honor. Everyone is happy. The world would be a better place if everyone chose to do the right thing.

If you choose to be Hindu, please remember that there is no easy way out. God is not an enabler, nor does She ignore the victim at the cost of a getting an easy convert.

Take someone who cheats others and makes a living through it. He is finally caught and now ashamed of what he had done, he goes down on his knees begging for forgiveness. Giving it will do nothing for the victim. Forcing him to pay back the money he had stolen will force him to earn an honest paycheck. He will be forced to take a good look at the devastation that he has caused—to look at the suffering that he has inflicted—and hopefully he will become a better person. The victims get their money back. Everyone benefits!

Remember, forgiveness is all about the criminal/perpetrator; Reincarnation is about the victim.

Nothing good comes out of being forgiven—it is the back door, it is avoiding a problem, hoping it will go away.

Taking responsibility for our failures, our shortcomings,

and working to make ourselves better is the right thing to do, the Godly thing to do. We have to work through our problems, not take the easy way out.

A Hindu must not even entertain the thought of asking for forgiveness. If after making amends, making things right by the victim, if the victim forgives you, well and good; but forgiveness must always be given, never sought, never asked for.

A personal story: some time ago a dear friend of mine asked me for some financial help. Call it brain-lock, call it amnesia, or maybe just call it heartlessness on my part, but I did not step up, I did not help this friend, a friend who had been unselfishly supporting me all of my life. Well, this friend is no longer alive, and each and every day I regret my actions. I can't take back what I have done; all I get to do is to reflect and wish that I had been a better person.

Do I want to be forgiven for what I have done? No, not at all. What I have done hurts so much that I would rather be punished for what I have done. But what I would really love would be a second chance—one more time, just one more time, I would love to be in the same situation again; and this time, I hope to react better, do better. And this is exactly where Karma and Reincarnation comes in: I will be given a second chance, I will have the opportunity to make amends. Thank God!

Reflect on your own life—has something similar happened to you? Have you let someone down in your life? Someone that you love, someone that you respect? Now you feel terrible, disgusted with yourself for not stepping up. If given the choice, which one would you take—forgiveness or a second chance to help, to make a difference? I would be shocked if anyone with a heart or with decent values would choose the former.

I say, *a second chance to set things right beats being forgiven every time! Tell me reader, which one would you rather have—*

forgiveness or a second chance? You show your character when you make the choice.

This teaching is about making you a better person. Reflect on your life. Yes we all make mistakes but we will also get a second chance. Look for it, ask for it and you shall receive. And this time, step up!

If a person is truly repentant, then that person will not ask for forgiveness. The truly repentant person will hurry to make amends, to set things right for the victim. The truly repentant person will realize what a horrible thing that he has done, the suffering that he has caused, and he will not sleep until the victim is made whole, the damage repaired, the pain abated.

That is true repentance.

Chickenators, Curtainators and Idolators

There is a huge statue of Abraham Lincoln in Washington, D.C. Tell me, have you ever heard anyone say, "Oh my God, I didn't realize Lincoln was so tall"? People are not stupid, right?

Then why do people think Hindus are praying to a statue, or that we do not know it is one? Hindus call the image of God a murti, and yes, we do realize that it is made of stone (or another hard material). Yes, we do know that it is not God.

There is an important difference between praying to God and praying before God. Hindus are praying *before* these murtis or statues; they are not praying *to* them!

You might see pictures of the Mecca—Muslims going around something that is behind a curtain. Non-Muslims are not allowed inside this curtained-off area, and cameras are prohibited. They say it is the rock from which Mohammed ascended to Heaven. But all I see is these people showing their respect to a curtain! Do Muslims pray to a curtain?

Do Jews pray to a wall? Are Christians praying to air? Or maybe a book? I see Christians saying thanks before they eat. Are they praying to food? I see them sitting around a table, their heads bowed, and in the middle of the table is a dead, burnt bird! Are Christians praying to a dead bird? Would anyone be foolish enough to say, "Are you praying to a Chicken God?"

Idolators, Chickenators, Curtainators, oh my!

We know that all of the above questions are ridiculous. No, Muslims are not praying to a curtain, Jews are not praying to a wall, and Christians are not praying to a book or to air or to food.

Hindus are not praying to idols either. We are praying *before* these things.

Hinduism is a religion that says God is everywhere. When Hindus show respect to animals such as cows, it is because of what they have done for us over the centuries. The cow gives us meat and milk, and it has helped us plough our fields and transport goods. Humanity moved from a hunter-gatherer society to an agrarian society with the help of the cow. I doubt humans would have progressed to where we are now without the cow's uncomplaining help. Hinduism teaches us to venerate those who have helped us—animal or otherwise—and the cow has definitely earned our gratitude.

Hinduism says that God is everywhere: Yes, God is in that tree, in that mountain, in the sky, in the river. There is no place where God is *not*. If you want to pray to God, you can do it right from where you are sitting, and God will have no problem hearing you.

One poet mused that she saw her lover even when she closed her eyes. When she opened her eyes, he was there as well! A devout Hindu sees God everywhere.

So why do we build places of worship? Are they needed? Obviously they are not.

However, we are humans, and we don't always do things that make sense. Places of worship and idols give us comfort. We feel closer to God inside those hallowed walls, with those idols. They are for our benefit—they are our weakness on display. Certainly God has no use for these things. The idols in Hindu temples help us focus on God, just as mosques help Muslims, churches help Christians, and temples help Jews and Buddhists. These things are not necessary, technically, and yet they help us.

There are no such things as holy places, buildings, or idols. Every place is holy, because God resides everywhere. It is we humans who have designated only certain areas as holy. It is our weakness that makes us think that certain things or places are above others. They are not.

In any Hindu home you will see idols displayed in the living room as decoration pieces. If Hindus consider these idols to be God and are praying to them, why are they showing them off as decorative pieces? Because that is what they are— simply images made of stone. By themselves they mean nothing. Idols, places of worship, pujas, chants, prayers, fasting, ways of dressing—all of these things by themselves are meaningless.

Some of the images of Hindu Gods are quite unusual, and there is a reason for it: Hindus are saying that God can take unusual forms. Expect the unexpected. Don't assume that God will come down in the form that your religion presents. Take Jesus for example: He was born in the Middle East, so he could have been short, brown-skinned, brown-eyed, and frizzy-haired. However, over time, as he travelled to the West, his image changed. The same is true of the Buddha: He was an Indian—not someone born with what we think of as Oriental eyes, as you see him depicted in many Asian countries.

We often shape God in our own image. But what if God surprises us? Will we throw Her out? If you are a non-Hindu and God comes before you in the shape of a woman, will you shut the door in Her face?

The Hindu idea of expecting the unexpected was put to brilliant use in the second *Star Wars* movie. The young hero goes in search of an elderly Teacher and instead he meets up with an annoying, funny little "creature". It is the very Teacher that he was searching for: Yoda! But the young hero does not recognize him because, like many in the audience, he was looking for a Teacher that resembled his previous one—a tall, gentle, kindly-looking, white, blue-eyed person. An old person with a white beard!

If you have a set view of God, you may not recognize Her when she comes before you— which is why, for example, Islam prohibits any image of God. We Hindus, on the other hand, have arrived at the same conclusion by flooding our faith with so many images that we are prepared to see God in unexpected ways.

Hinduism gives God many names. We call God Rama, Krishna, Durga, Allah, Jesus, the Buddha, and any other name from any religion in this world or beyond!

Movie stars and other pop stars are often called idols, and there is a clear reason for that: the nice, handsome hero who runs around in tights doing good all over the world, helping the poor and unfortunate, may be a heartless person in real life. If we fall in love with the hero image, then we are idolaters. We fail to see the real human being behind the hero.

So if God does not take on the pleasing image that we have created for Him, then we may end up rejecting God. On the other hand, an evil being can take on that pleasing form and make us commit horrible acts.

Those who claim that God can only be known by one name or form are guilty of idolatry, of saying that there is only one way (our way)! *These people then become name worshippers.* If the Parents of this God had named him Joe instead, today they would be insisting that Joe is the only true God! That's how ridiculous these ideas can get.

Why of why, do we seem to be brainwashed when it comes to religion? Does the greed for the good life trump everything, kill brain cells?

The other day I watched on TV as Syrian Parents bid good-bye to their son. He was going off to fight a brutal dictator who was using modern weapons to kill his own people. Their two other children were already on the front lines, fighting. Does it matter if these Parents were Muslim, Hindu, Christian, or atheist for that matter?

God Sri Rama has a place in his heart for such good people. Those who condemn others based on religion are the true idolaters. Those who run segregated Heavens are the true idolaters.

Idolaters are fixed on the externals, the rituals. Unfortunately, quite a few of these people are Hindus. Many people overemphasize the pujas, the prayers, the mantras, the japas, or the number of times God's name is invoked. They put too much importance on cutting or not cutting their hair, shaving their heads, growing a beard, covering their hair… Of course, all of these practices are harmless compared to the debate over what is the right name or image to use for God. Millions have been killed because people have insisted that the right way is their way and everyone else is wrong and destined for Hell.

God Krishna was once asked, in the manner that was customary in those days, "What is your name, and which village do you come from?" God Krishna answered, "*All* names are mine, and I will answer to whichever name that you choose to use for me. All villages are mine, so there is none that I call foreign." The way a person refers to God must come from the heart. It is not religion-based.

Hinduism asks you to focus on the true inner God—

Truth, honesty, compassion, ahimsa, dharma, kindness. Hinduism asks you to do the right thing and walk on the right path.

Do good, think good thoughts, and speak the good word!

Consider our attitude toward photographs. We all have photographs of our loved ones, perhaps on our office desks or in our wallets or purses. People laugh and cry looking at photographs of their loved ones. Do these people think that the photos are their loved ones? Most definitely not!

If I were to take the photographs of your family from your wallet and tear them up, would you not feel anything? After all, they are just photos, right? They don't matter, because we can always have new ones printed.

But you *would* get upset if someone did that. The photos represent your loved ones. They encapsulate memories and put a smile on your face. To see someone tear them up would hurt you.

The idols in Hindu temples are like the photographs of our loved ones. Idols are representations of our Gods. Seeing these idols invokes good feelings in Hindus, just as seeing the image of Jesus invokes good feelings in Christians and seeing the image of the Koran invokes good feelings in Muslims.

However, by no means do Hindus mistake these idols for God.

9. Karma and Reincarnation Mean that Hindus Are Not *Quitters*!

"Winners never quit and quitters never win"
—Vince Lombardi

"I failed my way to success" —Thomas Edison

I am watching the Olympics—young kids trying their best to perform, showing sad faces when they get a silver medal, striving so hard to be the best. This is what we see. What we do not see are the countless hours of practice, hard work, the countless number of times falling down, hurting themselves, but again and again, picking themselves up, and starting over once again.

In life you will fall many times. The winners, the heroes will pick themselves up each and every time and keep trying. The weak, the losers will give up, look around for help to arrive. The gymnast falls off hard off the balance beam. Her coach runs to her, asks her, "Do you want to continue?" "Yes," says the gymnast. The crowd cheers, sensing the young woman's distress. The end result may not be great, but the crowd gives a rousing ovation anyway. They see that this young lady could have quit, but she kept going, she didn't quit.

Imagine you are a young, very, very promising ball

player. Coaches from around the country are coming to your house, chatting up your Parents, urging them to send their kid to their college, promising great days ahead. They smile at you, talk to you sweetly. Finally you decide upon a college and start practicing with your new team. But all of a sudden the sweet, smiling coach has undergone a swift change—now, he is a yelling, screaming ogre, telling you to run faster, that you are no good, will amount to nothing etc. Life now becomes a tedious repetition of classes, practice and homework before hitting the sack—no time left for a social life. You are tired all the time, practices become more and more difficult, and you start disliking the very sport that you once loved. You think of quitting the game, and so you do. Suddenly life opens up, now you have all the time in the world! Now you can take your girlfriend or boyfriend to a movie, sit back and enjoy and think of the poor suckers, your former teammates going through tough practices while you get to enjoy life. Then the season starts, you are up in the stands watching your former teammates play. It's a great game, back and forth, the crowd cheering… in a nutshell, the person sitting in the stands chose Heaven whereas the players down on the court have chosen Reincarnation.

Death is like falling down. God asks, "Do you want to quit?" "Yes," say many. "Quit on life?" Many say yes, blinded by the prospect of an easy life promised to them by their religions.

The temptation to quit when the going gets tough is difficult to resist, especially if there is a delightful prize to be received if you do quit: Heaven. Heaven is for those who have quit on life, have said, "No mas," to life.

Can you blame them? In a popular TV show, the husband wants to go out and play golf, and the wife says, "Yes, why stay home? What is at home? Just bawling and needy kids, lots of housework, lots of boring responsibilities. Not fun at all. Better to just sneak out for a round of golf with the guys, where there is fun, fun, fun."

And that is the promise of Heaven: leave the earth, leave the world of pain, work, suffering, troubles, problems, jerks and headaches, and head on out to a life of joy and happiness. Fun, fun, fun for eternity!

These religions urge you to quit. Quit, they say. Quit, Quit, Quit. The joy of quitting, the joy of doing nothing for eternity, the joy of death!

Quit on life! Quit on God!

But while the husband plays golf, it increases the workload on the wife. If a teammate is injured or quits the team, the rest of the team's workload suddenly increases. If a co-worker quits and no replacement is hired, his former co-workers find their workload increased!

We all know that life does not get better without an incredible amount of sacrifice and effort by untold millions. Millions have lost their lives to altruism, risking their lives for total strangers. A policeman risks his life jumping after a suicidal person—a total stranger to him. Ordinary people will take a bullet if that means saving a child. People will stand in long lines waiting for hours to donate blood after a major terrorist attack. Firefighters will jump into mostly empty buildings risking their lives and sometimes losing them. Today, as I write this book, Libyans are fighting dictators, scientists are working day and night to find cures for deadly diseases, and millions have died fighting in wars— sometimes senseless wars, sometimes wars fought to preserve the very way of life held dear by their societies. There is a man in India who risks being killed trying to free child slaves. Journalists have paid with their lives for exposing the corrupt and venal. Women are fighting to get even half the rights enjoyed by men. I could go on and on.

Ordinary people risking their lives—who wants to do

that? Who wants to risk having life no more, to risk never again being able to set eyes on their soulmates and kids, to leave their families to struggle without them? Who wants to make the sacrifice of one's own life to benefit others, and not themselves?

The "good old days" were mostly a myth, enjoyed by the lucky few. Time was when those conquered in wars could expect mass rapes, killings and a lifetime of slavery. Women were relegated to second-class status. Black folks were bought and sold like cattle—an inhumane and terrible life awaiting them in a strange foreign land. People were tortured and killed for sport. Countries were conquered and exploited as colonies, their wealth looted and then given independence after they were picked to the bone and nothing of use was left. Some of these horrors are still with us now.

Few defenses could stand against the ravages of gangs intent on mayhem or diseases that stalked the land. Millions died due to lightning strikes of diseases, their young children left to fend for themselves. We have AIDS as a reminder of yesteryear's horrors. The vagaries of weather have brought starvation to untold millions.

Let us remember that in the old days almost everyone depended on agriculture for their livelihood. Very few had the luxury of working in non-agricultural endeavors. Today, maybe 2 to 3% of the American population is dependent on agriculture, compared to 97 to 98% in the old days. And we all know or can imagine the harshness of this life: back-breaking work every day for hours on end, no days off, no holidays, no vacations—farm jobs are the toughest jobs in the world. And these people depended on the rains; there was no fertilizer to speak of, so one bad season could wipe them out. One bad rainfall, one bad flood, one bad drought meant starvation.

Is it any wonder that our ancestors hoped for a better

afterlife and religions have rushed in to tell them what they wanted to hear? All except one. One faith stood out.

Times have changed for the better, and you'd better believe it. We do live in better times, and if we work hard and stay true to God (that is, stay true to our morals, values and principles, stay true to Truth, honesty and compassion), then our future will be better. Follow your dharma, commit to ahimsa (non-violence).

The day will come when we will conquer all diseases, maybe even live forever! Poverty and starvation will be a distant memory. People will live in freedom, live to pursue their hearts' desires.

This makes the weak and cowardly among us fearful. They are not prepared for the work or the responsibility. It is much, much easier to believe in a nice tooth fairy coming down to help us. One quick wave from her magic wand and we will all be living in paradise! What could be simpler?

Well, not all of us. Those of us who are foolish enough not to believe in tooth-fairy magic and insist on building a better world by hard work, sacrifice, effort, sweat and toil must be punished! You are not in the tooth-fairy camp? Well, eternal pain and torture await you!

But that is the coward's strategy, always using scare tactics. When a fort is going to be attacked, the coward wants desperately to run away and hide; but then everyone will call him a coward, ergo, he needs to provide some nice, noble-sounding reasons for the "strategic withdrawal":

a. The enemy is too strong, ten times our number.
b. The enemy has better weapons than we do.
c. We are not running away, we are moving away to regroup; better to assess the enemy's strengths and weaknesses.
d. This is not the right time to fight, right now is a bad time, we are not ready, we have been weakened, we

should wait till we are stronger.

And so, the list grows. There are times the coward succeeds in persuading others, but sometimes it comes with a catch. Some people disagree and want to stay and fight. If they are small in number, they are in great danger—no, not from the enemy attackers but from within. The coward cannot let them do this. He cannot let them stay and fight while he flees—they actually might win! The enemy may not be as strong as he had supposed, maybe fewer in number with inferior weapons. They could be defeated, or not even attack at all! But that scenario would be horrible for our weak and cowardly. For the rest of their lives they will have to live with the shame of being labeled as weak and cowardly. Women will snicker at them, people will laugh behind their backs. Children will make fun of them openly.

"The brave and strong must not be allowed to stay and fight," says the coward. "Fortunately their numbers are small. I can label them as traitors and connivers working for the devil, and then kill them all! That is why we must believe in the magic genie who will come down one day and save us all. Those who do not believe in the magic genie *must* be made to regret it."

Two people see the same thing, but in very different ways. The coward sees the oncoming battle and all he can see is pain, suffering, and loss of blood. All he feels is fear. The warrior sees the exact same thing but he sees an opportunity for glory, an opportunity to save his family and society, to achieve greatness, to go down in history as the great one!

And so, the coward runs away. Far away from the battle-field, he is safe. No more fear, no more pain or suffering. Heaven! Heaven is for such cowards running away from life.

Life has been seen as a sin, full of pain and suffering, with a sugar daddy God waiting elsewhere to keep us in comfort.

The coward is forever seeking the easy pastures; but all I see is death comforting them.

Death will keep them in comfort for eternity! Let us shout out loud: Do no quit on life! Do not give up on life! As much tempting it is to run away and hide, we must resist such temptations, for cowardice is never rewarded. The way forward is the only way, running back is never a good idea.

The warrior does not run away, the warrior stands tall in the face of adversity, the warrior will fight and conquer, will make God proud.

Your work here is unfinished. You are no *quitter*! For you, there is much yet to do, many threats yet to be conquered. This kind of work may not be for everyone. Most will choose the easy life. Most will believe the easy promises. This choice is for those who believe in making a difference, those who seek to earn praise *from* God! Such praise is not easily attained. Much sacrifice, much effort is needed. Is it worth it? Hindus think it is.

Let Hinduism give you a backbone, give you strength. Hinduism will separate the adult from the child, the strong from the weak, the warrior from the coward.

Caste

Let me start with my personal opinion, an opinion shared by millions of Hindus; Gandhiji is one of them. Caste is an abomination, a black mark against Hinduism, and I wish it would be gone! Racism, to me, is like caste. Many would rather have it gone, live in a racist-free world. But, just like caste, racism has defied many attempts to kill and eliminate it. Or take sexism: Most religions relegate women to a second-class status; but somehow the misogyny of religion is tolerated.

I compare caste to the pedophile issue in Catholicism

today or terrorism in the Islamic religion. Does Catholicism encourage pedophilia? Of course not! Does Islam tell its followers to go kill innocents? Of course not! But the underlying conditions within these religions and the society today have proven fertile ground for such evils to take root. Caste also took root in ancient Indian Hindu society.

Caste basically is another word for discrimination—such discrimination exists in other countries as well—someone please tell me why any living Jew of today deserves condemnation for something his ancestors allegedly did? Minority Muslim sects are deemed not Muslim enough in several Islamic countries and face discrimination. Of course, women and blacks can tell us the long history of discrimination that they have faced since time immemorial.

How did caste get started? How did people start dividing people up like this? People get emotional over this, but I believe that there is a rational, commonsense explanation for everything. Many do not realize this, but caste is not that uncommon. Japan in yesteryears had people divided into four categories: the shogun, the artisan, the farmer and the trader. Even Plato divided people into gold, silver and bronze. Frederick Nietzsche also divided people into three classes.

So, why do this? I believe that ancient people were simply trying to understand the world around them and put things into categories—not just people, but most everything else as well.

Hindus encounter the number four a lot in their daily lives: the four Vedas, the four seasons, the four Yugas, the four directions, the four dimensions, the four aspects of the Hindu holy word *Aum*. In marriage, Hindu couples promise to stay together in four ways: dharma (duty, work), artha (rich or poor), kama (love, sex) and Moksha (enlightenment).

It is possible that ancient Hindus thought of putting people into the same four categories was a good idea. We do that too, even today. A nurse is lower than a physician and must follow his or her directives. Putting people into categories based on the work they do is not wrong and is done today.

What was wrong was saying a person was born into a job, that he could not move into something that he wanted to do. Ancient India was not like this. The Teacher of God Sri Rama, sage Vishwamitra, was once a king, a Kshatriya, but gave up his kingdom to become a Rishi, a Brahmin (a learned person)—it is interesting to note here that the educated person (a Brahmin) was deemed higher than even the king! Amazing! The great-grandfather of the Pandavas, the heroes of the Mahabharata, an emperor, fell in love with a *fisherman's* daughter and married her! Sage Vyasa or Veda Vyasa, an important figure in the Mahabharata and one some Hindus regard as an incarnation of God Vishnu, was the son of a fisherwoman.

Examples of inter-caste marriages and movements abound in Hindu literature.

Slowly but surely, however, things changed. There was an economic advantage in keeping a certain occupation limited to as few people as possible, and some saw something actually good in it: it kept peace within the society. Yes, you could not move into certain occupations, but that also meant others could not move into yours! The son of a fisherman grew up with the knowledge that he could always depend upon a steady job.

Another explanation could be the question that dogs almost every thinking person: why are some people born in wretched conditions while others are born with silver spoons in their mouths? Most religions have refused to touch this question, for a good reason. If you are a non-

Hindu, ask yourself or your religious leader, why are some people born into a loving family while others are condemned to a wretched life? Why do some kids get a happy, loving childhood, while others fall victim to a pedophile, while still others are kidnapped and forced into prostitution? After the Europeans landed in America, over the years, over 95% of the Native Americans were steadily exterminated. Is there an answer for the steady persecution of Jews over the centuries? Hitler did not *start* the abuse against them, he was just a later manifestation of the bigotry that Jews have faced throughout history. I have posed this question before: A kid is abandoned, grows up without love, is unable to call anyone family, is beaten, abused, raped, made to steal and be used for other criminal acts—what did this kid do to deserve such a cruel fate?

If there is only one life, is it right that some people be born in the lap of luxury, be born as a prince or princess, a rich movie-star and enjoy all the pleasures of life while another is born in abject poverty and forced to see his siblings and Parents suffer and die right in front of him? Little girls stolen from their Parents and forced into prostitution? And the end result for both is the same—eternal Heaven? So, why the ultimate good fortune for some, while others endure horrific lives?

Seems unfair, doesn't it? If you were the person who got the raw deal, wouldn't you be asking God why?

Most religions stay away from answering this question, but Hindus dared to ask this question and tried to answer it.

There are three possible answers to this problem. Let us discuss the first two:

1. Blame God
2. Blame ourselves

It is hard for anyone to blame God. After all, God is our

creator, our Parent. Blame God for the terrible things that happen to us? Unthinkable!

And so Hindus came up with another explanation: the fault must lie with us. We are responsible for our fates. This is not so far-fetched as it may seem. Plenty of religions use the same explanation. For example, when I ask people who believe in some of these religions, who condemn me to Hell, "Why would a loving God do such terrible things?" their easy explanation is that it is *my fault*. God doesn't want to torture me, but it was my choice! We are more similar than we think!

I believe that most Hindus have missed the correct explanation, the third explanation: Hinduism is a Teacher faith; the Teacher will not interfere in our affairs. We choose to be born and work our way towards Moksha, so some of our births will not be so pleasant, others might be wonderful! I believe that all Hindus will experience all types of births, both good and bad! In one birth you will be born a prince or a princess, but in another you will face a life of poverty and hopelessness. Each life is like sitting in a classroom. Some classes will be very interesting with a good Teacher and subjects to our liking; others may be a sheer bore and downright excruciating to sit through. But all these classes will end up teaching us something, as will each life.

There has always been this question in science: Why is there something instead of nothing? Why is there life, matter in this universe? Why does the universe seem to be too finely tuned for our existence? For life? Well, the answer is that maybe we live in such one universe that is conducive for us! Multiverses! Yes, there is more than one universe! And some universes are empty, devoid of life; in others the physical laws may be different, with life forms adapted to those universal laws.

The same way, we too will be born again and again, and

will taste life in all its varied forms.

We hear or see horrible things happening almost every day, with God seemingly doing nothing to prevent such things. Why didn't God stop the Holocaust? Stop 9/11 from happening? Stop the World Wars? Stop the genocide under Stalin and Mao's rule?

For most religions God is like a king. Is God asleep on His throne? Is He uninterested—too busy to bother with us?

Only a Teacher faith gives the right explanation: God is there only to advise and instruct, this is our earth, we are the owners of this land, we must bear with the horrors and work to make this a better world for ourselves.

And so, we have a few explanations as to why the system of caste arose. It seems misguided to us now, and it certainly is; but we have the advantage of hindsight. Another thing to keep in mind is that society was different then. Draupadi, the heroine of the Mahabharata, had *five* husbands—certainly something we would not allow today.

Whatever it was, the reality is that caste was solidified. One was told that he or she was born in a particular caste, destined for a particular job, and that was it. As the modern age has arrived, the job classification by caste has disappeared but caste labeling still survives.

Most religions have their divisions, although they may not call it caste. We know the big ones: Muslims are divided into Shia and Sunni, and today we witness the horrors of that division; there are other minority sects in Islam not deemed Muslim enough and are being persecuted. Christians have divided themselves into Catholic and Protestant and many of them consider Mormons heretics and not Christians. Jews have been hounded for centuries over the alleged crime of one of their ancestors. When skin color alone makes one a criminal that is also a form of casteism, as is sexism.

Millions of Hindus, myself included, would love to see the end of this evil teaching, but it persists even in the modern age. What is keeping it alive?

Arranged marriages.

This is the advice that I give to all young Hindus: eschew arranged marriages and we can abolish caste within one generation! The evil tree of caste is being watered and kept alive by the practice of arranged marriages. Without arranged marriages, caste would have died out a long time ago.

Hindus have moved to other countries. For instance, there is a large concentration of Hindus in Latin America. They are not divided by caste. Why? When the number of people is small it is very difficult to find eligible members of one's own caste. One has the choice to either stay unmarried or marry a Hindu of another caste. As the inter-caste marriages increase, it becomes increasingly difficult to keep up the caste divisions. Caste has died out in these Hindu communities! What a wonderful thing!

One more thing about arranged marriages: They were never designed for adults. They were meant for kids or pre-teens. If we go back in time, a few thousands of years ago, people did not live as long as we do today. Inadequate nutrition and primitive medical practices meant that people died in their 30s or early 40s.

If people had waited until their 20s to get married it would have been too late. They would have died or been in their old age while their kids were still young. All this meant that kids needed an early start; they had to get married and start producing children during their teens if they wanted to have a chance of being around when their children could stand on their own feet. So marriages between pre-teens were common. But kids were still kids then, so adults had to step in and arrange the marriages.

Times were different then. People had to make tough

choices that suited their times. It is crazy to see people of today blindly following whatever was done in the old days! I think it is crazy that some people still do not believe in evolution and think the earth is 5,000 years old. And obviously some of these people believe Hindus are crazy for carrying on practices that no longer belong in the 21st century!

So, young Indians, please say no to arranged marriage! Show the world that you are adults, and let us kill caste at the same time!

10. Karma and Reincarnation Mean That We *Earn* Everything. A Hindu Must Never Beg nor Take Anything That Is Unearned

Do you hate the word *free*? If you are a strong person with good moral values, you realize that there is no such thing. When you were in school, if you got grades that were not deserved, you thought the Teacher had made a mistake. Are you the type to speak up? If you got something that you felt you had not earned, are you the type to refute it?

It amazes me to see this side of Westerners. From what I see, Westerners teach their kids to earn everything, to work hard, to pay for whatever they take, to never beg, to never take anything for free! And yet, when it comes to religion, it's OK to beg?

Is it OK to get a job because the boss took a liking to you and hired you even though you are not qualified?

Is it OK to get top marks or grades for a test just because the Teacher is fond of you, even though you submitted a blank paper?

Is it OK to win the match by bribing the referee?

Please tell me that it is not OK. Then it is not OK to beg your way into Heaven.

If Heaven is not earned, you must not enter.

Everything is always earned in Hinduism. Moksha is earned; it cannot be begged for, nor given. God's grace is earned, redemption is earned, and forgiveness is earned.

You ask yourself why people lower themselves to such disgusting behavior—that's the power of the easy life! Just like people fall for Ponzi schemes, the Bernie Madoffs of the world, the easy money and the greed, these make people lose sight of every value that they hold dear in life.

They shade it. They hide it under this so-called "devotion", or "Love of God." No sir, it is the love of the easy life. *That* is what they love.

I tell them God is here, God is right here, but God resides amongst the poor, the suffering, the disadvantaged. Being with God means staying amongst these wretched people, fighting for justice, dealing with pain and suffering.

But it is no surprise to see that I find few takers.

Have you ever begged for anything? There are those who have lost jobs and have had to depend on the kindness of others; they feel a great deal of shame and humiliation. They feel that they are no longer a person, no longer worth anything. There are many in poor countries, with no social security or a pension net, unable to work after an advanced age; they must depend on their children or on the kindness of relatives and strangers. Sometimes things do not work out, and it is a sad sight to see these once proud people, reduced to begging on the side of the street.

Begging emasculates you. You become disgusted with yourself, down on your knees, head held down, at the mercy of others. Is that your choice? In Heaven will you end up begging for your daily meal each and every day? These religions say that their God will not hesitate to torture billions of innocents for their "crime" of belief. Well then, you better brush up your "Yes, master, no, master," or else you may end up in the torture chamber. To be a slave for eternity—is that your choice?

When young people first step out into the adult world to start making a living, they have choices:

1. Find a job, work hard, earn your living, build your future;
2. Find a sugar daddy, beg, grovel, praise him, laugh at his jokes, become his yes-man and hope he throws down or gives you your daily meal.

In Hindi, we call these people chamchas—you see such people all around the rich and big sports stars—hangers-on who boost the rich man or woman's ego and hope to be kept, get the easy life. Are you really one of them? Has the greed for the good life reduced you to that level?

In the former the operative word is earn; in the latter, it is give.

There is nothing free in this world. There are no free lunches. "If it sounds too good to be true, it probably is" applies here. Evil lures you down the easy road, telling you that you can get everything by simply begging and showing remorse.

But that is not enough for Hindus. It is not enough for God. A victim ignored means justice denied: a victim raped twice. Neither is a favor to the criminal/perpetrator; he is being coddled, babied. If a Teacher were to indulge in favoritism and give good grades to an undeserving student, is she really doing the kid a favor? The student comes out of college having learned nothing. What if this student is a medical student and can now call himself a physician? How many innocent people will die needless deaths because of the blindness of the Teacher?

You can probably buy yourself a degree online from a fake university. Let's do that! Why go through the trouble of going to a legitimate college and slogging for years for a degree? Why do the work? Why make the Hindu choice?

A degree or a grade or marks that are unearned are fakes. Fake degrees, fake grades, fake marks—they mean

nothing, they do nothing for you. A Heaven that is unearned—that is begged for—is fake.

If only, if only, every human being on this planet would commit himself or herself to a life spent on the straight and narrow, to commit to a life of earning everything that they take, to realize that good things in life must be worked for, to eschew evil's "easy" life—then this world would be a wonderful, wonderful place!

In many of the world's successful countries the mantra is never to take anything for free. If you take something, make sure you pay for it. However, in many unsuccessful countries the opposite is true; these countries are plagued with corruption and backroom deals.

Most Parents teach the correct values to their kids: Earn it. Do not try to get something for nothing. Do not take the easy road. Even when you do get something for nothing, it is probably worthless anyway. For example, if your child comes home with an F or a failing mark on a test, would you recommend pleading with the Teacher for a change of grade or better marks? Would you recommend asking for her pity? And even if the Teacher gives in to your entreaties and changes the grade, does this mean that your child has learned anything? Did you just teach your child that even if you cannot earn anything by hard work and effort, you can get ahead by pleading or using other demeaning methods? Is that the lesson that you want your child to learn?

Has he become a better student? Has he learned his subject matter? In both cases, the answer is no. There are plenty of young men playing in the professional leagues who have a "degree" from a prestigious university—are they our role models?

And what message does this send to those who have earned their grades? They see a slacker who did not work hard, partied while he studied, and yet stands next to them.

What is the message that is being sent to those who earn their way through life? If we go down this slippery slope, what kind of a world will we end up with? In Heaven the good person stands next to the very pedophile that abused him or his own son. The brave soldier stands next to a mass murderer. Daily, a woman has to run into a gang that raped her and left her for dead!

In the beginning, God was perceived as a moral guide—a divine entity that would guide us through the toughness and roughness of life through the narrow prism of the good and just. But sadly, that view has changed: today to most, God represents the doorway to an easy life, an easy back door, an escape hatch from the troubles of life. Life's problems are not to be faced and conquered; instead you can turn tail and run away to a magical land.

We see that today in all the online avatars. Though most people play with these avatars in their various delightful universes for fun, for some they represent an escape hatch. Real life is hard, it is troublesome; the life of the avatar is easy: everything and anything is possible with just a click, a push of a button. It is tempting to believe in this magical land of cyberspace and the un-manifested.

Heaven is the original avatar land, the place to escape from the realities of life. But escaping or running away never solves anything. Real life is not any better after you finish playing on your computer; but the weak, the feeble will continue to run away from life, while the strong will face their problems and master them.

J. Krishnamoorthi, the renowned philosopher from India, commented on this issue— that people are happy to place their bets on the un-manifested, the unseen, rather than the manifest, the world that is before us. The far-away mountain looks so smooth; the grass is always greener way over there.

The reason is quite simple: real life does not change with

the click of a mouse. Real life is hard, it takes a lot of hard work, patience, perseverance, determination and sacrifice. In real life the good things have to be worked for, earned, the happy Heaven must be built. In the fake eternal life, Heaven comes pre-built.

To use a sports analogy, ask a player to choose from either playing and not winning a championship or sitting on the bench, injured, and winning a championship. The vast majority would choose the former. There is no glory in being handed something.

The Parents who encourage their kids to beg and plead have missed teaching a great lesson to their kids: to accept a loss with grace, dignity and class; that we must strive to get up after a fall. Instead, they teach them not to worry after a setback, that there is always a backdoor way to get in. There's no need to earn your wings, there are other ways of getting them.

This game is played out in most families. The mother plays the "bad" mom, while the "good" dad (in some families the roles are reversed) lets the kids stay up late, watch inappropriate programming, and let their homework and chores slide. Who is really the "bad" Parent here? Who is really doing a good job of teaching their kids the right values?

It is easy to be the "nice" daddy, right? It's tough to be the responsible, "bad" mommy. Easy to make wonderful promises: this God is just waiting for you to die, just get down on your knees and cry, and this nice God (they make sure to tell you that he is very merciful) will forgive you and off you go to party!

"Bad" Hinduism reminds you of your responsibilities, values, ethics, asks you to do the right thing! It reminds you of the victim down below who is still waiting for justice. A God who looks to you to be strong, to do the right thing! A God who treats you like an adult, a strong, ethical person who will step up when things get tough.

At some point in your childhood when you learned that there is no Santa, that there is no tooth fairy, you slowly became an adult. Well, certain religions insist on still keeping you a child, still ask you to believe in a Santa waiting above with bags of goodies. Hinduism is not one of them. Hinduism is not a "genie religion".

The world is conquered by those who refuse to give up— who keep getting knocked down but keep getting up again and again—and not by those who seek underhanded ways to win, who take the back-alley way to achievement.

Hinduism is anything but absolutist. It is not for nothing that this faith is called tolerant, accepting. We are the first ones to say there are many paths to God, not just ours; but on this one issue there can be no debate: the place beside God must be *EARNED*! This issue is not about God but it is about your core values and principles. If all your life you have always worked for everything that you have, never taken a handout, then this issue is clear as day to you.

At the core of the matter lies the heart of a person. His or her principles, values and ethics are shaped by it. No matter how much you implore a coward or a weak person, they will hesitate to walk the path of God.

Perhaps, yes, Hinduism is too hard, too harsh for some people. A God who coddles and enables God Sri Rama is not.

Hinduism Is a Faith, Not a Religion

Faith is for all; religion is for the few.

Religions divide us; faith will bring us together.

I am asking for a change in paradigm. Let the world's teachings be divided into faiths and religions. Those who lay stress on the "us," character, conduct, ethics, morals, spirituality, the life here, this world, this society are faiths. Those who lay stress on the "I," hereafter, belief, X God, Y God, prayer, rituals and conversions are practicing religions.

A child has faith. Faith is more about character, conduct, a clean heart. If religion is just cheap talk, faith is more about action, work. Belonging to a religion is about joining X religion, wearing the garb, reading scripture, etc. Belonging to a faith is more about doing something to make a difference, whether it is working in a soup kitchen or walking to raise funds or writing an exposé on the corrupt and venal.

Religion makes one selfish, it's all about how one can practice the easy life; whereas faith is putting others first, working for God. *Anyone* can have faith. There's no need for religion, no need to convert, no need to declare one's affiliation. *Anyone* can volunteer at a humane shelter, anyone can give blood, anyone can clean up the local beach, anyone can build a home, anyone can deliver meals to the elderly…

While religious people debate endlessly about who created this world, what they look like, who do they favor, who will he punish, etc., with faith you have no such worries. By doing good, one is with God. Unfortunately this is not enough for most people, which leads to the establishment of religions.

Atheists are the key. Those religions that welcome atheists are faiths because they are saying that character alone matters to God. Religions that mock and keep out atheists are basically cults that think rituals are all that matter to God. Their focus is outward, the belief, the prayer, the scripture, the dress—all rituals that mean nothing to God.

These people serve religion, not God! RELIGION WORSHIPPERS!

We are all born atheists. At birth we have no idea of God. Well, our mothers are Gods to us at that time; and then as we grow older, we discover faith. Faith is characterized by innocence, Truthfulness, a clear heart, a heart that loves all, will extend a smile and a cheerful and shy, "Hi," to even the likes of a Hitler or Stalin. A heart where God would love to take permanent residence – but alas, we grow up and discover religion. And some religions preach hate, put up walls between us: "Only us", "We are the only ones on the true path", "Everyone else will be tortured, must suffer". These are the words of evil—hate being nurtured and cultivated. Call me amazed and dumbfounded by such brainwashing going on now in the 21st century. We were supposed to have progressed, created a "modern" society. But such hate finds fertile ground because it is looked at askance by a friendly media and "good" people.

God flies out of such hearts. There is no room in there for Her.

Listen, any fool can embrace religion. As we know, a mass murderer can hide in a church or a temple or a mosque. As we know, a pedophile can deliver moving sermons. Any fool can change religions. How long will the ceremony take? Two minutes? Any fool can study the holy books and recite from them. Any fool can close his eyes and pray, chant, get down on his knees and beg, grow a beard, shave his head, hide his hair; these are *all* cheap, easy rituals.

They do nothing to bring you close to God! Nothing!

Rituals give us comfort, they make us happy. But to think they will make God happy is ridiculous, ignorant. It is like buying vegetables to make a curry, putting them near the stove and then going to sit in the living room and watch TV. You come back to the kitchen after a couple of hours and what do you see? Have the vegetables cooked themselves? Is there a delicious dish waiting for you? Of course not. Rituals are the same way, and to expect results from them is the delusion of the weak.

Being with God is tougher, harder. We keep running into these words, don't we?

Discover faith. Discover spirituality. Dump religions of hate.

People foolishly think that simply praying or chanting will please God. But without doing good works these are only a waste of time. Kant raises the bar by insisting that one must do good works as a duty, as a job; doing them once in a while when we have some free time doesn't count for much in his book.

Hinduism is a faith. This is why we don't encourage or work obsessively to get converts. Faith has nothing to do with religion; faith has everything to do with character and conduct.

This is why Hinduism asks you to focus on the inner God, which is your character, your values, your ethics. This is why we have so many millions of Gods, so many strange images of Gods, all of them sending the message that it is not the God that is outside that matters, but the God within that matters—the God that we discovered as children.

Imagine a path that each and every one can follow – *everyone*! Anyone can choose to live his or her life on the straight and narrow. There's no need to join a religion. Finally we discard religion, all the infighting and killing, and discover faith and spirituality! No more separation, no more going to different places of worship, no more divisiveness.

Let us consider exchanging God Rama's name for Truth, Krishna is honesty, Jesus is compassion, The Buddha is ahimsa (non-violence), Allah is kindness, Mahavira is dharma and so on. Now we don't have to fight. We can pray to all Gods! Everyone can join! Everyone! All Gods will be dear to us. No more fighting!

11. Karma and Reincarnation Mean God Is Within *Us*

You are taking a nice long walk through the park, and you see a wallet lying by the side of the road; you open the wallet, and to your surprise, the wallet is full of cash! Times have been hard for you, and you could really use the money.

Do you try to find the owner and return the wallet with all the money, or will you simply pocket the money and throw away the wallet?

No one needs to know what you had done. No one will find out. The cash that you need desperately is very tempting. What will be your decision? Will you do the right thing?

But what if you are caught? What if the money is traced to you? Will that affect your decision? Will punishment, derision make you return the money? Or will the prospect of a reward sway your decision? Is this how you finally make a decision—because of the fear of being caught and punished? Or are you hoping for a nice reward if you do something good?

Here's where you should listen to the God within, your conscience, and do the right thing. As we have been discussing all along in this book, the emphasis in Hinduism is about doing the right thing. Most religions stress reward or punishment—a deliriously joyful Heaven or a horrific, abusive Hell. Hinduism stresses neither; there is no Heaven and there is no Hell (thank God).

Will you listen to your conscience? This money is not yours. It is *unearned!* There's that word again: *earn*. The money has to be returned. No, there is no reward for returning the money, and obviously you will not be punished nor ridiculed.

But what if the wallet belongs to a known criminal or despicable person? Will you cheat a criminal? Will you steal from a thief? Will you steal from your place of work if you feel that the corporation that you work for lies and cheats? Or will you say, it does not matter what others do, it matters what *I* do!

People focus on the wrong thing; they focus on a being "up there" somewhere, watching us, and they think that if they just praise that being, things will be okay. They focus on behaving like a slave. They focus on how many times we pray, how we pray, and where we are praying, instead of focusing on the God within.

These peoples' morals come from the outside, not from within. They do the right thing only because of an external threat; if given the license, they will kill, cheat, abuse and do whatnot. Apparently the only thing that is stopping them from going on a murder spree is the threat of being cruelly punished.

We have a saying back in our country: "For a human, use words; for an animal, use a stick." Because the animal may not understand, you may have to use a stick to make it do what you want. These people are saying we are no better than animals: we need the threat of being beaten and tortured in order to walk on the straight and narrow.

Do not tell them the stories of Rama, Jesus or the Buddha—those who walked on the straight and narrow path, the lives of whom humankind should emulate. Instead read to them the stories of criminals who got what they deserved. Stories of burning in Hell and torture, is what they need.

Talking about the inner God—Truth, honesty, ethics, values—this won't get you money or power, because *anyone* can do these things. An unbeliever can be honest. An unbeliever can be a good person with high morals and values working to make a difference in society.

The inner God is for the strong, for the God within us. But that does not mean we get magic powers; it only means that we must do the right thing, tell the Truth, lead our lives on the straight and narrow.

The inner God cannot compete with the outer God. There's no magic or miracle here, nor is there a promise of the easy life. After all, the outer God comes with magic, miracle, the easy life, no more having to turn in an 8 hour workday, no more worries, just lean back and enjoy! And what does the inner God come with? Why, nothing but a conscience—an inner voice that asks us to do the right thing. No prizes on which one the weak lazy bum will pick.

Do people think God is a fool? Imagine yourself—just an ordinary guy, a few friends, acquaintances, family, and maybe a few detractors. Some of these people barely give you a nod as they pass you on the street, some cross the street so that they don't have to talk to you. Well, one day things suddenly change—you have hit the lottery! The news spreads like wildfire. Well, suddenly you are the most popular guy on the planet, it seems. The guy who barely acknowledged your existence?—why, you are now his best friend! The guy who crossed the street so he wouldn't have to talk to you? Now? He comes to visit you and calls you his buddy!

I don't have to draw you a picture, you obviously have figured out why all these people "love" you all of a sudden. It's your money that they love, the money that will give them the good life. Unless God is a fool, I am sure He can figure out why all these people claim to love a being they have never seen, have no clue what this being looks like, have zero evidence of any his powers or his existence.

Tell me, is it not the good life that is promised is why you claim to "love" God? True love does not come with conditions, nor the expectation of a reward.

At one time I was challenged by someone on YouTube—"Why do you Hindus pray to a cow or a tree (The Tulsi tree is revered by Hindus)? They can do nothing for you!"

For which I say, "Exactly!"

Learn to say thanks to God. Stop asking God for this or that, stop making selfish demands. Stop thinking God is a sugar daddy, good for nothing but the giver of the good life.

Just put yourself in the place of this lottery winner. Do you think he will eventually get tired and upset about the constant demands for money from his relatives and "friends"? Seen only as a cash cow, respected and "loved" only as long as he gives them what they want? Do you really want God to feel the same way? Just a Sugar Daddy, a meal-ticket? Is this all what God means to you?

Our mentality needs to change—for too long we have been weak, looking upwards for the knight in shining armor to come save us. It is time for the strong to step up.

The day we become strong, we discover the inner God.

Hindus greet each other with *namaste*, which literally means *I bow* or *I greet the God within you*. Time and again, Hinduism has stressed that God is within us. We don't have to look far or go out of our way to find God—She is right here.

The Hindu God is immanent, right here with us. For some other religions God is "up there", transcendent, somewhere else, in the land of the dead. Every Hindu is familiar with the popular image of Hanuman with his chest ripped open to reveal his God Rama within. The symbolism is clear: God is within us, each one of us. Or to be more precise, the goal of Moksha is to make God reside within our little hearts.

God is within us. The light is within us. We are the light. We are the hope!

The question is, "Do we want to find this God within us?" Am I worthy of God? Have I conducted myself in such a way that God will be proud of me and call me Her son/daughter/student? Or have I behaved in such an awful manner that God would be ashamed of me?

Be a child of God. Find the God within you. Open your heart and let God walk in. Do not let religions teach you hate. Stand up and condemn religions that do. Focus on the inner you, not the outer you. Focus on leading a good, clean life. Tell the Truth, be honest, help others, then you *will* be with God. Whether you are an atheist or a theist, it does not matter. Character matters.

The God within simply implores you to do the right thing; there are neither rewards nor punishments. Well, yes, there are some rewards: the reward of feeling better about yourself, the reward of feeling good because you did the right thing, the reward of having contributed to a better society.

Living in a happy, great nation is no puzzler. There is no magic in this. If citizens of any given society treat others the way they would like to be treated, do the right thing, follow the rules of the law, embrace ahimsa, are kind and compassionate towards others, and yes, *earn* everything that they have, then, yes, that society will be a paradise to live in.

It's not possible to have a policeman around every corner. The best societies function well because of their inner God. Nobody has to threaten them with dire consequences to do the right thing; they do it because it is the right thing to do. They listen to their inner God.

Why is it that in some countries, if you do not pay a bribe, nothing gets done, while in others, things get done without bribes? Why is it that in some countries women can walk around in the dead of the night, while in others they are afraid to walk in daylight without a male escort?

Listen to the God within you. Listen to your conscience, and let Truth guide you to do the right thing.

Hinduism is not for the lazy, for retirees. Hinduism is for those who want to work, for those who want a part in creating a just and peaceful society. Let us realize that this is not about creating a rich society. Yes, money is useful and comes in handy, but the *behavior* of the citizens of any given society goes a long way toward creating a happy society.

In Hinduism paradise must be built, Heaven must be worked for.

When I wrote about Moksha, I discussed seeing the inner beauty (Moksha) vs. the external beauty (Heaven). Sadly, we all fall for the external attributes. Most of us pay lip service to the notion of seeing the inner person, the inner beauty, the good within each one of us, etc.; but most of us are still affected by the external. Let us all agree that seeing the inner beauty is a good goal to have, even though we may fall short of it many times.

In the movie "Star Wars", the young hero mistakes a great Teacher for a little buffoon. At first, all he saw was the external attributes, the short stature, the ugly pixie-like face, the old, bent age. It is one of the most thrilling moments of the movie when the young hero realizes that the great Teacher that he had been searching for all along was standing right before him. Why was the moment so thrilling, so memorable? Because we all saw the inner beauty, the God within, of this strange-looking creature. Now we have glimpsed Moksha.

If given the choice of being born to rich, handsome Parents who have no time for you or poor, "ugly" Parents who shower you with love, how many of you would choose the former? Not many, I presume.

Many have entered into marriages based on looks and wealth, but those marriages quickly fizzle out. We may all be attracted to looks and wealth, but in the end, without love and affection, relationships will not last.

It is the person who is always kind, helpful and gentle who will be loved by all.

You are walking along the street and you hear a big commotion. Then you see hundreds of people running towards you, screaming and yelling. They are all running away from something, their eyes wide with terror.

But like the hero in the movie, you stand, confused; you want to run away with them, but you are also curious as to what it is that is making these people run away. And then you see it: a huge beast, a horrible creature, maybe 50 feet tall, spewing fire through its mouth, destroying and killing anything standing.

It is making its way right towards you! Do you stand your ground and fight it? Or run away? The weak look up, hoping for divine intervention; but, as a Hindu, you realize that this is your problem. You alone must face it.

Fantasy? A science fiction story? Or are you in a new computer game?

No, this is reality. It happened. Both on 9/11 and 26/11, hundreds of people were running away from troubled areas, while others—policemen, soldiers, firefighters—were rushing towards these areas, running towards the terrifying beast.

I am sure a lot of them were thinking, "Is this the day I die? Have I seen my loved ones for the last time? Will I never get to say goodbye?"

But that did not make them run back. They pressed forward and fought the beast. Some paid for it with their lives. That was the last day they were alive.

These are just two instances. There have been millions of such instances in human history—of brave, good people running into danger to save the rest of society. Recently, brave young Muslims in Egypt and Libya faced down brutal dictators. These good people did all this because they listened to the God within, their conscience. It is because of such people that we move forward to bigger and better things in the future.

Whom will you choose—the God within or the God above? The God above promises a comfortable life. Choose the God within, and you will come back after death once more to drink from the nectar of life. Once more you will work for a better earth. Once more you will continue your life's work.

Be part of the future or disappear into the dark and become just a statistic?

Be part of the future or be part of the past?

The God above makes you weak. Well, those religions appeal to the weak anyway, encouraging their believers to get down on their knees to pray for the savior to come and make the beast go away.

The God within makes you strong. You realize you have nothing to be afraid of—God is within you. When you stare down the evil beast, you stand tall and straight (as they do in movies). With the God within, there is no magic, there are no miracles. There is just tiny you, just flesh and blood.

And a tiny little man, Gandhiji, brought down an empire, and he did not even use any weapons to do it. Another man following in his footsteps, Martin Luther King, Jr., awoke and healed the conscience of a nation. Throughout history great men and women, fuelled by the God within them, have brought tremendous changes to their societies, altering the course of history.

And throughout history evil men have silenced the God

within them and brought tremendous pain to those around them. Religions have not stopped mass murders, massacres. Religions have not stopped slavery, caste; instead, religions have stoked these horrors.

This is the fight we cannot lose, we *will not* lose.

The God within makes you stronger, tougher. This is exactly what the world needs right now.

Satanic Saying

"The only thing necessary for the triumph of evil is for good men to do nothing."
—*Edmund Burke*

Focusing on religion and its rituals has promoted hate within us. I am encouraged to see that more and more people are labeling themselves as spiritual and not religious.

In the past, if you were of a different religion, this was enough to get you killed. Even today, sadly, this situation remains. America was settled by people who were fleeing religious persecution. These people had a great opportunity in front of them, to put to bed the religious hate once and for all. Unfortunately they missed that opportunity.

Today, in America, you may not get killed for your religious beliefs, but you are certainly abused for them, for being different. There are religious "nut jobs" running around, threatening good people with Hell. God discriminates on the basis of religion? Amazing. God would torture you because you did not call him by the right name or because you did not belong to the right religion? And yet, we are supposed to have freedom of religion.

This is a satanic saying, period. To condemn people based on their religion is pure evil. These people are with Satan, not God. There was once an evil man who did exactly that;

his name was Hitler. He set apart and condemned people for their religion. He made them wear armbands that set them apart by religion and then had them brutally killed. It didn't matter whether the Jew was a good or bad, young or old, male or female. Their religion alone condemned them to a brutal death.

Apparently for these evil folks, their "God" will do the same thing. He will set me apart for being a Hindu and will then torture me for eternity for my "crime".

"God" is a Hitler? One cannot go any lower than that.

Are there concentration camps up there? Is there an Auschwitz, a Buchenwald, a Treblinka up there? Will we be starved, beaten, raped and gassed to death? Is that what awaits the rest of humanity—set apart, boarded onto railroad cars and sent off to gas chambers?

If reading this makes you feel sick, that is my point.

Hitler did not start the hate against Jews, this hate has been taught for centuries and is still being taught today. When they saw a Jew, they didn't see a human being with loved ones, a father, a brother, a wife, a daughter, a grandchild—all they saw was religion. Many blacks in the US are quite familiar with people moving to the other side of the road when they see them—these people see skin color, not the human being. When "God" sets apart people by religion, these religious leaders are saying God is exactly like the above folks—he doesn't see people, he sees only religion—religious divide and hate is the result.

How could *any* religion teach this? How could any follower of these sick religions not speak up? How could they remain silent? Like Hitler's supporters, were they content to think that they would be exempt from the horrors of the gas chambers?

Where were their ethics and values?

Think of your own loved ones. Can you imagine how

heartbreaking it would be to lose one of them? And then imagine, as you grieve for them, that a stranger comes to you and tells you that your loved one is being tortured in a concentration camp forever—for the crime of their religion!

In Mexico they honor the Day of the Dead, a day when they commemorate their loved ones who have passed on. But some are unluckier than others. There are those whose loved ones have simply disappeared, with the drug cartels being the most likely suspects for these disappearances, killing and throwing away their bodies where no one could find them. The mothers and fathers of those that disappear refuse to believe that their loved ones are dead. They could move to other locations, but they stay in their old homes, hoping against hope that their loved one will someday walk in through that front door.

So much pain, so much suffering! Imagine telling this poor mother not only that her son is dead but that he is being tortured by someone for his crime of religion?

What kind of evil does that? What kind of evil teaches this? And what kind of evil gets such support in this world? For God's sake, this is the 21st century!

These people are throwing the rest of humanity under the bus!

What happened to my freedom, my freedom of religion? Democracy? I can have it here on earth, but in "God's" presence it is absent? I am now subject to one-man, despotic rule? "God" is primitive, backward? These religions came into being when kings ruled, one-man rule was common, and there was no democracy. By believing in these satanic sayings, these people are confirming that their religion is man-made, primitive and backward.

They are also saying that "God's" heart is small, shriveled; there is room in it only for the few. Heaven is segregated. Let me repeat: Heaven is *segregated*! As in the times when blacks looked up to see signs reading "Whites Only," Heaven has a sign: "X Religion Only"!

Hitler said there was only room for a supposed "pure Aryan" race in his Germany. These people were saying "God" only has room for a few "pure" people in his Heaven. *The same sick ideas!*

These people are happy to proclaim that they are going to Heaven, a land of pure joy and happiness, to enjoy for eternity, in the presence of God. What could be better? What more could anyone want? Nothing! Right? Wrong! *Our* socks are filled with goodies brought by Santa, but that is not enough; *their* socks must be filled with coal—nay, filled with biting snakes, scorpions, bugs, diseases, and misfortune must visit them and they must suffer! This is the concept of Hell, the place to which these "God-loving" people condemn those who are different.

So much hate! So much anger! I ask why. Why can't you be happy that you are going to Heaven; why all the hate directed at others who may not be like you?

It puzzles me no end why good people willingly participate in this evil. Do people become inured to hate? Do they see the hate and evils of others but not their own?

Collective Punishment

Under Hitler, Jews were collectively punished, it didn't matter that these people were young or old, good or bad—they were not seen as people, all different, with different ideas, personalities, but more like animals, most people do not see animals having different personalities, they are seen as one unit. Today, some people say that in Israel, Palestinians are seen that way.

Some religions tell us that God sees people the same way—our character, conduct, ideas, aspirations, loves do not matter—ALL Hindus, ALL Buddhists, ALL atheists are to be condemned—seen as one unit—collectively punished for our "crime" of religion! What is behind this idea? Hate. Easier to hate when people are not seen as individuals but as a collective—"All blacks are criminals", "All Jews are greedy", "All Mexicans are…". Once reduced and condemned this way, then it becomes easy to hate and abuse.

It is clear to me that a loving God would never treat Her children this way, divide Her children in such a manner—what is clear is that it is a religion, eager for converts, abusing the very notion of God, has turned a loving God into a cruel master, one to be feared, forcing conversions on innocents.

It is one thing for a drug dealer, prostitute or a gigolo to lose their morals when tempted with cold, hard cash but it is an amazing sight to see millions of highly educated, moral, intelligent people to lose their morals just by the promise of an easy life that awaits them after life. Such brainwashing being done right before our very own eyes! Why are not psychologists studying this effect? Have they been brainwashed also?

One of the great stories of Hinduism concerns an elephant named Gajendra. As with most religious and philosophical stories, the underlying message is important, and not the story itself. Once, this elephant was caught in trouble, unable to free itself. It called upon God Vishnu to come to help him, and God Vishnu rushed to help. Now, by what name did the elephant call God? What religion did the elephant belong to? That's the point of this story: God is not offended that you do not belong to the "right" religion or to any religion for that matter. God is not offended that you did not call Her by Her "right" name. More important things matter to God. One must not cheapen God by giving importance to such cheap, religious, bigoted tricks.

Let us discover faith and spirituality, not religion. In religion, let us leave the dogma, the hate behind.

But I do see a lot of good people abusing others. Check out some Hindu religious videos on YouTube and you will see bigots of other religions spewing hate, using threats of Hell. Never, never will you see Hindus doing the same thing (this is another thing I am thankful for in being a Hindu). This faith has never taught such hate.

Such hate disturbs us. Who is teaching this hate? Why is it so common in some religions? The media seems undisturbed by such hatred and continues to ignore it; good people of these religions also look the other way, maybe because in the past, violence has worked. Hate fills one's mind, leaves little room for anything else. There is no room in a mind filled with hate for intelligence, compassion, honesty, acumen, gentleness or kindness. The one thing you can do after reading my book is to let go of this hate, let go of the hateful thought of Hell. Let no one be condemned to Hell, not even Hitler! You may think you are punishing an evil man, but you also abuse God when you do so. You bring God down to the level of a Saddam or a Stalin. You make God a torturer.

12. Karma and Reincarnation Mean That We Hindus Choose God, Choose to Stand by God.

This may seem self-evident. After all, do we not all stand by God? No, not really. We may want to be with God, but to stand by God, to stay with God? That's another matter.

Tell me, did any of the great heroes in history lead a nice, comfortable life? No, not even one. All these people strove against injustice, poverty and hopelessness. Their lives were spent in hardship, poverty. And yet we say they were with God. How can that be? Most religions tell us that being with God in Heaven means living in a land of milk and honey. And yet we see these great men and women who were with God enduring pain and suffering.

This is what it means to be with God. This is the sacrifice that you must commit to in order to be with God. Choosing Karma and Reincarnation is for the strong, the committed— those souls who choose to remain with God.

The mark of a true devotee is asking nothing from God.

What is God's work? God's work is helping the less fortunate, working for the welfare of animals, helping preserve our environment, making our planet livable for future generations, working to find a cure for diseases that kill us, breaking new frontiers in science. All of this is God's work. Where does it happen? Here!

It stands to reason that where there is God's work being done, there is God!

Let us repeat: where there is God's work being done, there is God!

God's work is being done right here on earth. No work is being done in Heaven. It is here; it is right here. Again, where God's work is being done, you will find God. If you do God's work, you are with God! Where God's work is not being done, there is only death.

If it's not YOU, who will?

Where there is no God's work being done, there is Death! Here is the conundrum in front of you:

1. Fall for the easy promises of most religions, go for the easy life (eternal death aka Heaven) and be without God, or

2. Choose God and follow the footsteps of those above. The second choice will be difficult. This way is not for the faint of heart, not for the weak, not for the coward.

Let me change the paradigm for you: to be with God means to face pain and suffering, the exact opposite of what every religion teaches you. If this frightens you, please stop reading this book right now and move on with your life without Hinduism in it.

God needs our help.

This might seem a strange thing to say, but yes, God needs our help. This is our land, our earth, these are our problems to solve; and as Arjuna says to God Krishna, if God Herself comes down and starts to make things better for everyone, then what is the use of our doing anything down here? Why not just give up, sit down and just wait for the magic moment?

So many good people in history have given their lives

so that the rest of us can have better lives—is that all for nothing?

When a Hindu dies, he comes right back in another life. We choose to stay. We choose Mother Earth. We Hindus choose to stay and make things better rather than chase fairy-tale castles in the air to live in. People do that nowadays. They build elaborate avatars for themselves in online worlds; the avatar lives are much better than real lives, but most of these people do realize that this is just a fantasy, that it is not real.

But it is very tempting, is it not? And most religions make it very easy, sometimes just a matter of a few minutes of conversion. You are the same person of two minutes ago; but now, strangely, instead of staring at the depths of Hell, now you are off to the land of magic and revelry. Such Heavens come very, very cheap.

When we are children, we dream of a gift-bearing Santa. But at a certain age, our Parents tell us that it is all a myth, that nothing is free, nothing is magical, and that all those gifts were paid for by our loving Parents.

Once upon a time, women waited for their knight in shining armor; today, not so much. Today, such a notion is considered insulting to woman.

What has changed? The weak became stronger. The little child is now strong enough to hear the Truth. The "delicate" woman is now a strong, independent woman capable of realizing her own dreams without anyone's help.

Hindus realize that real life is difficult. There is no knight in shining armor coming to save the day. The earth will be a Heaven only because we chose to stay, stand and work for a better day. We face a lot of problems today and none of these will disappear by themselves. Someone has to stay and fight. Someone must be willing to stay and fight for a better earth. Hindus have chosen to do so.

Once you decide to stay, you have no choice but to fight. Just making a living is a struggle to most people. Sometimes you lose hope, and some people choose to kill themselves.

But it doesn't have to be this way. Life can be better for everyone; and believe it or not, life is getting better day by day. Life for our elders was much, much tougher. But they persevered, worked hard and handed down to us a much better life than they ever dreamed of having for themselves. It is our duty to carry the torch forward.

Sadly, few are willing to come back. It is like a tour of duty for them—a short jail sentence—and then they are done. They have done their duty, they have completed their sentence, and it's now time for them to enjoy a life of ease. To them, Hindus say, "Good luck. Sweet dreams."

Hindus would rather build the dream castle with their bare hands and backs. They would rather work and make this earth a paradise. A ready-made Heaven is a false Heaven; it does not exist. You want paradise? What are you waiting for? Let's build it! You want a life of ease? Earn it!

There is nothing new here. These are the very values and principles that you teach your children. And it is these values and principles that form the core of your soul, the very values and principles that bring you closer to God. If everyone chooses to abandon ship, who will be left to save the unfortunate, the old and the very young?

What are your goals in life? What drives you? Are you involved with a charity? Raising funds for a good cause? You do realize that the battle is never-ending? Tell me, if given the chance would you:

a. March alongside Martin Luther King?
b. Go to jail with Gandhiji?
c. Stand with that young man in front of a ten-ton tank in Tiananmen Square?
d. Work alongside Mother Teresa?

e. Rush into the burning buildings on 9/11?
f. Close in on Hitler and Berlin?
g. Assist Einstein?
h. Be the first to receive a call from Alexander Graham Bell?
i. Walk with and learn from the Buddha?
j. Research and find a cure of cancer?
k. Help and assist Mozart?
l. Research alongside Marie Curie?

If you answered yes, then you have chosen life! You have chosen to be with God! For such opportunities will come again and again; they came in the past, they will do so also in the future. Do not be foolish and embrace eternal death, be left with regret and pass up your chance to shape and participate in the future of humankind!

You will pass all this up to sit and do nothing in Heaven? You will turn your back on God?

Make the right choice: choose God.

In many religions there are quite wonderful stories of God's emissaries being sent down to help man, but in Hinduism there are no such emissaries. God Herself comes down for us! Maybe Hindus are special? LOL.

You may have seen plenty of movies with this theme: the lonely hero finds himself in a village that is about to face a dire threat. Perhaps a horrible creature or an evil army is about to attack the innocent village and destroy it and kill all its inhabitants. The hero has the option to go away—this is not his fight, he is a stranger here, just passing by, he does not have to put himself at risk, this is not his problem.

But the hero eventually always decides to stay, does he not? But then that is how he becomes a hero. A hero does not walk away and abandon those in need.

You also have the same option: once you die, you can

forget about life on earth. It is now someone else's problem. In life, perhaps you were fighting to cure cancer, walking hundreds of miles, working, networking, and spending your free time and money to find a cure. Well, that is someone else's problem now—or is it?

In life you may have dedicated yourself to helping animals. Surely, animals are the greatest victims of man's greed and desire for a cozy life. You spent your life helping to find a home and shelter for abandoned dogs and cats, helping to preserve a habitat for endangered animals, helping to end their hunting and destruction. Well, you are now dead. It is now your time to relax and be happy. The work to feed and shelter these mute animals is someone else's—or is it?

Your country is about to pass a horrible law that will negatively affect innocents. You have resolved to fight this draconian law. You have spent time and money, invested countless hours in this fight—this is your life's work. Is it now time for someone else to carry this fight forward?

Journalists have dared to expose corruption and nepotism in their countries. And some, sadly, have paid for it with their lives. More than ever, they need our support—but is it no longer my problem?

There are many, many stories like these. All over the world, good people are fighting for a better earth. The fight will go on. Such people will make the world better.

What will you choose to do? Put your life in the mirror behind you and run away or choose to come back, choose to continue to make a difference? If you choose the latter, then you choose life. Choose the former, you choose death— eternal death!

Tell me, dear reader, why would any sane person choose eternal death over life?

Don't let religions cheat you out of life by believing their wild promises—realize that it is quite easy to make these promises, any fool can make them and in fact several religions say the same thing. Obviously they can't all be right and so to cover up their lack of substantiation, they resort to the all too familiar threats. In the end they cheat you out of life and you end up with nothing but death—yes, only death is eternal, and only then you realize that these religions are not entirely wrong—death *will* deliver you from facing pain and suffering. Even if such a place exists, remember the famous axiom: *life should be big, not long.*

Death = Heaven; life = Reincarnation.

Yes, life is here, and only here. Only here do you fall in love, only here do you dream and become another Mozart, only here will you fight to defend your country, only here will you dream.

Yes, Heaven is no place for dreams.

Imagine that, in Heaven there are no places to conquer, nothing to look forward to, nothing to achieve—you go to Heaven to retire, to die.

Life is where you dream—as a child you dream about that toy or about ice cream, then later you dream about maybe being first in class, meeting that special boy or girl, getting into that great college, and then having that dream career. There will be heartbreaks and disappointments along the way. Not everyone's dreams will be fulfilled.

Life!

If you choose Heaven, you will be forever forgotten.

I know that life can be brutal for a lot of people—thousands of people committing suicide is a testament to the brutality. But giving up is no answer. Choosing death is no answer. Yes, it gives the perfect opening to weak religions to exploit this pain and suffering and to promise an easy life, but please realize that these are but empty promises. A ready-made instant Heaven up in the sky is not real.

Only life is real.

Hindus and all those who choose life have been given a special Gift: we can elect to stay and continue the fight, to continue our life's work—God's work.

You too have the chance to become a hero, to impress God! Take the chance. Do not disappoint God.

Stand your ground. Stand shoulder-to-shoulder with God and fight the good fight.

Here lies your opportunity, here is your chance to make God proud of you, here you can bring light to the world, here you can make all that pain and suffering go away or die fighting it. Come back and try again!

Will you choose God?

The Nanny God—A Dangerous Idea

It is perfectly natural for people to hope for a pleasant after-life, and this hope gives the perfect opening for religions to step up and make nice, easy promises. Of course, God will forgive you. Of course, you are going to a pretty, happy place full of joy and happiness. How can anyone check these Ponzi scheme promises?

That's not good enough? Don't worry, God will come down soon, all the signs point to it; just give a quick wave of the magic wand, say, "Am Phat," and you have instant paradise!

Problems arose when bad things happened. The gullible populace rightly wondered why God did not do anything, did not come down and make things better. The religious leaders were in a fix—how to answer this question? Aha! Enter the scapegoat! See that guy who does not attend our services or looks different? He is the problem; God stays away because he is in our midst!

And so the killings started.

Millions were killed, millions were scape-goated — innocent people dragged out of their homes and killed right in front of their children. The religious leaders, drunk with power, desperate to hold onto that power and the accompanying wealth, exhorted their followers to kill and burn.

And they continue to this day. The Taliban whip women because they expose some skin, beat men because their beard is not of the proper length. See, correct these and surely God will be pleased and Her blessings will rain down on us!

We see and read daily about the bombings and killings of internecine wars within these religions.

At some point the blame must also shift to the "gullible" public, which is not so gullible after all. Anyone ready to kill his friend, his neighbor, just because he is told that X is a problem deserves some blame, and we must include the media in this as well (hiding the identity of the perpetrator, covering up for the criminal, etc.).

The problem is man's weakness. Time was he was at the mercy of the natural world. Life was harsh, terrible; and old age was the worst affliction.

Enter the Nanny God!

Why work? Why work hard, sacrifice, do anything when magic God can solve all our troubles with a little shake of the magic wand? An, "Am Phat," can solve all our problems. Any day now it will happen. Why do anything?

Once man has been weakened, become greedy, then he plays right into the hands of the religious leaders. Now they have him. Now the carrot and stick are in place. The faithful are kept in line.

Such reliance on a Nanny God makes us weak, keeps us weak.

To me, terrorism is the direct result of this Nanny God idea, the idea that one can get the easy life of Heaven simply by belonging to a religion. We see that real life is hard, some countries have fallen behind others by refusing to change, stuck in their old mentality of women remaining at home, large families, hatred of science and education—but on TV and the Internet they enviously see the modern world enjoying themselves, distancing themselves further. Unable and unwilling to change, the easy promises of a nice easy life is very, very tempting. And so they check out, violently!

But I fear a greater danger.

I fear the day a calamity might strike earth. Scientists talk about climate change; many are convinced that a catastrophe will happen. Millions will die due to coastal flooding, millions will be thrown out of work, and crops will fail, bringing even more starvation. But that gives the perfect opening to some religions. They do it even today; they will set up shop in these terrible times, warning, threatening people: "God is angry because you did not hear him, you refused him; now he is punishing us." In such times when people are weak, it is easy to frighten and force them to join the religion. Then, I fear, will come the killings. For the weather won't change. The bad storms, tsunami and the extra hot weather will still be with us. People will wonder why God is still angry with us. And then these people will point to the atheists or the people of other faiths and say that they are the problem. As long as these "unbelievers" remain in our midst, God remains angry! And so, the mass murders will resume.

This is why I urge all good people, atheists, those of other faiths, to speak up against these horrible ideas.

The weak are dangerous; it is the weak who won't hesitate to knife you from behind, shoot you from behind, call ten to one a fair fight.

Then there is the story of a warrior who was once challenged for a fight. He was seen going to the place of combat with two swords in his hand. When asked what the second sword was for, he answered, "Just in case my opponent does not bring his."

We need to be strong. The world of the strong will be a just world, a world where there will be peace and prosperity.

13. Karma and Reincarnation Mean That We Are the Strong, the Good, the Brave

Frankly, who would choose Reincarnation? If this book is an attempt at proselytizing, I doubt that it will be successful. While some Hindus and most religions talk about an ease of life after death, Reincarnation offers you more of the same: a lifetime of struggle, a lifetime of work, daily conflict, lots of pain and suffering.

How do you gauge the heart? How do you gauge character? You do this by observing the way one reacts to adversity, by the way one responds to a challenge.

This is an appeal to the strength within you, the good within you and the courage within you—in other words, the God within you. God needs you. God needs you down here. God needs your help. Do not fall for the sweet words of evil. Realize instead that being with God is not a bed of roses.

Notice I did not mention religion. People do not need religion. They need God.

Almost everyone seems to be looking towards God as some kind of Santa, the giver of gifts. Almost all religions portray God as some kind of benefactor, she will do this for you, She will do that for you. Alas, few stop to ask, "*What can I do for God?*" You do that, and suddenly your whole perspective changes. I understand you will be happy in Heaven, I get that. If your personal happiness is all you can think of, if you are so self-absorbed, then you can stop reading right here—this faith is not for you. This faith is for those who think of others. Are worried about the happiness of others?

If there is such a thing as Heaven, I am asking you to turn away from that. It is a false Heaven, a Godless Heaven. I ask you to choose God, the God who is right here, right here on earth.

If you are a person who spends her time working for the welfare of animals, God needs you down here.

If you are a person volunteering to go fight for your country, Hinduism asks you to re-enlist.

If you are a person who is raising money for the cure of a disease, then God asks you to keep going. Do not stop until the job is finished.

If you are a scientist or researcher eager to make new, astounding scientific discoveries, Hinduism says, "Come on down, we need you, we have a job for you."

If you are a person who spends his spare time working in a soup kitchen, God says, "There are yet hungry people still waiting to be fed."

If you are a person who hears of a terrorist attack going on and rushes to that place to save innocent people, God thanks you.

If, by your mere presence, the life of a dying child is brightened, Hinduism says, "There are more young children to hug."

If you are a person hurrying to your volunteer English-teaching job for adult immigrants, God says, "Your students are patiently waiting for you."

If you volunteer to clean up the garbage on your favorite beach, Hinduism says, "Garbage is piling up!"

If you donate money to build schools or buy school supplies in poor, needy areas, God says, "There are plenty of kids hoping to go to school."

If you are a person fighting for democracy in your country, Hinduism reminds you that the job is not yet done—there is much more to do.

If you are a journalist writing about the evils of modern life, the corrupt and venal people of this world, God says, "Keep going."

If you do not want to put down your tools, if you do not want to retire, Hinduism has lots of work for you.

If you are itching to fight for a good cause, sacrifice yourself for the betterment of everyone, God wants you close to Her.

If your heart bleeds every time you see animals or people suffering, Hinduism says, "Come, let us work to make things better."

If a thousand years after your death you want to be remembered, Hinduism says, "Choose Karma and Reincarnation."

If you want to participate in the golden future, to help humankind reach the stars, God says, "Come on down."

If you want to continue your life's work, Hinduism says, "You can keep going."

If you are a person working to end sexual slavery and human trafficking, God says, "I need your help."

If you want the earth to remain pristine and healthy, Hinduism says, "We need you down here."

If you want to be the first person to walk on Mars, come on back!

If you want to earn praise *from* God, Hinduism says you can only do that here from earth—only through hard work and sacrifice.

This is what Hinduism offers you: a chance to make a difference once more, to fight the good fight, to stand bravely in the face of adversity. God needs you down here. The world needs you down here. After all, you do realize that evil and bad things continue to happen after your death, right? Here's the choice to make: No more any of my business OR I want to continue the fight.

Back in the 70s the Hindi movie "Deewar" was a huge hit. In this movie a young man, frustrated by the cruelties of life, takes the wrong path, the criminal path. He is tremendously successful, but he keeps his criminal activities hidden from his family (well, it is a movie, after all). Meanwhile, his younger brother becomes an honest police officer. Well, you can see where this is going – the young police officer is assigned to find the master criminal, and he finds that it is his dear old brother. The family is torn apart, with the mother siding with the younger brother. The two brothers meet at one point and the older brother berates the honest younger one: "I have fast cars, a big house, money, all the luxuries of life! What have you got?"

"I have Mother," replies the younger brother. The mother here is a metaphor for God.

Choose wisely. Choose to be with God.

Few want to walk with God. Walking with God is hard. Walking with God is like doing the right thing. Doing the right thing is always hard. It is very tempting to take the easy way out. When you resist and do the right thing—even if it not advantageous to you—that's when you know you are with God!

Hinduism says that God is like a Teacher: She's always there to help and advice, but the hard work is yours to do. You must be willing to work for a better earth. Why stop now? Why leave things halfway? Let us continue this exciting journey. Stopping now would be like Darwin writing his book but never publishing it! It would be like the Apollo astronauts turning back to earth midway to the moon!

Have you ever watched a prize fight? You always remember

the fighter who keeps getting back up after being knocked down. This is a good metaphor for life. In life you will certainly get knocked down. How many times are you willing to get back up?

Children are weak. Children are fragile. They are not yet strong enough to take on life's problems. Hence, the stories and movies made for them are full of magic, miracles, prophecies and genies. No real life here, no long hard struggles, no sacrifices, and no bitterness in the end. The good guys always win, the bad guys always lose, and there is always a happy ending.

No one should have any problem with the good guys winning, the bad guys losing and a happy ending, but how this is accomplished is a bit troubling: it is always through nice and easy magic—the magic beanstalk, the magic genie, the magic carpet. Yes, such stories are appropriate for children; childhood is a time for dreaming, but when such magical stories are carried over to adulthood, then it becomes a problem.

Heaven is such a place, a place for adults who don't want to grow up, who dream of a nice, easy life being cared for, for eternity. It is far easier to believe in such things. There is no burden on you, the weight of responsibility is off of your shoulders, the earth is someone else's responsibility. You can relax and enjoy yourself.

But this is not how you thought when you were alive. It was your responsibility, this was your earth, your society, your country, your world, that needed good people to work hard and sacrifice everything. And people have! Recall the young man who stood before the tanks in Tiananmen Square! What a brave if not foolish thing to do, standing before a ten-ton behemoth. Imagine dying under its wheels, the slow excruciating pain of death. And sadly, that might very well have been his fate. How many others died that day? Fighting, losing their lives for a cause they very well knew was hopeless?

We can't let those sacrifices go in vain. We can't leave the fighting to others. Wait, let me correct myself. Yes, you *can*. You can let others do the fighting, you can look the other way. *But I hope my book finds the few who don't want to sit idle, finds the few who will reenlist: those who want the glory, the opportunity to grasp the cup, the cup of greatness!*

This is *our* fight to win. The earth has a lot of problems, but our forefathers had it much tougher. Things are better now, but in some cases things are worse. For the first time we humans are capable of wiping out the entire human race and much of the life on earth. We are capable of doing a lot of damage. With the rise of terrorism, a single human being can inflict so much pain on others. A few men taking control of a few airplanes almost brought down the greatest nation on earth! The more deadly, the more powerful evil becomes, the stronger we must be. We must be willing to sacrifice more, to work harder, to overcome more setbacks.

Heaven is a primitive, backward idea—a safe place to run off to, away from all the troubles mentioned above, a place for the weak and the cowardly. Show God that you are not one of them.

God demands more from us. We must become stronger, braver. Let the good in us guide us to great heights. Let us show God what we are capable of. Let us make God proud of us.

Want to Be with God? Get Ready to Face Some Tough Times

I give you a conundrum:

Pain, Suffering, Life, God;
No Pain, No Suffering, Death, No God

Now choose.

People ask, "How can I find God?" Do they really want to know? What are they really after? They have parked God in a nice, joyful Heaven, just where they want Her to be. Many religions insist God is not here, that She is "up there" somewhere. God being here presents a problem: here is not such a great place, here is pain, here is hardship, here is suffering.

Here, if you want a nice life, it has to be worked for, slaved for, sacrificed for. In life, we realize that nothing good happens without hard work, perseverance and dedication.

Why is it that food that tastes so good is bad for us?

Why is it that food that tastes so bad is so good for us?

Why is it that lying on the couch wasting away sounds so good?

Why is it that getting up and working out is so hard?

Why is it that getting an education is so hard?

Why is it that dropping out is so easy?

Why is it that destroying anything is so easy and only takes but a few minutes?

Why is it that building anything worthwhile takes a lot of time and effort?

I am sure you are onto the pattern here.

Let's discuss the last two from the list above. How long did it take Michelangelo to paint the Sistine Chapel ceiling? Months, years? Tell me, how long do you think it would take a crazed individual to destroy it all? Minutes?

Then think—how long will it take you to get to this mythical Heaven by confession, expression of regret and begging for mercy? Two minutes?

How long will these take: accepting the responsibility for what you have done, coming back, making amends, doing the right thing? A lifetime? Several lifetimes?

Beware of the easy, breezy religions—those that sweet-talk you, offer you sweet nothings. In the end, you will have nothing. You might be an upstanding person, a child of God, one who has morals, ethics, one who is always doing the right thing; but the prospect of the easy life has turned you into a slave, down on your knees, begging to dump your responsibilities and run away through the back door. The easy life has made you comfortable with the idea of torturing innocent people for their beliefs!

They have brainwashed you and you are letting them destroy you!

Want to be with God? Well, tighten your belt, stand up straight and get ready for some rough times.

This is not what the weak want to hear.

I get discouraged at times writing this book. Am I speaking to a deaf audience? Is it still a weak world? Are there any strong, brave people out there for whom this book will resonate?

If the world is still a weak world, this book will be a colossal failure.

Think of the great people in history: the Gandhijis, the Mirabais, the Schindlers, the Harischandras. Did any one of them have an easy life? None! Not one! *We talk with reverence and call them great souls—strange, not one of them ran away from pain and suffering, in fact, they did the total opposite!*

They all chose to side with God, and they all lived a life filled with pain and suffering. They chose to spend their lives fighting pain and injustice, trying to relieve the suffering being inflicted on their fellow human beings.

If you want to be with God, you will be drafted into battle against the injustice of this world. You will be working to make this a better world for future generations, and for the current generation as well.

Don't want to? Well, there's always death. Eternal death.

You can decline to be with God.

Few people want this job. Few people elect to be with God.

We are all biased to some extent—this cannot be helped—but let us realize that being biased, choosing to close our eyes to the horrors perpetuated by our religion means that we move further away from God. Instead we move closer to the antithesis of God.

You have heard this question: if a tree falls in the forest and there is no one to hear it, does it make a sound? And the answer is no, it does not.

Everyone knows that the Nazis killed six million Jews. Few know that they also killed more than half a million gypsies. These are the trees that fell and did not make a sound, because there was no one to hear them.

The 95% of Native Americans who were killed did not make a sound either.

The 300,000 Kashmiri Hindus who were ethnically cleansed from their own homes—they have lost their voice also.

The point of looking at all these horrors is to ask: where was God? Only a Teacher-faith can explain why these things happened: God is there for us, for advice and encouragement, but the earth is ours to shape whichever way we want. The course of humanity is to be laid out by our own hands. If horrible things happen, then we are to blame.

There is so much work to do here. There is so much need is down here. Yes, it is tempting to run away to greener pastures, but beware: a place without God is never a good place to be. Those "greener pastures" are nothing but mirages. Heaven is a mirage.

Hinduism will not sweet-talk you. It will not make enticing promises. It will not tempt you with sweet nothings whispered into your ear.

This faith is for those who are willing to embrace Karma and *work*. You are required to stand tall with God, shoulder to shoulder, head held high and to face down the problems life throws at us.

There is so much pain here, so much hardship here. God takes all that pain, all that suffering into Her heart. Let us lessen that pain, let us share in Her hardship, let us lighten Her load.

How many will step up?

There is no rest for the good, for the strong. There is no rest for God's people!

I am not interested in sitting in a corner of Heaven rocking in my armchair. I want to be down here. The earth might yet turn into a horrible place, climate change might yet come true, terrorists might yet succeed in killing millions, all sorts of horrible things might yet take place, but there is no other place I would rather be.

God can count on me.

If there is a bright future for humankind, all the troubles of life a thing of the past, then I want to be here forging that bright future, making that bright future happen, giving a helping hand.

I want to be part of the future, help build it, not live in the past.

Make God proud of us! What a great opportunity!

14. Karma and Reincarnation Mean That We are the Chosen People

Many are called, but few are chosen.

Let me rephrase the above: Many are called but few choose to suit up.

Okay, this is going to be cheesy: ask not what God can do for you, ask what *you* can do for God.

Most people beg for a handout from God: "Gimme this! Gimme that!"

The Hindu stands apart. He or she sees God surrounded by people with their hands out, begging. Poor God. Everywhere She looks there is someone asking Her for something.

The Hindu takes all this in—he decides God needs his help. "I can help," says the Hindu. There is much to do here on this earth. And so, when a Hindu dies, he or she comes right back. There are so many tales of suffering—little children out on a picnic with their families, getting lost or being taken away, crying themselves to sleep, crying for the comfort of their mommy, the same mommy distraught, looking for her lost child. Who is going to put up fliers? Who is going to help with the search? Who is going to comfort the grieving family and this little child? God is with this family and that little child but She needs our help. Will you ask to be chosen?

"A child is lost in the woods. Who wants to go back and search for him?" asks God.

"Not I," says the seeker of Heaven.

"Me, pick me!" says the one who choose Reincarnation.

"A dictator is bombing his own people, killing innocent women and children. Who wants to go back and fight for him?" asks God.

"Not I," says the seeker of Heaven.

"Me, pick me!" says the Hindu.

"A disease is ravaging the country, killing millions. Who wants to go back and research a cure?" asks God.

"Not I," says the seeker of Heaven.

"Me, pick me!" says the Hindu.

"An old sick dog is abandoned on the road by his human family. He is in shock, bewildered. "Who wants to go back and take care of this sick dog?" asks God.

"Not I," says the seeker of Heaven.

"Me, pick me!" says the chooser of Reincarnation.

"A family loses their breadwinner in an accident. They are forced out of their home and take refuge in a shelter. The children go to bed hungry. Who wants to hug these kids and take care of them?" asks God.

"Not I," says the father of these children!

"Me, pick me!" says the Hindu.

God can count on us.

Please do not misunderstand the title of this section. We are the chosen not because God favors us but because we choose to work for God, stay with God. We choose to come back. And this option is open to all. Anyone can choose to come back and work for God. Religion does not matter.

When you choose to run for office and are elected, you must realize that you carry a special responsibility. You have chosen to serve the people. You have been given the power to effect meaningful change in people's lives. Your decisions must be weighed carefully, as they will impact the lives of innocents.

As you have chosen a career in public administration, so have people chosen you to serve them.

When a Hindu chooses Karma and Reincarnation, chooses to come back to earth, willingly chooses to fight all the problems that the earth and its inhabitants face, come good, bad or worse, the Hindu has chosen to stay and work, to sacrifice for a better earth. As much as he or she has made this choice, God, in turn, has chosen him or her as Her special ambassadors.

Don't be a taker. Be a giver.

The man I admire most—as millions do—the man who walked with God, is Gandhiji. He inspired Nelson Mandela and Martin Luther King, Jr. His whole life was spent in the service of others. Unfortunately he did not get the chance to enjoy a well-deserved retirement. Gandhiji was a giver, not a taker.

The strong, the good are the givers, they are with God; and it is these people who choose to come back, who choose Karma and Reincarnation.

The weak are takers, they think only of themselves. Heaven makes perfect sense for these people. There is no work to be done. They can simply lie back and enjoy—for all eternity. But I seriously doubt that such a fantasy world exists.

Are you a person who will abandon your loved ones? Abandon your responsibilities? Your work is only half done: there are debts to be paid, responsibilities to be shouldered. Will you take the easy way out, if given the chance? Will you just cry for mercy, have everything forgiven, and then off you go to a happy place? Left behind are your debts; left behind are your wondering loved ones; left behind are your responsibilities; left behind are those who depended on you and are wondering where you went.

A dog thinks it is part of the family. Dogs are ready to die for their human family, but some of them find that their love is not returned. Some of them find themselves let out of a car on a lonely country road, only to watch the car speed away. They run after the car, trying to catch it, but the car is too fast for them. They watch it disappear over the horizon. The poor things never blame their human family; they whine and look bewildered, their hearts broken, and wonder what has just happened.

And so it is with your responsibilities, so it is with those who had depended on you to finish the job. It turns out all you were looking out for was for yourself. *God offered you a chance to abandon everyone and make yourself happy and—shame on you— you took it!* Unfortunately you will find that there is no free lunch, that there is no Heaven for the selfish, the cowardly and the weak. God has better things to do than cater to such people. All they get is death—eternal, useless death!

Karma and Reincarnation give you a chance to make a difference. Take it. *Stop looking at life as a burden, but as a golden opportunity.* It is only here that you can make a difference in the lives of others. It is here, by your actions, where you get to live a thousand or more years. Gandhiji may be dead and gone, but he lives in the hearts of millions and will continue to do so for years and years.

Come on, life is not *all* bad. There are plenty of joys in life; it is a matter of fighting for them, working for them and making them happen. That's the trouble: good things just don't fall out of the sky, you have to make them happen!

Karma and Reincarnation put you in control of your destiny. Stop dreaming of being a burden on God; be an adult and stand on your own two feet. But being an adult is tougher. It is easier to be a child—the worst you have to deal with is a stubbed toe, and there is always a loving person to console you. And that is precisely the concept of Heaven: a place where there is a nice old gentleman ready to take good care of us; we won't even have to worry about a stubbed toe!

Being a Hindu means choosing to be an adult and to accept all the accompanying responsibilities and worries that come with adulthood. We may not be able to stop all evil. Recently the country of Norway was hit with terrorism, with a madman running around killing innocents. A bomb exploded in a crowded place in Mumbai. How can we stop attacks like these? Maybe we cannot; so we have to be strong, take the blows and remain standing.

Can you find the strength to take a body blow and come back for more? It is very tempting to give in to the promises of a comfy retirement home waiting for us, and let others deal with the pain and suffering. *We did our part, now it is for others to carry the torch forward?*

Not everyone thinks this way—while his fellow presidents enjoy retirement and play golf all day, former President Jimmy Carter works tirelessly to bring hope and joy to millions of unfortunates and the poor, setting up schools, building houses, travelling the length of the globe to reach out to the needy, helping as much as he can.

He has a choice: (A) enjoy retirement, take in a ball game or travel the country making millions through speaking engagements; or (B) work for the betterment of humanity. He chooses B.

This is a man who was chosen by God; this man would be the Hindu that I talk about: willingly taking responsibility, willingly stepping forward, willingly moving to the front, willingly embracing Karma and Reincarnation.

And there are millions who think like him, millions of good people all over the world, from all walks of life, from all religions and the non-religious as well, who go out of their way to help others, who do more than their share, who bear more responsibility than their fair share.

Are you the person who is disturbed by images of famine—images of starving children? You rush to help. But after you are gone, have famines gone away? Have little children stopped starving to death? Who will help them? Hindus will! We come back; we work. We will make things better.

A woman has taken in dozens of children orphaned by a tsunami. After she is gone, who will carry on her work? There will be more tsunamis, more orphaned children. Will this mother choose to come back and hug those kids again?

A teen resolves to fight human trafficking. A man in India is risking his life trying to save children from slavery and bondage. The man is Hindu. He knows that, after he dies, his work will not stop. He will come back and resume his work. Will the teen resolve to do the same?

Well-meaning, ordinary people set up soup kitchens for the down-and-out. After they die, is it over? Or do they choose to move on? Hinduism asks these kind folks if they would like to come back and continue their life's mission. If you were one of these folks, what would you say?

A bright young award-winning chef quits his international job, comes home and starts feeding the poor and destitute, using his meager savings. He is dependent on his Parents for his own food and board. He is Hindu, so he knows he can continue this work forever and ever. If you are in the same situation, will you choose to come back?

An elderly lady keeps traveling to the murder capital of the world to keep her hospital open. Once she dies, who will continue her work? Will the hospital—and other hospitals like these—close? If you were she, would you choose to come back?

These are the people that God needs down here. These are the people making God proud. These are the people who we hope choose Karma and Reincarnation.

It's not What-you-Know, but Who-you-Know?

In real life, whether you are up for a promotion or are applying for a job do you not expect to be judged based on your body of work? Your accomplishments, your resume? Why then do certain religions preach that it is not what-you-know, but whom-you-know that matters? God doesn't judge you based on what you have done with your life, your accomplishments but uses a simple, primitive system of whether you call him by the right name or not? Why, oh why, do we continue to blindly accept such teachings? Where does our intelligence, education go? Does religion kill brain cells?

I need a job—is it—do I know anyone who can help me get a job? Or is it—do I have the necessary qualifications to land a job?

I want to attend med school or Yale—is it—do I know anyone who can help me get in? Or is it—do I have the necessary qualifications to make my dreams come true?

Remember, in the olden days the first question probably ruled the day. People had few qualifications, so it was mostly about knowing someone who could get you a job or gain acceptance. But times have changed, have they not? And that is the question that this book poses—*when it comes to religion, are we still stuck with old ideas that do not belong in modern society?* It is strange that there is not that much difference between an uneducated terrorist and a highly educated, well-read New Yorker.

In a recent commercial, a young girl asks, "How about being accepted for who you are?"—I ask the same—should that not be the right thing to do? Shouldn't God be accepting a person for who he or she is?

Is it because the lure is simple? Quite easy to simply join a religion—takes 2 minutes of our time. Much harder to lead the good, moral life—are we then giving in to easy promises being made? No need to work hard, no need to earn—just join us and we will get you into heaven? Get in the back door way?

Have we not changed over time? Women at one time were not allowed to vote, told to stay in the kitchen. Blacks at one time looked at the sign on the door before entering an establishment. Today, married couples, Parents of a family can be of the same gender.

Yet, the dominant religions of the planet are locked in the attitudes of the past. Some of their ideas should be an insult to every modern citizen but yet they see no reason to change, because of the silence of good people, the media.

15. Karma and Reincarnation Mean That All That Matters to God Is Character

Character is not everything; it is the only thing.

Okay, I took liberties with the above. But it is true. Character *is* the only thing that matters.

Only fools think that a two-minute conversion will get them close to God so they can enjoy the easy life. God "judges" us by our entire body of work through a whole lifetime. From childhood to old age, what have we done? Have we told the Truth, been a good citizen, strove to do the right thing?

But see, here is the quandary: being "judged" for what we did over a whole lifetime vs. just two minutes of ritual? You can see why the weak and the lazy would gravitate to the two-minute conversion and the easy way to the easy life.

For a child/student of God it is character that is paramount. A student understands that before you get an A or the top marks, much work needs to be done. It is like seeing a beautiful house or a great building: everyone stares at it and applauds, but beneath that great exterior lies the true foundations, the unsexy iron beams, without which the great building would not be possible. *Before* you get those top marks or that A, what lies before you is endless and relentless studying, sacrificing and setting goals—then only then will you achieve success.

You must be worthy of God *before* you meet God—only those who are worthy, only those who have made the necessary sacrifices, the great achievements will reach God.

At the end of the day, values and principles matter, both here on Earth and in the afterlife, before God.

Let us take some examples: a person like Mother Teresa worked day and night for the betterment of the poor and unfortunate. Did she have time to think of herself? Could she take the time to pray and thank God? Would God think any less of her if she were an atheist? I think not. She was doing God's work and that's all that matters—that's all that *should* matter. It is easy to pray, easy to sing praises; but to do actual work is hard. Doing hard work should be celebrated and acknowledged.

Or take Gandhiji. The majority of his time was spent in jails or fighting for independence for Indians. He had little time to think of himself: in his own words, he could not care less whether he was going to Heaven or getting Moksha. His days were spent deciding a million things: writing, cajoling, speaking, hugging and pushing for the rights of Indians. He had little time for religious issues, to go to a temple, to pray to God.

There are millions of people who regularly pray, go to a place of worship. In the end, who benefits? Themselves—just their lonely selves. Selfishly, they think only of themselves: how they can get to Heaven, how their afterlife can be better, how they can be happy. They think praying, spending time in a place of worship, belonging to religion X will get them the easy life; I don't think they care a whit about God, their "love" for God is false love, the real love is for the easy afterlife.

What matters to God is what you have become, what you

have chosen to do with your life. Has it been for the betterment of society? Is it a loss to your community or society if you are gone? Have you helped others? Have you thought less about yourself, and more about others? Instead of thinking of how you can get yourself to a nice Heaven, are your thoughts more about how you can make a difference in the lives of others?

Actions speak louder than words. But, as we know, actions are harder. To talk is easy. To sing praises to God is easy. To belong to a religion is easy. To pray is easy.

Working to make a difference in the lives of others is hard. Putting others first is hard. Taking time out from your personal life, time that can be used for your personal enjoyment, and using that time to give to others—that is hard.

Instead of praying to God, instead of going to a place of worship, you choose to go to an animal shelter and volunteer your time and love to those wonderful animals, or volunteer your time for a cancer walk, or help guide young children after school—in fact, anything that is more about others than your single self.

Which person would be closer to God? The one who spends his time praying or the one who is helping? It is the latter that is close to God. Religion does not matter—character does. You could be a Hindu, Christian, Muslim, Jew, Buddhist, atheist or agnostic—your choice of religion or lack of it does not matter to God.

When you help others, give your time and money to a shelter, realize it is this act that God appreciates, not whether you are of X or Y religion.

I realize that a lot of people will be shocked by what I am saying here. Millions of people love going to places of worship. Singing, dancing, chanting and praying helps to calm people and gives them joy. Am I saying that these are not enough? Yes, I am lifting the bar higher. You have barely started. In fact the real work has not yet begun. It is as if you have decided to write the next great novel and all you have done so far is turn on your laptop.

The Hindu religion says that once you die, only your soul rises to meet God. The soul has no body, no religion, no gender and no baggage of its earthly life. No more are you an American, Indian or Russian. No more are you a vegetarian, a carnivore, a republican or a democrat, a physician, a homemaker, a sailor, a mother, a father—all these are things in your past. All that matters now is the good or bad that you have done in your life.

A Hindu story: In a village there lived two men. One was a very "devout" person of God, daily visiting the temple, offering prayers to God, asking Her for more success in his activities, his trade, beseeching her for more money. But he never helped anyone in his life. Beggars learned to walk away when he came along. His debtors found that they were dealing with a merciless, heartless man.

And in the same village lived an atheist. This atheist mocked the very concept of God, laughed at the religious people and made fun of them and their Gods. But he spent the majority of his life helping others. He chose to make a difference in the lives of those around him.

It is the latter that God Rama welcomes with open arms. It is character that matters to God Sri Rama.

When some people promote religion over values, ethics and principles, you can be sure that they are not working for God—they work for *religion*, an endeavor that has benefitted them immensely. If character is all that matters, religion ceases to matter; and then they kill their golden goose. Decide for yourself if you want to participate in this charade.

Dr. King dreamed of a day when a person would be

judged not by the color of his skin but by the content of his character. It is sad to see so many believe that God judges us by our religious affiliation.

Changing religions is easy. Building character—now that takes work. It takes time.

When you choose to do God's work, please do so because you want to, not because you think that will make God happy or that you will one day be rewarded (while there is nothing wrong with thinking that way, it is better not to expect anything back when you are giving).

It is Hinduism that says God is within us. This does not mean that a super being resides within us. It is a metaphor. When you talk Truth, when you are kind, gentle, and have the heart of a little child, *then* God resides within you.

"Namaste": I greet the God within you.

Teaching speaks to our character. It asks what kind of a person you are rather than what religion you belong to. There is so much hate, so much abuse, so much killing going on in the world because people believe one's religious affiliation is the only thing that matters.

Here we go—make your choice—would you rather be defined by your actions, character or the religion you belong to?

Why Do Hindus Not Actively Proselytize?

Because Hindus believe that God is everywhere, that God is for *ALL*. We are *ALL* God's children, **no exceptions**. Hinduism is a unifying faith, it does not divide. Changing religions is like putting on different clothes; you are still the same person, nothing has changed.

Real change starts with your character, not with your outer trappings.

Changing religions is like changing your socks when you go out to an interview. Do you think that alone will get you the job? Is the interviewer that stupid? Of course not! Will your tennis game improve because you changed courts? Of course not! Then how come you think God is stupid enough to reward you based on religion alone? I have to say I am amazed at the brainwashing some of these religions have accomplished with otherwise intelligent people.

Listen, God couldn't care less about what religion you belong to.

God couldn't care less about what name you use to call Him or Her.

God couldn't care less about which holy book or scripture you read.

God couldn't care less about the way you pray or do not pray.

God couldn't care less whether you pray to one God or many.

The above are simple, cheap *rituals*! They mean nothing to God.

You hear people say they have book X or book Y or heard something and have converted to religion X and now follow this or that God. Let's follow this train of thought logically. There are three things such a person will do:

1. Convert to this religion (ritual)
2. Pray, read scripture, quote it (preaching)
3. Do good, tell the Truth, help others (action)

Tell me, which of these things will help you get close to God? Not the first two, obviously; but these two are the ones that are trumpeted by modern religions.

And it is these two that give religions their power and wealth.

But it is the third thing that Hinduism says will bring us close to God, not the first two, which are just cheap talk and rituals.

Picture a soup kitchen with volunteers helping the hungry and destitute. There are about 50 people there. Are they all of the same religion? Of course not. Some are Hindus; others are Christians, Muslims, unbelievers. What brought them together? Not religion, obviously, but a love of God, of humanity, a need to make a difference. It is the third thing from the list above that brought these diverse people together, and this is what scares most modern religions. For if it is Karma (action) alone that matters to God, religions will lose their power and wealth!

Hinduism emphasizes action—Karma. If we want to get close to God, it is through our actions, not because of some religion.

Let us suppose you are at a party and are introduced to someone—Tom or Krishna. You exchange pleasantries, chat for a while and then leave. Later if someone asks if you knew Tom or Krishna—what would your answer be? Would you not say, "Yes I have met him but don't really know him?" You don't expect to know a person just by their name or what they do, do you? There is more to a person than that. So, then why do you think God only knows you by your religion? Why do you think God will reward you because you got his name "right"? Your character, conduct, hopes, desires, accomplishments, failures, all the things that you did in your life do not matter? Only religion matters? Can we be that brainwashed?

You were born without a name, your Parents went through a list of names and finally picked one or maybe two and that's what they named you. What if they picked something else? Would that change you? How did you pick your friends—at what point did you pick a person as a friend because of his or her name? Divorce your spouse and then you meet a wonderful person but you reject her because her name is not the same as your former wife? Did you first pick your spouse because of their name?

Lincoln, Newton, Einstein, Shakespeare—why are these people loved and remembered so long after they are gone? Because of their names? Or because of what they accomplished in life?

How did you get a job? A promotion? They gave you the job or the promotion because they liked you name? Seriously? But you think God will give you the easy life because you got his name right? Seriously? The prospect of an easy life brainwash millions that much?

Do not be a NAME WORSHIPPER! God is more than just a name!

Let's recall the story of Gajendra, the elephant who cried out for God's help and the story tells us that God Vishnu rushed to his help. What name did the elephant use?

Just because an atheist murderer takes on a religion, does he stop being who he was? Just because a religious pedophile switches religions, does he stop abusing young boys? Of course not. It is his character that must change. The pedophile, murderer or rapist may have accomplished the first two items from the above list, but he has discarded the third, the most important one on this list.

And that's what is most important to God: your character. Changing religions will do nothing. According to Hinduism, after death your body stays down here to be burnt and vanishes into the air. It is your soul that will stand before God. That soul is your conscience. An evil conscience will be shriveled and dirty. A clean conscience will be pure and clear.

As I write this piece, the word ISIS has become famous recently for all the wrong reasons—these are a group of so-called Islamists who are using violence to stamp their brand of Islam on others in Iraq. Convert or die! They became more famous since they attacked Christian villages in Iraq, forcing the people to either flee or convert to Islam.

But are their ideas so new? Unheard of? Here in the US, I am told that unless I convert, "God" will torture me without end. Couched in a nice language doesn't lessen the evil intent. Religions, claiming God as their own, fostering and encouraging an "us" vs "them" mentality, religious division and hate. And this is what some Hindus fear that our faith will also descend down to if we actively start proselytizing.

Obama declares that ISIS must be destroyed—one of the reasons is that it uses violence to impose its brand of religion on others. Hmmm, I am being told that a being is waiting for me upstairs that will impose its religion on me using unspeakable violence, and amazingly, millions of people have no problem with such horror. Only religion, it seems, is capable of turning good people into such zombies. Not much of a difference between an uneducated terrorist who dreams of pleasures of the flesh in the afterlife and a bright, educated person brought up in a democracy in the free world—only religion can brainwash such disparate people equally well.

Some Hindus become upset when you call them Hindu. They say this is a misnomer. These people insist that the true name is *Sanatana Dharma*. These Sanskrit words translate to *Eternal Truth* or *Eternal Right Way of Conduct*. Now is that any kind of a name for a religion? *Exactly!*

The God who has no name or all names, God Sri Rama, is Krishna is Jesus is Allah is Buddha is Durga is....

Hinduism: the religion that has a funny name—or no name at all!

There's no need for names. Discover spirituality. Discover the God within.

Let me say it again: the Hindu way is tougher, harder.

If you wish to be Hindu, you must change your character: become a giver, not a taker. Being a Hindu does not mean you have changed religions. You can still pray to Jesus or Allah or Buddha or any other deities or Gods. Hinduism wouldn't be Hinduism if we insisted you stop praying to these Gods.

But of course you have to change your attitude. No longer must you think praying works; it is actions that count. No longer must you fear God, no longer must you behave like a slave or servant, no longer must you think of sneaking out the back door.

No longer will you "pray" to just one deity. You will realize that all names are God's names.

16. Karma and Reincarnation Mean a Hindu's Goal is Moksha—An Awakening of the Mind, Soul and the Heart—to Be Touched by the Hand of God!

Let us differentiate between Heaven, as it is popularly understood, and Moksha. Heaven needs no qualifications; it is a destination you can reach by begging. But Moksha is always *earned*—it is never, ever begged for; it is a goal that you must work for. Moksha is a state of mind. It is not a place, and it is certainly not a place to run off to. It is enlightenment, knowledge, a pure heart. It is said that the Buddha had attained enlightenment while sitting under the Bodhi tree. Moksha is something we work for right here, on earth.

It is about reaching a state of mind that transcends but at the same time embraces life and reality. While the concept of Heaven is about leaving everything behind and running away, Moksha, Karma and Reincarnation are about embracing life and working towards a better physical and mental state.

Let us suppose you have gotten lucky and won millions of dollars in the lottery. You are now rich beyond your dreams. You can now buy anything your heart wishes—the fast car, the big house, a big boat, fancy clothes, sex, all the expensive food and drink that you want, lavish vacations… fun, fun, fun!

But you are the same person as before. You hear beautiful music and wish you could play like that musician, but you can't. You see a beautiful movie and wish that you could be the director or the writer who wrote the wonderful story! You still can't understand most scientific articles or books. You see a great painting and wonder how the painter could come up with such wonderful brush strokes!

The former—fast cars, food, drink, sex—can be bought or received as a gift.

The latter—art, music, intelligence, etc.—has to be earned.

The former is Heaven, the latter is Moksha!

Here's the Golden Rule: Heaven=pleasures of the flesh; Moksha=pleasures of the mind, heart and soul

Think about it. If you beg before a king or a rich person, all he can give you is money, land and riches you can use to buy drink, sex, the good life and all the pleasures of the flesh.

But get close to the likes of Einstein, Tyagaraja, Gandhiji, Socrates, Mozart, Plato, Oskar Schindler and the Buddha, and what can these great men and women give you? Just imagine the treasures of the mind these great souls have.

To have the intelligence of an Einstein, the mind of a Gandhiji, the heart of a Mother Teresa, the talent of a Tyagaraja, the guts of a Schindler...can you imagine what that would be like? Now you are on the path to Moksha.

Those who seek Heaven seek a reward that delights the flesh. Those who seek Moksha seek to uplift their hearts and minds.

Some Hindus hold the wrong view that Moksha means a state free of sorrow and misery, which is absolutely untrue. Absence of pain and suffering means an absence of life! To be alive means to face life's ups and downs. Moksha gives us the power to navigate life's wrong turns with equanimity, like a ship that navigates the ocean's choppy waters with ease.

The goal of Moksha is the pursuit of big dreams; pain and suffering are constant companions on this journey. In a Teacher faith like Hinduism, the goal of a Teacher is to shape her students into productive citizens. The Teacher challenges your brain, develops your intelligence, turns you into a strong adult, so that you may face the problems of life with equanimity, perseverance and become successful. All the Teacher can do is to give you tools for success. The rest is up to you.

If you want to move forward, become an adult, take control of your life, shape your life, shape the future of humankind, then choose Moksha.

If you want to go backward to your childhood, back to the womb, choose Heaven.

Aspire for a bone, a bone is all you get.

I just don't see it. I just don't see God playing nursemaid to billions of self-absorbed people who want to sit and do nothing while God caters to them.

There are only two kinds of existence I can imagine in such a "Heaven"—one is as a life spent as a ghost. With no body, you'd have no more hunger or bodily pains. Memories of your past life would be totally erased. This looks more to me like a condemnation, not a commendation: day after day, night after night of a life (if you can call it that) without memories, without any human contact, without participation in anything, without working for anything. You'd be just an observer unable to understand anything, your brain completely blacked out. That would be your "Heaven." Seems more like a Hell to me, but this is what you chose.

But why would God give the gift of life to some and not others? So, if Reincarnation applies to all, then I can see the seekers of Heaven, the easy life, coming back as bugs, let us remember, the lower life forms do not get the gift of pain and suffering. Life as a bug, a dust mite say, would be quite good—they live in your bed and in your carpets, no concerns or worries, no work, happily munching away at your dead skin cells!—Heaven!

No one in his or her right mind would choose such an

existence over human life, but there it is—the greed for the good, easy life makes one make crazy choices. God will not stop you from making stupid choices, all God can do is to give you the intelligence and the education to make informed, educated choices. If you let yourself be brain-washed by religion, then it is your fault.

Moksha is the awakening of the mind, the heart and the soul. It has also been described as being one with God. To be a God! I describe it as being touched by the hand of God. Buddhists describe it as the path to enlightenment—a path that never ends. Enlightenment is never fully attained. For the path is long and never ending. Knowledge is a vast sea that never can be fully absorbed, never can be crossed. One can only journey in it. One can only dance on the path, feet tripping over in joy, with a song in one's heart.

I lied when I said earlier that Moksha is a goal. Moksha is a never-ending journey—a journey for knowledge and enlightenment, walking side by side, step by step with God.

I am going to go off on a tangent here, but please bear with me. Have you read X-Men comics? Have you watched the "Star Wars" movies? The *Lord of the Rings* trilogy? The Harry Potter movies? Who is the leader in all these films? Yes, there is a young hero, but he is always guided by a wise person. The leader of the X-Men is not the one throwing fire from his eyes or a person with claws or a woman who can conjure up storms, but a guy with a brain! A wise old man who cannot even walk.

Intelligence beats all. The leader is always the one who is the most intelligent of all. Hinduism is more relevant today; the world has steadily moved from a brawn-dominated world to a brain-dominated one. Have intelligence, have brains, have the necessary education, and you can conquer the world!

Being touched by the hand of God, the blessed ones,

people like Gandhiji, Socrates, Einstein, Tyagaraja, Mozart were very special people, but such specialness had to be earned. One must be willing to walk through fire, walk with God. When the going gets tough, one must be patient and calm. One must fight through, for God is with you. These people reached for greatness, they strove to be extraordinary human beings, they dared to be God-like just as Sri Rama did.

How do we earn blessings from God? First, let us not seek to run away from pain and suffering. We must realize that these are part of life. One can easily go online and buy a degree for a few bucks. There's a guy sitting in his basement printing out fake degrees, as many as one could want. Why go through years and years of schooling? Why bother working hard, making sacrifices, spending endless hours studying, preparing notes, dealing with deadlines, when you can get it all with just the click of a mouse? But we know that this fake degree will not get us anywhere. Take this degree and seek employment and employers will laugh in your face. At the end of the day, things that come easily and are cheap are just that: easy, cheap and totally worthless. The things that are worthwhile come with a lot of hard work, a lot of sacrifices, a lot of pain and suffering.

Just by joining a club (religion), do you think you can get free food, drink and sex for all eternity? Are you that gullible? Well, you are not alone, it seems millions of highly educated people fall for these easy promises.

Haven't you heard people always saying that one should see the inner person, and not fall for the outer beauty? What is beautiful is the inside, the good heart and not the external shell, which over time will fade. How many follow this dictum? Well, that is what Moksha is all about: the ability to see such pure hearts, the ability to see the inner person.

But first you must prove worthy. You yourself must have a clean, clear heart. There are many greats in the Hindu lore—MiraBai, Madhava, Sankaracharya, Kabir. Many Hindus mistakenly believe that it is their singing or praying to God that got them close to God, to Moksha; but I believe it is their pure hearts, the hearts that held no malice toward anyone, that made them worthy of God.

The other day I stumbled across a video on YouTube. Indian TV and movies are very popular in Pakistan. Millions of Pakistanis avidly watch Indians in their daily lives; well, at least what passes as a daily life in the made-up world of TV and movies. Pakistanis are mostly Muslim, and they are watching Indians, mostly Hindus, go about their daily lives. Well, in the YouTube video, this little kid, a Pakistani Muslim, is shown praying to Hindu Gods. This little child's pure heart has not yet been corrupted by adults. He saw God in everything.

I want you to be under no illusions. As you can see, Moksha is the dead opposite of Heaven. Most religions make it look easy to get into Heaven, but attaining Moksha is difficult. Like King Bruce, we Hindus will be reborn again and again. We will try and try again. How long might this take? Ten lifetimes? A hundred? A thousand? Or maybe it will never happen? Remember, nothing is promised, but what a wonderful journey will it be. Anyone who loves reading can attest to this: the joy of learning is the greatest joy of all.

This journey will test us. It will test our mettle, our commitment.

People talk about the bliss of Heaven, but bliss for whom? How many? Just one person, one selfish person. Can you find bliss in the laughter of a child? Can you find bliss in making sweet treats for young kids or buying them gifts? Can you find bliss in their shrieks of delight? Can you find bliss in helping others, in saving a frightened animal, in making life better for total strangers? Can you find bliss in curing a frightened young child, in making her Parents shed tears of joy?

Well, you can't do that while sitting in Heaven, only here. Only here on earth can you do that. Such bliss is possible only down here.

King Bruce, here I come!

To be a Hindu means to be special, to be that special person who has made that choice. It means that we chose the hard way, we chose to earn something rather than take anything unearned. I am sure many of you can relate. It means we chose to do the right thing even if the journey is long and hard. It means we chose to stay with God and work for a better earth. We are like Atlas: the weight of the earth is on our shoulders. The last part is a result of our choice; when we choose to stay on, we have no choice but to work for a better earth, or perish trying. Let others choose to run away and hide; the Hindu will stand firm alongside God.

You have to be willing.

Are you? One cannot be a hero without jumping into the fight, without risking life and limb. To wish to be safe is a normal reaction, but only a hero will put his life at risk for the betterment of society, for the sake of others.

Think of how many police officers risk their lives daily fighting crime. A routine traffic stop can turn deadly in an instant. Think of the firefighter who goes to put out a small fire that suddenly turns deadly, or the soldier who goes to clear a roadside "rock" and discovers—too late—that it is a bomb.

Do you think that these police officers, firefighters and soldiers and their families never thought of an easier, less risky life? As we all know, there are much easier, far less dangerous and far more lucrative jobs than these. But then, if everyone thought this way, who would protect us? Who would save us from danger?

We hear so much about the great ones who risked their lives, but we hear little about the foot soldiers who bore the brunt of the first bullets fired. Their names have been forgotten, except by their near and dear ones.

The choice is clear: believe in the easy promises of charlatans or turn to God. The path to Moksha is difficult; it is a difficult choice to make. It is very tempting to make the easy choice: the nice Heaven awaiting us, an easy life for eternity!

Who in his or her right mind would choose to do the opposite? Many have, many do. Hindus have chosen to protect the rest, to save others from danger. Hindus have chosen Moksha, the higher goal.

Pascal's Wager

The 17th century philosopher and mathematician Blaise Pascal speculated that belief in God is better because you gain if you believed and you lose if you did not believe.

To me, both the above conclusions are wrong.

First, let us take the last conclusion that if you did not believe, you lose. Why is that? Recently we had an election here in the U.S. Many people did not believe in Barack Obama, and they did not vote for him. Now that they have lost, should they be discriminated against? Shot? Abused? Their legs broken?

Thank God we live in a democracy.

What seems clear from Pascal is that his era was not a democratic one, nor were his ideas democratic. Live under the likes of a brutal dictator like Saddam Hussein and these words make perfect sense! Haven't we all heard of brutal dictators holding sham elections and then being elected by a huge margin, because their people "loved" them so?

In these countries if you voted against the strong man like Saddam and were found out, they would come and break your legs—or worse.

According to the likes of Pascal, you better believe or else!

It shows the power of religion that even good people can be brainwashed into working for a strongman, a Saddam. It shows that kings ruled during the times when these religions came into being, and these religions simply elevated their local king to a God level: God made in the image of a strong, brutal king.

Pascal's first conclusion does not make any sense either. Is he is saying that if you believe you are rewarded? Yes, the people who support the strong man, the dictator, will be rewarded. Sycophants will be rewarded with plum positions and big contracts. Toadies will be rewarded with wealth under a Saddam's regime.

God's place is a place for flatterers, toadies, grovelers and sycophants? Is there no place for honest men and women who tell it like it is? No place for those with principles, values and ethics? Character doesn't matter? Ethics and values do not matter? These religions say so. To them, what really matters is whether you are loyal to this king or not. A pedophile, a mass murderer can get into Heaven and enjoy themselves; while at the same time a Gandhiji or an Einstein could be tortured, beaten, raped and sodomized, their legs broken—under a king's rule!

It is this mindset: once you have lowered God to a king and yourself down to a slave or servant, all your values change.

Hinduism has consistently said that God is our Parent/Teacher, that we are *all* God's children/students.

Now imagine God as a Teacher. A kid in his class has clashed with the Teacher. Perhaps the Teacher is leaning towards the Democratic Party while this kid is a republican. Maybe the Teacher is a Bears fan and this kid is a Packers fan. Anyway, the Teacher has given a test and now he is ready to assign grades. Should he give this kid a lower grade because he spoke up, because he did not "believe" in him or chose to disagree with him?

A good Teacher would never do that. Marks or grades will be given according to the quality of the returned paper. You better believe that the Hindu God is a Teacher!

What is *quality* for God? Character! The works (Karmas) that you have done in your lifetime. How you spent your days. Have you done good works? Have you striven to do good, to help others? Did you treat others well? Did you strive to tell the Truth, to do the right thing always?

These are the things that matter to God; and as you can see, these have nothing to do with any particular religion. As you can see, even atheists can lead lives in a clean, honest way, God's way.

Works (Karma), not words, matter.
Pray to God with your actions, not words.

And there you have it: religions value belief over good works, because belief is where the money is, where the power is.

If even atheists can be close to God, then what use are our places of worship, holy books and other religious artifacts? If no one comes to places of worship, if no one buys religious trinkets, then how do we get their money? How do we keep our power, our hold over them?

And what power! Some time ago, in a backward country, a woman was accused of a crime and was sentenced to death by stoning. One of the stoners was her own son. Her own son! This is not an isolated incident. In the past, neighbors collaborated with religious leaders in dragging out their friends and neighbors to the gallows. Religious leaders came around, pointing out the heretics, those who didn't attend worship, those who spoke out, and their neighbors helped catch and kill their own friends and relatives! Imagine the Buddha being dragged out, beaten almost to death and hanged until he died!

As they say, it takes two to tango, two hands to clap. Without support, evils like racism, fundamentalism, religious bigotry and the caste system would have collapsed long time ago.

And so the drumbeat of evil continues. Even today we have people supporting Pascal's wager, warning others to kowtow or else. Thanks to modern times and democracy, their actions may have changed, but the mentality remains the same. The sickening ideas still remain in circulation.

17. Karma and Reincarnation Mean the Victim Should Not Be Left to Suffer. Coddling the Criminal While Ignoring the Victim's Voice Is Wrong

God takes away sin? What about the suffering of the victim? THAT is not taken away? If you had a choice, which one would be more important and the first to be taken away, is it the sin or the suffering? The criminal is the one that is made happy, forgiven? The victim is ignored, left to suffer?

A lot of religions aggressively proselytize. They know that telling a would-be customer what he or she wants to hear is more likely to result in a successful conversion. These religions are happy to cater to the criminal/perpetrator (a category most of us belong to—who among us has led a clean, Godly life?). We all have made our share of mistakes; and so, these religions are happy to tell us that a nice God awaits: one who is happy to overlook our mistakes, happy to forgive us for our transgressions—after which we happily go off to the land of Oz!

Almost every proselytizing pamphlet is filled with promises of what "our" nice God will do for you.

The pedophile does not have to come clean to the world, ask for forgiveness from his victim, turn over a new leaf and work to help other victims (this is what Hinduism requires you to do); all he needs to do is beg God! Now, isn't that easy?

A Bernie Madoff, one who has cheated innocent elderly

men and women, doesn't have to pay back all the money he stole (again, a Hindu requirement).

The easy-breezy religions! Telling you what you want to hear: *Don't worry, just confess on your deathbed and off you go to that paradise waiting for you! Hooray for the criminal/ perpetrator!*

Do you see the missing person in this scenario? The victim!

One thing that strikes me as quite odd is that most religions pay little or no attention to the victim. All their attention is directed towards the criminal/perpetrator, towards making sure he feels better.

And the poor victim?

Who?

Who is that? What is his or her fate? Has the victim's hurt gone away? Has the victim been compensated for their loss? It is as if we are talking gibberish, as if we are talking crazy, by asking such questions.

What is frightening to me is that in over 2,000 years not even one person has asked about the victim. Not even one? Have people been brainwashed to that extent?

When you make a mistake and your mistake has hurt someone and you feel remorse, shouldn't you feel bad for the *victim*? Instead you are encouraged to feel bad for yourself. If that was you, wouldn't you be rushing in to set things right? If you lost control of your car and hit and injured someone, shouldn't your first priority be to take the injured to a hospital, pay for his treatment and then ask for forgiveness from him?

Assume someone had assaulted you or your loved ones, your daughter perhaps or your aged father. He is caught and brought before the judge. Without even looking your way, he begs and pleads the judge to forgive him. And the judge says, "Okay, you are free to go"!

Has your jaw just dropped to the floor? And yet, when a religion says this is what will happen after death, you sing this judge's praises?

Let me get this straight—God pays more attention to the sinner than the victim? He is more concerned with the pedophile, the murderer, the abuser, than the one who is suffering? So, if a pedophile of this religion abuses a young boy of another faith, say a Hindu or an atheist, God will nicely forgive the pedophile and proceed to torture the young child for eternity? Is your stomach churning with disgust yet?

You are a policeman. You come across a terrible scene. A gunman has just mowed down innocent men, women and children with a machine gun, but someone had thrown a chair at the gunman and now he is on his knees clutching his head. Your first priority is... to make sure the gunman is okay? You ignore all the victims dying, bleeding to death, and rush to the gunman, embrace him and make sure he is okay? Are we in the Twilight Zone?

Again, someone, just one person, please speak up! How many of you readers have taken courses in ethics, values and principles in school? Can one of you speak up? Please? This is not about God. It is about a *religion* using all the carrots at its disposal for conversion purposes, making easy promises to lure converts.

What values are being taught here? Are these the values of today or are they primitive, outmoded values?

A recent famous case: the University of Penn State was rocked by a pedophile scandal. What was heartbreaking was that the so-called good people, people in authority, people guiding young men and women at a prestigious learning institution, could behave so unbelievably callously without regard to doing what is right.

To recap, one university official started using the university facilities to conduct his nefarious activities, using his access to the sports facilities provided by the university, enticing young kids with the lure of unprecedented access to the famed football team, and then abusing them. When the Truth came out, the top officials got together, and decided to do nothing. I speculate this is what must have happened: the pedophile apologized, cried, begged and vowed never to do it again. Just reflect on this for a minute. Eerily, this is what religions say is good enough for God. Just cry, beg and apologize. The criminal was not apologizing to his victim, no sir. He was apologizing to his superiors, those who could make him suffer, ban him from the university, go to the police or press and/or press charges against him. In the back of his mind was he also thinking, "If I am kicked out of the university, will there be no more boys to entice?" And so what happened at Penn State? Did the abuse stop? No sir, it *continued!* The criminal was back at his game, abusing more children.

This is why this is so wrong: talk is cheap, anyone can cry and ask for pity. When he was apologizing to his superiors, vowing to never do such things again, was the pedophile intent on deceiving? I think not. I think he was genuinely sorry, genuinely upset about his behavior. Think of resolutions that you may have made in your life, resolutions to lose weight, cut down on your drinking, stop smoking, start exercising, etc. How many did you keep? But when you made those resolutions were you not serious? Yes, you were! Of course you meant to do all that with all your heart. But saying and doing are two different things, aren't they?

Karma and Reincarnation, my friends, is DOING!

That is why they say talk is cheap, actions count. The Penn State authorities should have gone public, should have called in the police and pressed charges against their employee. If they had done so, they actually would have done this man a big favor: he would not have abused any more boys, maybe he would have sought help sooner. Everyone would have known who he was. Steps would have been taken to make sure he would not abuse any more boys. And yes, we keep forgetting the third party, the innocent victim here, aren't we? Penn State authorities were happy to get the criminal's side of the story. They didn't think it was necessary to call on the young boy, the young victim, to get his side of the story.

Religions are saying God does the same thing. Descartes was wrong. God does cheat. God cheats the victim of justice. God has no time to hear the victim's side of the story. God has no time for the pedophile's victim.

Mercy and Heaven for the criminal/perpetrator, but neglect and Hell for the victim?

Pandering to criminals/perpetrators and brutalizing the innocent once more is not justice! A criminal is tried, but if there is no victim to lend his or her voice to the proceedings, is it really justice? The judge and criminal come to an agreement without the victim's input? Is that justice? The criminal feels bad for what he had done? Great! But what is that? Has justice been done just because the criminal now facing serious punishment suddenly discovers that he has been wrong? Isn't this a bit too convenient?

This is not right. Things must be set back to where they were. The victims must be compensated for their loss. Then and only then can we say that justice has been done. But there's a problem. Doing this is hard.

Hinduism asks you to do the right thing, make God respect you, be proud of you. Please choose the harder option, the right option. Karma and Reincarnation, Hinduism, puts the victim first. Every Hindu knows that if you die without paying off all your debts, you must come back and repay. That is the right thing to do. This is Hinduism. Being with God or finding God is not going to be easy. It will be hard. You will be asked to adhere strictly to the Truth, to do the right thing, and above all to stick to your ethics and principles. It is those who show unflinching adherence to Truth who will find themselves with God.

Most of us do not lead lives on the straight and narrow; few of us devote our lives to the betterment of humanity. Few of us can stand proudly and say, "I walked in God Sri Rama's footsteps." We all have a few skeletons in our closet—perhaps not major crimes, but we all have done things that we are not proud of.

It is these feelings of guilt that are being exploited by some religions. They tell us what we want to hear: nice God is ready to forgive as soon as we show some regret; no follow-up action is needed. There is no need to ask for forgiveness from the victim or the world at large, no need to work to make amends.

The poor victim hearing such nice words is twice-raped: once when he is brutalized, and twice when he learns that "God" and his perpetrator have come to a cozy agreement—one that does not involve him, does not involve his input.

Accepting your mistakes, owning up to what you did means not asking for forgiveness, *not* seeking a way out!

If you have an option to declare bankruptcy or repay your debts, no matter how long it takes, how many will choose to do the latter?

Sometimes I hear feeble responses: "Yes, the victim was compensated, amends were made, but we are asking God for mercy anyway." Huh? For one thing, nothing was heard from the victim about making amends; second, if you had made amends, then the question of asking for mercy does not arise. You paid back your debt; then why are you down on your knees begging for mercy? What crime have you committed? The reason you are down on your knees begging is because you have cheated your victim; and sadly, as you get down on your knees and keep begging, you continue to cheat your victim. Your victim is twice victimized!

Hinduism does not coddle the criminal.

Break something? Apologize, yes, but you must replace the broken item! You must make amends! You are at a rich guy's party. You are enjoying yourself, but a momentary slip means an expensive vase or item gets broken. The rich guy takes one look at you and says, "Forget it!" How does that make you feel? You know why he said to forget it: he thinks you are too poor to make up for the loss. He took pity on you. But shame on you for asking for pity. Whether that owner pities you and asks you to forget it or asks you to pay for the item does not matter. There is only one way to resolve the situation if you are a Hindu. You *must* replace the item. There is no other way.

Similarly, if in your life you have done wrong things, have hurt people, have debts that have remain unpaid, stop feeling sorry for yourself. Cry later, cry inside, but first there is work to do. Asking for forgiveness benefits just one person: you.

Hinduism says that if you have a debt to pay, why not honor that debt?

Maybe try thinking less about yourself and a bit more about what you can do for others, a bit more about what you can do to alleviate the pain and suffering that you have caused. What is important, what is the right thing to do here, is to make sure that what has been broken be put back right, that what has been taken away be given back, to wipe others tears first before you wipe yours.

The first question a Hindu asks God is, "How can I set things right? How can I make it up to my victims?"

And the Hindu will not do this while on his knees either. A Hindu *stands tall* before God, his held high, his back straight; no asking for forgiveness, no sir. Forgiveness must be earned! Only one person can forgive us, and that is not God! God is not qualified to forgive us. Only one person—the victim—is qualified to forgive us.

God is the third party here. The issue is between you and the victim, no one else. Who is God to poke His nose in this business? Listen, God is not the one that was robbed, beaten, raped, sodomized, abused. That person is the victim; and he or she is still hurting, still waiting for you to make amends.

Once when my nephew was a kid, he asked me permission to do something. I was a bit puzzled, why is he asking me and not his mother or father? My sister who overheard the conversation laughed at me and said, "He is asking you so that you would say it is okay."—These people are doing the same thing—the victim might not forgive so easily, so they think they take the easy way out and religions are happy to promise it to them—one coward encouraging another coward.

But the whole idea is wrong; why are we even thinking of being forgiven? Our first thought should be to make things right. We have been bad, we have been thoughtless, but we have changed. We have become better people. Now it is time to do the right thing, to make things right for those who have been hurt by our actions. Whether they forgive us or not is immaterial. What is important is that we make up for the loss caused by our actions.

Shouldn't we be excited to get this opportunity? Excited to right a wrong? Make the victim happy, make the victim whole once more? The idea of Reincarnation makes us look at the same situation in a whole new light—let us seek enlightenment, not forgiveness! If you made a mistake turning in your homework at school and Teacher says it's okay, you don't have to get it right, will you ever learn anything? The only way is to do it right, but then it also depends on whether you want to learn or not, correct? If you have no interest in school, in studies or bettering yourself, why correct your mistakes? There is no need—hence you see why Reincarnation benefits those who seek to get better, to be enlightened, those who seek Moksha.

And that is the chance that God gives us through Karma and Reincarnation—behold the power of Reincarnation.

We note here that if there is no Reincarnation, as some religions preach, then there is no way of compensating the victim, so then begging seems the right course of action. But for the life of me, I just don't get how using violence on a criminal will help the victim (Hell), I do not view God as a torturer, nor do I think that cowards will be rewarded, and so death is the final answer.

These days we hear so much about all these killers who have caused so much harm to innocent people—the young killers in Colorado, the killer in the movie theatre in the same state, the killer in the Wisconsin Sikh temple, the cold-blooded murderer of children in Newtown. Are all these killers going to be simply forgiven if they beg and grovel? Where is the justice for their victims? Most of them were young, just starting out in life, dreaming big about starting a family, having children, accomplishing great things. All those dreams were snuffed out! And what about the living victims? The relatives of those killed? Someone has lost a son, a daughter, a best friend, a father, a mother, an aunt… the list goes on and on. These people then have to live with the heartbreak till they die. Where is the justice for them?

In Hinduism you don't get to beg your way out. You must repay.

You made the mess, *you* clean it up! Don't you even dare thinking of sneaking out the back door!

The one who sneaks out misses a great opportunity: an

opportunity to become a better person, an opportunity to become strong, an opportunity to be a hero and yes, an opportunity to make this a better place to live for all of us. God is testing you to see how you will react to adverse situations; will you seek to sneak your way out, head for the back door, find the escape hatch? Or will you be a Hindu and head for the front, the battlefield?

Be a Hindu. Nail that back door shut! Remember, there are no shortcuts, not in life and especially not in front of God. Some Hindus think that taking a dip in the river Ganges will purify them and that all their bad Karmas will be washed away. Nice and easy! It saddens me that most religions have fallen prey to the weak. Even Hinduism could not escape.

A clean conscience, a clean heart is what will bring you closer to God. No amount of begging or taking a bath in a holy river or doing a puja or chanting a mantra or confessing will get you anywhere close to God.

Heroes don't cry for pity. Heroes *stand tall* (there's that word again). Heroes look you in the eye. Heroes do what is necessary to get things done, to put things right.

Heroes do these things first, *then* they ask for forgiveness.

Maybe I am being too harsh on some people. Most religions do not believe in Reincarnation. They believe in a cozy Heaven or a cruel Hell. They give you a choice to either go down on your knees and beg, or be tortured for eternity. Faced with such a "choice"—as if someone has put a gun to their head and said, "Do this or else!"—do they really have a choice? Followers of such religions have no choice but to beg and grovel.

But Hindus and those who believe in Reincarnation *do* have a choice: ask for forgiveness or go back and repay. Choose to go back and work to make amends, and watch God beam with pride!

Lord Jim

One of my favorite stories and very relevant to this book, the novel *Lord Jim* by Joseph Conrad is a must-read for every Hindu.

The book tells the story of Jim (his last name is never revealed), a sailor, who makes a mistake. When the time comes for him to be a hero, he fails completely. But God gives him a second chance to prove himself, and this time he grabs this chance with both hands. The second chance ends with him taking a bullet, but Jim never flinches. His well-wishers urge him to run away, to build a new life (Heaven), but he refuses. He chooses to do the right thing and ends up losing his life.

When the person who is suffering is a loved one, and they are suffering because of something we have done, no one would want forgiveness. We would all want a second chance—a second chance to put things right, to come through this time. It is the same second chance that Karma and Reincarnation gives us.

Those who choose Karma and Reincarnation might be put in the same position as Jim. They could be walking into a worse life than they had experienced. Will you choose to stand tall and take the bullet? Hindus do not believe that being born is a waste, where we grow up with the fear of going to Hell, our ultimate destination being a kind of "retirement home". Hindus believe that life has a purpose, a meaning.

We are children of God. Much is expected of us. We give back to God. We are destined for great things. On our shoulders falls the responsibility of steering humanity into a great future. Walk the path that Lord Jim did. Stand tall before God and make Her proud!

18. Karma and Reincarnation Mean That We Do Not Believe in Miracles, Magic and Prophecies

"There is no secret ingredient. It's just you."
—from the film KungFu Panda

Hinduism says there are no miracles, there is no magic man; it is just *you*! It is all up to your lonesome self.

Don't we all love magic? Saying, "Am Phat," and getting things done? Why not? With magic there is no hard work, no sacrifice, no dealing with setbacks, no uncertainty, no waiting for a long time—just a snap of the fingers and things get done in an instant. Where's the downside? This is how people are lured in to the idea of Heaven, a ready-made magic land of happiness and joy.

Fact is good things in life don't just show up at our front door, nor do they fall on top of our heads. They have to be worked for like a dog, sacrificed for. The weak have neither the strength, the willingness nor the patience, to put in the time and effort, it takes to become a success. And so enter the magic genie. You just have to show this magic genie that you are a spineless jellyfish, and the genie will do a quick wave of his magic wand and presto! Paradise! Enjoy!

Today the earth faces a lot of problems. Some people say the jury is still out on climate change, but a solid majority of scientists worldwide agree that it is inevitable. What will happen then? Hot, ugly weather, withering crops, entire countries under the oceans, millions displaced. Utter devastation! But if we pray hard enough, the magic man will arrive. Everything will be set right as before! Yay!

What if terrorists get hold of nuclear weapons and threaten to wipe out major cities around the world, causing immense devastation and destruction? Not to worry, here comes the miracle man to make the evil people go away. In an instant, their weapons vanish and they are set to be tortured!

Where are we now? Are we in comic-book land? These religions keep us in perpetual childhood, perpetual weakness. We remain like children, afraid to become adults, afraid to question. How many good people have sat silently while the priest went on a rant?

Myths, fantasies, magic and miracles are *too* perfect, *too* instantaneous. That's how you know they are fake, just myths. Real life is not the life of a Cinderella. Real life is not perfect; that is how you know it is real life, not fake.

In real life change is constant—nothing lasts forever—no wonder they say, "the only constant is change". But fairy tales do not change—10,000 or a million years from now Cinderella will still be losing her shoe, the ugly frog will still turn into a prince—but that is how we know they are fairy tales

The coward wants a magic sword and a magic shield. He thinks, "I can point the sword at them and they all will die. As long as I have this magic sword, no one can kill me. As long as I have this magic shield, no one can harm me. The magic cloak that will make him invisible." This is the coward's way, perpetually looking out for himself so no harm can come to him.

The magic sword is a myth. The magic *anything* is a myth. If it were just an ordinary sword, would you still fight? Do you have the heart of a fighter? It is a testament to your character that you are not some helpless maiden screaming for her savior to come save her.

Children's stories are filled with magic, miracles. This is understandable. Children are weak, at an age where they cannot grasp the concept of earning money and paying for something. They go to a store, Mommy says, "Tell the nice man what kind of ice cream you want," you do so and the nice man simply gives away the ice cream. What a nice man! Simply magic!

If such a thing as a Heaven really does exist, then the residents can only be children. For only children do not have the capacity to worry about things. If you are an adult you will always worry: "What became of my children, my family, my country? Are they well? Are they in trouble?" Remember, in Heaven you cannot have these thoughts. In Heaven there are no worries, no pain or suffering. So then you become a perpetual child. Some being will take care of you, feed you, clothe you, then pat your behind and tell you to go out and play. Yay!

Yay?

But can we afford to stay children all our lives? When will we grow up? This is the task Hinduism has taken on, to make you grow up and become an adult. There is no magic man coming. There is no magic fantasyland waiting after death.

This is it. What you see before you is *all there is!* It's just you. It's all up to *you!* Can you handle that? Are you strong enough for Hinduism?

An interesting observation about sports: of all the sports, baseball has the most players who believe in all kinds of good-luck charms, lucky apparel, lucky routes to the stadium, lucky gloves, lucky hats, etc. But why baseball? Why not other sports? Scientists and researchers have speculated it is so because baseball is the hardest sport to play. A great hitter hits the ball once every three times he gets to hit. If you could hit the ball half the time you are at bat, you would be in the Hall of Fame. My opinion is that it is not necessarily the act of hitting the ball that is difficult, but the rules are set up in such a way that makes it very, very difficult to hit the ball. The bat is thin and round, it is difficult to get ahold of the ball and you must only hit the ball in specific areas, areas manned by fielders armed with outsize gloves that make it easy to catch the ball.

Whatever the reason, the harder it is to succeed in any sport, the greater the reliance on good-luck charms. *The more a person feels helpless, feels the odds stacked against him, the more he will rely on magic and miracles,* thus opening the door for religions that promise an easy way out.

One can understand why our ancestors rushed to embrace these kinds of religions. Life was much, much tougher. Natural disasters were not understood. Early humans were helpless against them.

Are we *still* weak and helpless?

Almost every religion has a "miracle man". Sadly many Hindus, and even some Buddhists, have fallen for this easy out.

Doesn't a miracle man sound wonderful, though? What is wrong with believing in miracles? Don't we all pray for them? When faced with stress or illness, do we not pray for a quick release? Yes, many of us do. Praying and believing are signs that we have good hearts, that we can't bear to see pain and suffering and wish that they would go away. Our intentions are good.

The popular movies of today are all about magic men (and some women, but mostly men): the guy who gets hit by lightning and suddenly becomes super-intelligent, or the guy who gets bitten by a spider and suddenly gains magic powers. His fat, flabby body is transformed overnight into a lean figure with rippling muscles. He dons a snazzy suit and off he goes to fight crime.

Let's follow the movie script and imagine what it would be like to become a super healer. A bug bites you while you sleep or you get hit by lightning, and suddenly you gain super healing powers.

One day you are walking in a hospital and a child breaks away from her mother and runs to you. She hugs you tightly. The mother and the nurse rush over and try to disentangle the child from you. The more they try, the more the child clings to you, all the while crying and refusing to let you go. You finally dissuade the mother and nurse and pick up the child. You talk to her in a comforting manner and take her to her hospital bed, where she refuses to go to sleep unless you promise to stay right there with her. After a while the child falls asleep. The mother breathes a sigh of relief and thanks you for being so helpful. "This child never liked strangers before," she says. "She's always clinging to me. It's odd that she was drawn to you like that."

You go home and forget about the incident. However, your life is about to change dramatically. The doctors at the hospital find that the child has been miraculously cured. The disease that they were unable to cure—the disease that was slowly draining the life out of her—has vanished! It's a miracle!

You wake up the next day to find the mother, the child, and her family at your door, along with a bunch of TV cameras. The mother can't thank you enough for what you have done. The child shyly gives you a hug. The rich father is ready to write you a big check. The TV reporters have dozens of questions for you.

Now the real trouble begins.

In the middle of the night, you are awakened by the persistent ringing of your doorbell. You open the door to find that your whole yard—in fact, the whole street—is filled with hundreds and thousands of people! You cannot see the end of the crowd. All of the healthy people are either carrying a sick child or holding on to a sick person. They are beseeching you to please, please touch their child, grandmother, father, uncle, friend...

You are happy to oblige. You have been given a great gift and have accepted the responsibility of it. You hug each and every person. A long time goes by, and suddenly you look up and it is 10 o'clock in the morning. You have not had your breakfast, showered, or even brushed your teeth. You want to take a break, but the crowd at your door has not diminished at all.

Eventually the government gets involved, airlifting you to a huge hall adjacent to an open area so that you may continue your work. You take a few breaks, but most of your time is spent curing people. Tears come to their eyes when they see you. They begin to call you God. You are famous—people are streaming in not only from your own city and country, but from all over the world. Airlines are overbooked, all with one destination! Even people with minor ailments are rushing to see you.

Now for the bad news.

Hospitals have shut down. Funding for medical research has dried up, and all the labs doing research have been forced to shut down. There is no longer a need to find cures for diseases! Drug stores have shut down as well. Millions of people are out of work. Even graduates of medical schools are unemployed.

Isn't this situation a good one? After all, millions of people are now cured thanks to you. However, these millions go on to have more children, and the earth's population—which was already near a breaking point—is now overwhelmed. Unless researchers find new ways to increase food yields, millions of poor people will face starvation... all thanks to you and your miracles!

As some people say, be careful what you wish for. The wish for a Heaven—a place without worries, without pain and suffering—might turn out to be a life of the spirit only, without earthly memories. Not quite what you expected!

Heaven is a myth. A place without pain and suffering is a myth. If there were such a place, it would have no soul. We may think that a person who remains unperturbed by life's ups and downs is fortunate, but he or she could very well be an uncaring person. If you are a caring person, you feel others' pain. *You feel suffering, and you are a better person because of it.*

Gandhiji chose to endure frequent jailings and starvation because he cared about others. The Buddha walked away from his palace because he cared about others.

When you care, you want to do something about people's problems. However, magic is not the solution.

Does God treat the lazy and the hardworking equally? Imagine that your son is struggling with his studies and you stay up late at night to help him. You are proud that he is putting in long hours, working hard, and not giving up. The test results come in: he gets a respectable B. Later you find out that another student, who did not even study and turned in a blank paper, chanted and prayed to God for a good grade. God was pleased and used his magic to turn the F into an A!

Is it foolish to work hard, make sacrifices, and face uncertainty directly? Do those who try to satisfy God's ego with empty praises get rewarded? In this day and age, asking religions to teach morals and ethics may seem like a lost cause.

However, the above scenario does not actually happen in real life. Hardworking people do get rewarded, and those who put their faith in chants, mantras, and magic charms face disappointment. Nevertheless, magic is still appealing to the weak, because they do not want to work hard. Ideas such as Heaven, Hell, a forgiving God, mercy, magic, and miracles come from weak minds.

Hinduism firmly believes that God does not cheat the hardworking.

Karma and Reincarnation force you to become an adult. There are no miracles; there is no magic. There is no Superman to save the day, and no tooth fairy comes to make up for our suffering.

Karma and Reincarnation force you to grow up. Hinduism forces you to grow up. Problems don't go away just because you wish them away or wish for a magic man to come drive them away. If you ignore them, they only grow. You have to face them and fight them.

This is the reason that Karma and Reincarnation have been mocked, and not just by other religious people: with Karma and Reincarnation there is no instant magic, no miracles, no ready-made Heaven. Good things happen because of plain hard work! What a downer!

Again: Hinduism is harder.

Here's another example: Your child is very sick. She has cancer. You now spend every day in the hospital. Your brave child, your entire family, and a team of doctors are all fighting this awful disease. Do you pray to God for help? Yes, we all do. What do you pray for? A miracle? A miracle to save your child? What if one is granted? What if a miracle happens, and the disease that is ravaging your child mysteriously vanishes? You are overwhelmed with joy. The doctors are left scratching their heads, but you couldn't care less because you have your little child back. Happiness!

As you leave the children's ward, you notice the others—

the other mothers and fathers, the other little children. They didn't get a miracle. Their eyes are red from crying, their ache has not gone away, and their pain remains.

That is the problem with miracles: they affect the individual. Millions of people play the lottery every day, and the lucky person who wins it has just experienced a miracle!

Miracles are for individuals. Most religions preach to the individual. They are aimed at the selfish individual.

Hinduism asks you to pray for a *cure* instead of a *miracle*. A cure will benefit everyone, not just one person. How is a cure different from what happened in the previous example? A cure is found by researchers who work day and night trying to find a way to defeat the disease. It is a long, slow, agonizing process. First a way to fight the disease has to be found; then it has to be tested, tested, and tested again before it can be used for everyone.

We don't live in a magical world. We live in the real world... well, adults do. The weak, the cowardly, the childlike—these are people who want to live in a magical world, and religions have sprung up offering them just what they want.

Will the problems that beset the earth go away by themselves? Not at all. Who is going to be willing to stay and fight? The selfish look out for themselves alone: they have been offered a nice place to stay with no worries, and they stop there.

You become a Hindu when you think of others—when you put others first.

We *all* want a nice, joyful world to live in, right? Who doesn't? *Here's the choice—you can either run away to it (Heaven) OR stay, and work to make it happen right here (Karma and Reincarnation). Heaven is like that miracle, it affects one person, Karma and Reincarnation is like the cure, it affects us all!*

Will you stand tall in the face of adversity, with no help

coming, no magic to save the day? Just you—puny you?

Magic and miracles are so tempting, so nice to believe in. However, there is only one way (as you know by now): the hard way, the difficult way.

The real essence of Hinduism is to be great, to aspire to doing extraordinary things. However, you will be great not because you are gifted, but because you can outwork anybody.

While reading a book on Buddhism I was elated to read that the Buddha also warned against believing in magic and miracles. He said, "If you believe in miracles, you cannot be a Buddhist." What a wonderful statement!

But alas, some Buddhists and Hindus could not resist making him into a magic man who performed many little miracles.

Great men teach us a different lesson: depend on yourself and your own inner strength. When you do so, you become a stronger, better person. What else is a religion for? To make easy promises?

Say you get bad news from your physician. You have cancer growing in your body. If you are a non-Hindu you can turn to God and ask Him to perform a miracle. "God," you say, "Take away this pain. Take away his hurt."

As a Hindu, though, you do not get to ask for a miracle. All you get to ask is for mental and physical strength and guidance to fight this disease and its accompanying pain. It is your battle, your fight—not God's. You are not alone; you are but one among many. Either everyone wins or no one wins. If there is going to be a miracle, let it be for everyone. Let the doctors find a cure that heals everyone, not just you.

The same rules apply to all problems facing humankind, to the innumerable threats that make life harsh for us: problems must be faced by us and overcome by us alone.

Do my words scare you? Do we have to face life's harshness

alone? No, we are not alone. God is with us, but we must not run away from a fight. To cowards, God means not having to fight. Their God will demolish their enemies; their God will end their troubles. Hinduism asks you to be a leader, a hero. All you get from God is mental and moral strength and guidance—the problems do not go away. You still have to face them; you still have to fight them and conquer them. You might fail at times. You will not always succeed.

Why Are Children Considered Close to God?

Does a child know anything about religion? Nothing! Can a child recite sentences from the holy books? Perhaps she can, like a robot, but does she understand any of it? Not likely. Can a child perform prayers and sing holy songs? Yes she can, but again, she will do as instructed by her Parents and elders and may not understand what she is doing.

A child growing up in a Christian household will think Christ is God, and a Muslim child will think Allah is God. A Hindu child will think all Gods are Gods, and an atheist child will not bother with any prayers or Gods.

At the same time, we know that all these innocent children are close to God. Why?

The answer lies in the difference between the outer God and the inner God. What matters is what's inside you. A child's heart is clean and innocent, without hate or malice towards anyone. A child is ready to love and share that love with total strangers—to do good, to help others.

This is what matters to God: What is your character? Are you a good person? Will people miss you when you are gone? Do you strive to do the right thing, to help those in need? Do you do good because it is the right thing to do? Will you help others without expecting anything in return?

Every child is born an atheist. We are *all* born atheists.

But at the same time, we are all born close to God! When we grow up, we discover religion. At that point, most of us become followers of religion rather than God. It is sad that a lot of us choose to drop God and embrace religion instead.

This is what does *not* matter to God: the religion you profess, the God to whom you pray, the number of times you worship in a day, the garb you wear, or whether or not you grow a beard or shave your head.

19. Karma and Reincarnation Mean It Is Best to Teach, Not Punish—to Seek Justice, Not Vengeance

It is sad that some Hindus believe in the concept of Hell. This makes God seem more like a Saddam Hussein, a Hitler, or a Stalin—senseless despots who killed and tortured to get their way.

God Sri Rama is a loving God. The Hindu God is a Teacher. How can you accomplish anything by inflicting a beating on a defenseless child? Is that how a child learns? Remember a Hindu's goal: Moksha—enlightenment, knowledge. How do we get on the right path? Through the use of violence? A Teacher's goal is to make his students better—to help them learn to become better human beings, to make society better as a result. The use of violence will not achieve these things.

Even a dog can teach us something. Have you ever tried to hit a dog in order to make a point? Has it ever worked? Yet for the longest time we hit our children so that they would do things our way. Yes, we get our way, but they learn nothing. Instead they learn to fear their Parents. When you use violence, all you get is fear. This is why the concept of fearing God is so wrong: It says God is going to use unmitigated violence against you. Hinduism has never taught us to fear God!

The concepts of Heaven and Hell came out of primitive

and backward times. Life was harsh in ancient days. The world was very violent, with little law and order, so people developed the idea of a harsh place where evil people would be punished: a place of pain, a place of torture, a place where proper vengeance could be extracted for all the pain that evil people had inflicted.

However, over 7,000 years ago, one religious faith begged to differ, saying that it is better to teach than to punish. We must not confuse vengeance with justice.

Even more recently, punishments have been harsh. Talk to any elderly person. They probably recall a time when their father gave them the belt—such a harsh punishment meted out to innocent children! But those were the times then.

Today, Parents have changed; now hitting a child is considered unacceptable. If you hit a child, your message is, "This is what I say! Do it!" You may get your way, but the child never learns right from wrong. Therein lies the sad fact of using violence: you get your way and it is easy to do, but it accomplishes little. Are these the values any Parent or religion should be teaching?

Which of the following is harder to do: gain weight or lose weight, lie on the couch or exercise, watch mindless TV or pick up your school books, eat junk food or food that is good for you, destroy something or build something? The answer is easy in each case: the latter of course! In the same way, sending someone to a tortuous Hell is easy. Working with that person—making him see the waywardness of his ways—is difficult.

I truly believe that God has endless patience. God is loving and would never hurt anyone. God will lovingly and patiently teach a person and make her better. If it were your kid that had committed a crime, what would you do? Use violence, or make her a better person using love, kindness and endless patience? The latter path is Karma and Reincarnation. Everyone deserves a second chance, and that second chance is Karma and Reincarnation.

Today's Parents have realized that teaching is better. Parents have an opportunity to teach the child, to make him aware of his actions. The child learns, the Parenting is better, and the Parents learn to resolve issues in a better way. They bring up a better child: a child who learns to think and figure out issues. Everyone benefits!

For example, say you want to make your child more careful about crossing the street. "Why?" asks the child. "Because there is danger—a car might run over you." The child still might not understand. An endless number of questions follow—frustrating, long conversations that don't seem to go anywhere. This is the downside of teaching: it is time-consuming, it takes a lot of effort, and it may not work—or at least the method that you have chosen may not work. So you have to come up with a new strategy.

How tempting is it to simply say, "Because I said so!" In the old days, a child would be threatened with physical punishment. We recognize this tactic: it is our old friend, the concept of Hell. We figured out that hitting a dog solves nothing before we figured out not to hit a child. How sad.

However, times are getting better. In advanced countries, being caught hitting a child can result in time spent in jail. We have finally learned the value of teaching.

Imagine a 7,000-year-old faith with the same values. Karma and Reincarnation is God Rama's nonviolent way of teaching. *No Hell in Hinduism;* you are not brutally punished for your crimes. Most Hindus are under the erroneous impression that we will get punished for our mistakes in a past life by being born as an inferior person or animal, or that something bad will happen in this life as punishment. They are wrong.

What they are describing is vengeance, not justice. "An eye for an eye," as we all know, makes the whole world blind. Imagine a Palestinian or an Israeli rocket falling on the other side and killing innocent kids playing soccer. What should be the recourse—to kill the other side's children? To target a school and kill Israeli or Palestinian kids? Would that be considered justice?

Violent religions have violent Gods! Violence is not God's justice.

Let Hinduism stand apart from these hateful and violent religions. As we know, Hinduism stands for tolerance and acceptance. Let it also stand for nonviolence. The Hindu God is a loving, teaching God.

There is a great African proverb: "It takes a village to raise a child." We are not just the product of our genes but a product of the society that we grew up in. Both "nature" and "nurture" are factors. Parents, siblings, aunts, uncles, Teachers, and strangers: all play a part in bringing up a child.

Be aware of your conduct. A child is watching.

It is true that a child born with a "silver spoon" in his mouth (to a rich family) will have a better chance of growing up to become a productive member of society. A child born in poverty, growing up under terrible circumstances is more likely to cause harm to society. Growing up around violence, in poverty, a child is more likely to turn violent.

Should we not take responsibility for such a child—for such a situation? Is the village or society not responsible for the violence, and for the harm caused? How then can we justify Hell? Hell punishes the *individual*. It takes vengeance on the individual.

In a larger context, why are some countries around the world so successful and others not? Why is a country like Japan, poor in natural resources, able to provide a comfortable living for its people, whereas other countries that are blessed with natural resources, such as Iran and Iraq, struggle with violence and poverty?

A country that is blessed with great natural resources may sound like a wonderful thing. However, countries where great natural resources have been discovered have been beset by wars and gang lords intent on exploiting the wealth for themselves with help from other countries. Countries like Saudi Arabia, that have done a good job of making sure their oil wealth flows back into their country for the benefit of their people, often find that they are saddled with a populace that becomes lazy, unwilling to study or work hard to acquire skills that would be needed if the country were to run out of its precious natural resources. This is the curse of a free and easy Heaven.

While most religions focus on the individual level, Hinduism asks you to broaden your horizons and think of your family, your friends, your society, and your country. At the individual level, when a crime is committed, the criminal is caught and punished appropriately. The criminal is often put in jail or given other punishments. In certain countries physical pain has been used, to the point of cutting off hands or stoning people to death.

However, if you talk to an economist or a minister at the government level, you will hear a different perspective. Imagine a crime-ridden neighborhood, perhaps your own. Will the crime be reduced simply by beefing up the police presence or by investing in surveillance cameras? Is it enough to simply lock up the "bad" guys and throw away the key? Do you think these solutions will be effective?

They will not. What is needed is hope; what is needed is education. More schools, better housing, and better jobs are the key. What the young man or woman turning to crime needs is a better education and the prospect of a good, honest job with which to earn a living.

Your perspective changes when you take ownership of your society and your country. As the president or government in power often realizes, punishment is not the best solution. The better way is the more compassionate way. You can catch more bees with honey than with vinegar. You get more done using the power of knowledge than using the power of the gun. As the saying goes, the pen is mightier than the sword.

Following this way is not easy. Knowledge is not as quick; the pen is not as efficient. The sword is quick, and the gun is even quicker. Shouting at a child to get your way is faster, quicker, and less stressful (at least less stressful for you, the Parent).

It is hard to reason with a child and help her see the error of her ways. It is equally hard to shape a society that has lost its way. It takes time, effort, intelligence, patience, and sacrifice. Sometimes it doesn't work. In those cases, we have to go back to the drawing board and try once more.

We talked earlier about how there is no concept of Hell in Hinduism—how Karma and Reincarnation do not mean instant punishment by being born again in dire circumstances or as an animal. So then, does a criminal in a past life get punished in this life by some unfortunate incident? Is this why bad things seem to happen to some good people? Were they bad in a previous life and Karma punished them for it in this life? No, a thousand times no!

Let us go back to what Hinduism tells us about God: that God is a Teacher. When a student skips class, does not turn in his paper, or indulges in a drunken orgy over the weekend, does the Teacher punish him? Not at all. The Teacher treats him according to who he is: an adult who is responsible for his own actions. If the student skips class and does not study, who ends up being hurt in the end? It is the student who suffers. It is the job of the Teacher to make the student realize the error of his ways; punishment does not do that.

Similarly, Hindus do not believe in punishment or the infliction of physical or mental torture or pain. The path to Enlightenment is always open, but the believer must decide to walk on that path. The believer must come to God because she wants to, not because of fear of retribution or the lure of a reward.

The more people walk away from Truth, honesty and compassion—from doing the right thing—the more they punish themselves in the end.

After a criminal dies, he comes right back in another life. No punishment is meted out. Like a student who fails a class, he is simply asked to try again and do better next time.

Gandhiji used to stop violence when it broke out. He took full responsibility for the actions of unruly followers who could not control their passions. He was acting as a leader; that is what leaders do. Hinduism asks you to be a leader. Anyone can be a follower, but it is leaders who change society.

Responsibility for changing society makes people uncomfortable. It's much easier to play the "blame game". However, if you want things to get better, be a Teacher rather than a judge.

No matter how evil a person is, a Hindu never wishes Hell upon that person. Let God deal with evil people in Her own way, but we should never wish pain and suffering on others. I know this is difficult. It seems normal to believe that those who do inhuman things must pay for their crimes; but if we think about it, at some point we ourselves could do something inhuman. How many of our fellow creatures on earth have paid dearly for our benefit?

When images of Jews boxed up in stifling rail cars are shown on TV or in a movie, all of us are moved. Sad music plays in the background and we are reminded of the horrors of man's cruelty and inhumanity. Later we may be driving home and pass a truck carrying tiny squawking little chicks in the back. They are boxed up in crates in over 100-degree heat, separated from their mothers, with no food or water. If this were a movie, upbeat music would probably be playing. Yes, we too can be cruel. When will we realize that animals can feel pain?

A Teacher encourages you to think—to become a better, more informed, and more intelligent person. Most religions are quick to dole out terrible punishments at the same time that they offer you a way out through the back door. In Hinduism, there is no back door. Do you want out? Hold your head up high and use the front door. Only the coward sneaks out the back door.

The faith that follows the Teacher puts more responsibility on your shoulders. It treats you like an adult and encourages you to become a better person: truly a divine faith! The goal in Hinduism is Moksha, enlightenment. It does not come at the end of a stick or a whip. Pain does nothing to increase your knowledge.

Hinduism Means Democracy

"Tell the king. The king will fix it," equals *I don't have to do anything. I can just sit or doze off, go about my life and not worry.* What does this remind you of? Heaven, of course!

It is disappointing to hear some views, especially common in third-world democracies like India that spout a love for the strong man. As they say, democracy is messy. Things don't move as fast as in a country run by a despot or in a communist country like China. People are tired of being poor, of having corrupt and inefficient governments. When they see from afar pictures and videos of dramatic changes in a country like China they wish for the same.

The exception is when the magnificent new building or

the fancy-looking new highway goes right through your house and this great despot or communist government gives you only one day's notice to clear out of your home. It is then you appreciate democracy.

This is the frustrating Truth that these people do not seem to understand. Just like seeing a faraway mountain and admiring how smooth it looks and then comparing it to your nearby mountain and saying your mountain is not as good as the faraway one.

Even examples of powerful men like Saddam Hussein, Hitler, Stalin, Mao and Mugabe do not deter them. The case of Mugabe is very interesting: once hailed as a hero by his own countrymen, today he is just as hated as he was once loved by the very same people. Ensconced in their heavily guarded "castles", these dictators cease to hear the painful cries of their countrymen.

Another surprising fact is that we Indians live next door to a country that has known very little democracy since independence and has very little progress to show for it. Today, that country is rife with sectarian and terrorist killings.

Yet the allure of a strong man endures. Why? Because for much of human history we had a one-man (man, not woman) rule: the king, the master, the village head. The religions that dominate the planet today have simply moved him upstairs into the Heavens. Just as the king was the protector, the benefactor, so is their God. Pray, beg and be rewarded. These religions are stuck in the past, and it boggles my mind that highly educated people seemingly accept such primitive ideas.

Such ideas will also endure in the hearts of the weak, the lazy. The one thing the strong man does is to take away the responsibility, the hard work and the discomfort that comes with having to make hard decisions. In a democracy, the success or failure of a country lies squarely on the shoulders of its countrymen. This is not so in a country ruled by a despot or a strong man. It is the strong man—or in the case of a communist country, it is the party—that will make all the decisions. We have the examples of the former Soviet Union and East Germany where people were taken care of, everyone had a job and the state took care of their people. How did that work out?

What we see here are two kinds of societies. One is top-down with the king, the dictator, the communist party making all the decisions. The populace in such societies has no other option but to put their head down and obey.

Tell me, what kind of a society do you think a Heaven might have?

For much of human history we have had a society ruled by kings and authoritarian regimes. Democracy is fairly new. It seems we have people still locked in primitive societies by their religions, still following old, outdated ideas.

For much of human history one man, the king, was the answer to all our problems *He will come and fix everything!* It is amazing to me to see that these ideas are still held by a vast majority of humanity. But now the king has become a God. God will fix everything. He is our savior!

Democracy is a bottom-up society. The power and the decisions lie with the people or their elected representatives. Whether a democratic country succeeds or not depends entirely on its people. The people are responsible for electing the leaders, and they are responsible for the state of their societies. A Teacher faith teaches democracy: any problem that arises, you need to fix it. If you want Heaven, paradise, get to work. Don't go around looking for a magic-genie sugar daddy to come make it for you.

As a Hindu, when you die you come right back to this earth, to an earthly life. Here, you live in a bottom-up society. Here you will live as a free man, unafraid. In Heaven there is no freedom and there is no democracy. Is it worth it?

Thousands of people risked their lives to flee the former Soviet Union and East Germany and do so today from the likes of North Korea. They end up in democracies. Suddenly they find that they will have to fight for a job to make a living. There is no more cradle-to-the-grave catering society. Does even one of these people ever want to go back?

In a democracy, the power as well as the responsibility lies with the people, and it is that second word *responsibility* that a weak or lazy person does not like. He likes the idea of someone else doing all the work and taking all the responsibility. If the strong man does good things, the weak countryman will benefit. If the strong man turns out to be a Mugabe, then the weak man has someone to blame his troubles on.

Hinduism puts the responsibility squarely on the shoulders of its followers, as we saw from the very first point made in this book.

No, there is no bail-out God. God is not an escape hatch, God is not an enabler. You made a mistake, you correct it. You made a promise, you keep it. Regrets won't do. Talk is cheap, actions count.

God will not help you cheat the victim. Not in Hinduism, no sir!

By teaching that God resides within us, Hinduism teaches us to realize that life's problems are ours to solve. Hinduism does not want you to look up to the Heavens for answers. God is within us. We are the answer. No matter how dark things get, getting down on our knees and praying for a magic man to come down and set things right will not work.

If the state of our nation is poor, only we can set it right. If the state of the world is poor, only we can make it right. The population taking responsibility and ownership is the first step towards a democratic society.

Hinduism is a Teacher faith. God is there to instruct and advise, and that's it. In a classroom, the Teacher will encourage a lively discussion. She may raise an issue of the day and ask her students to discuss it. One student may stand up and give an opinion and immediately another might get up and give a completely contrary opinion, while a third may do the same. This is how democracy blossoms. Young people get to hear different viewpoints and also realize that each and every voice must be heard and respected.

Hindu India remains to this day an amalgam of hundreds of faiths. In other areas of the world, there was a time when, if you held a different view of faith, it got you killed. Even today sectarian killings by different branches of the same religion continue unabated. Imagine the plight of the minority religions in these countries, how frightened and cowed they must be, always fearing for their lives.

Only in Hindu India was a Buddha allowed to freely propagate his views without fear of violence and torture! The leaders of Buddhism, Jainism, Zoroastrianism, Sikhism and countless other faiths and views could freely air their views without fear of retribution.

They say that the British brought democracy to India. I say India was always democratic. Hinduism taught India democracy. There was a time when the leading followers of Hinduism, Buddhism, Jainism and other faiths of India sat together and discussed and debated religious tenants. They personally may not have liked each other or barely tolerated each other, but never in India's history has one religion set upon others in an attempt to kill and wipe out that religion. The oldest of these religions, Hinduism, has taught these follower religions well. You may not agree with us and that is your right. There are several paths to God, not just one, and we hope you find God in your own way!

Hindus are fond of saying that religions are like rivers all flowing and ending at the same destination: the ocean, the metaphor for God.

That's so true is it not? Most of us will find God in our own way. Personally, I see God in Truth, and Truth in God. No image or name is necessary for me.

Hinduism is not a "my way or the highway" religion.

Could a faith that says religions are like rivers all ending up in the same ocean, the same God, be anything other than democratic?

Another aspect of a democracy is the freedom that it gives to both men and women. In most religions women are second-class, an afterthought. It is evident in places of worship even today. The higher positions of authority are reserved for men.

Hinduism remains to this day the only religion that prays to a female form of God. Like the male trinity of Gods, Brahma, Vishnu and Siva, there is also the female trinity of Gods in Hinduism, Saraswati, Laxmi and Durga.

The iconic image of Ardhanariswara, the half-male, half-female form of Gods Siva and Parvati teaches us that men and women are equal partners. Imagine that, and this faith is 7,000 years or older!

Most religions abuse atheists but not Hinduism. A religion that teaches there is more than one way to God is a tolerant and democratic faith. A faith that teaches that character alone decides whether you are with God or not cannot and will not condemn atheists. The facts bear this out: Samkhyas are Hindus, but their philosophy is atheist. Many views all find shade under the umbrella of Hinduism.

One can see the effects even today. There is not one non-Christian leader in the West, not one non-Muslim leader in Muslim lands. Hindu India, until recently, had a Muslim president (since retired), a Catholic woman born in Italy as its leader, and a Sikh as the prime minister! All three top posts held by non-Hindus! India will always be a democracy as long as it remains Hindu.

It makes me sad to see some Hindus give up their faith so easily—they marry a person from another faith and we Hindus seem to be the ones who give must give up ours, 2nd class citizens, whereas the other party gets to carry on as before. What really cuts me up is that Hindus are tolerant, we don't cast you into Hell for not being a Hindu, religion is not what is important here, whereas these other religions will not be so nice. Are these people not moving from a democratic faith to a non-democratic one? We say we cherish democracy, we love the freedom it gives us, plenty of people who lived good lives under dictators and communist countries, chose to give up their all to flee and live in a democracy but we see the opposite happening when it comes to religion.

20. Karma and Reincarnation: Because the Pain Is Here, the Suffering Is Here

The guy under the influence of drugs is floating in a happy dreamland. Do you want to be that way for all eternity? Of course not; that guy is running away from life, just as those who run after Heaven are.

A woman in a coma is not suffering. Do you want to be that way for all eternity? The answer is yes, if you do not want to have a life!

Yes, pain is here, suffering is here, but so is life. I want to stay, work, sacrifice, make things better, make God proud of me, and yes, have a life! Can you relate?

Does this idea surprise you? One does hear it in our daily lives but not from religions. Many religions promise relief from pain and suffering, away from here, in Heaven or some other magic land far-away from here, but of course, which is described as a beautiful, lovely place where no pain or suffering may enter.

This is what most religions promise: Yes, a lovely fantasyland awaits. Let us go! Let us all run away! Nice God has nothing better to do than cater to our every need and keep us happy and content.

As a child we are catered to, but as an adult we are on our own. We must work, strive, and struggle to make a living. We learn in real life that nothing is given unless we work for it.

Some give up. Life is too hard for them. This is where "nice God" comes in, the fantasyland comes in. The fantasyland came first, God came later. After all, you have to have someone to manage the fantasyland. So religions jumped in to exploit this need: "Look what our God can do for you!" Like an evil politician's hot air, their pamphlets are filled with nice, lovely promises about a beautiful fantasy island to run away to after death. Or they say, "Just wait! God is going to come down and make that fantasy happen!"

Are we going to be stuck in the past? Our ancestors were weakened by the tough living conditions of their day. It is understandable that they hoped for better days in the afterlife. Few of us accept death. Few of us accept that this is all there is. We tell ourselves that there must be something better after this life.

Yes, life is harsh even today. Young children are forced to become surrogate Parents to their younger siblings after both their Parents died of AIDS or their single mother is dead because of a botched self-abortion. Young kids are dropping out of school, going to work or even into prostitution, because their families are too poor. One such tragic story involved a young woman from Eastern Europe who was lured into another country on the promise of a job and then was forced into prostitution. After a few years, she managed to escape and reach home. What awaited her at home was poverty and sick siblings. It was shocking and heartbreaking to see and hear this young woman deciding to go back to the same hell that she escaped from so that she could earn some money and help out her family.

The pain is here, the suffering is here. Will you choose to come back and help stamp out forced prostitution and poverty?

Let us assume you are the breadwinner of a family and that

you are barely making ends meet. You, unfortunately, die in an accident. In most religions, your destination is Heaven. What about your family? Do you think about them? How will they survive and make ends meet? Will your children be forced to beg? Will your wife or daughter be forced into prostitution? Maybe even your young son?

For most religions, these are inconvenient questions. These religions do not even address them, nor do they care to: *It's not your business anymore. Your next stop is Heaven. Party! Enjoy! Eat cake and enjoy yourself, while your young child starves and goes to bed hungry.*

Enjoy while your loved ones are suffering?

Not if Hinduism can help it.

Through the teaching of Karma and Reincarnation, Hinduism asks us to not run away and to stop building fantasylands "up there" to run away to. If life is harsh let us work hard, let us make it better. Running away won't make problems go away nor will running away solve the problems of the world. Will poverty, hopelessness go away? Will diseases vanish? Will dictators go away?

Yes they will—for the coward and the selfish—they put their troubles behind them. Is that who you are?

By running away from life you will avoid lots of pain and suffering. You will also never taste the joys of life. People who want just the joys but none of the pains are running after fool's gold. They choose death.

The coward who runs away and hides is free from facing all the troubles of life. That is lure of Heaven. This is why so many intelligent, good people fall for it. That's the sad part, leaving everything behind. But then the coward who runs away is letting others fight for him. Where a warrior is set to face one attacker, now he has to fight two of them.

No, not for Hindus. We will not leave things unfinished, goals never achieved. We stay till the finish, the end! We will finish what we started!

Facing one's troubles is harder and tougher. Hinduism is harder and tougher. It asks you to be strong, to be brave. Stand strong, hold your ground and face your problems. Attack them, defeat them, and conquer them!

The pain isn't going away. The suffering isn't going to go away just because you ran away. The pain and suffering are still here. The problems of the world are still here. Joblessness, homelessness is still here, poverty and hunger are still here. Rapists and pedophiles are still here. Cancer is still here. Loneliness in old age is still here. Dictators and guns are still here. Inequality is still here. Suffering animals are still here. I could go on and on.

That is why asking for forgiveness is so wrong. The guy asking for forgiveness is looking for a way out because he knows the victim is still suffering and the debt remains unpaid. He is not interested. He wants out. He is not interested in making things right because there is too much work and much sacrifice involved. Religions have rushed in to give him the way out. *God will take away your sin, don't worry. You can walk away from this problem that you created.* I don't see this unethical behavior being rewarded. All I see is this person ending up in the arms of death!

Not everyone is running away and not all religions encourage you to run away.

Hinduism asks, "The pain is here, the suffering is here—where else would you rather be?" The warrior eagerly looks forward to battle. Whereas, all the coward can think of is saving his own hide. One has to look at this from a different perspective, the perspective of the strong, the hero, the warrior.

A glorious future stretches before us, but that future has to be built.

I was amazed and shocked when I saw the Dalai Lama

on YouTube talk about resting in Heaven. His people have been fighting for ages for independence and a homeland for themselves and he wants to leave that all behind? Leave the fighting for someone else? Doesn't he want to participate? Continue the fight? As long as Tibet is under occupation the work is not yet done. The fight must continue. That is the central tenant of Karma and Reincarnation: Do not leave things unfinished! The Dalai Lama must come back and he must continue the good fight.

Tibet will be free. It may not come soon enough, but it will happen one day and the Dalai Lama wants to sit and watch it happen from above? To thankfully experience the great joy and happiness, along with his countrymen and people all over the world, he must be here! All that joy and happiness in a far-away Heaven cannot come close to being here, hugging his fellow countrymen and women, shedding real tears of joy, the heart beating so fast you think it will burst at any moment. This is real joy and real happiness and not the fake happiness and joy of a Heaven. This joy is earned! This happiness is earned! We made it happen and we worked for it and get to enjoy the fruits!

This is a choice you must make.

Before we go further, let me ask the reader a question:

Why do you want to be happy?

Millions turn to religion in their quest for happiness, and since this book is about religion, this might be a strange question to ask.

First, millions of unknowns are doing their best to create a better world. Second, there are the well-known names, the people we all know who jumped right in and embraced a life of pain and suffering.

There was Gandhiji: Stay in South Africa or London, keep my head down, practice law, make a nice living, and be happy, or go to India, involve myself in the freedom struggle, get jailed, maybe killed, bear pain, bear suffering?

There was Martin Luther King: Shut up, keep low, say nothing, keep quiet and try to make life better for myself, or speak up, stand up, speak for the oppressed and humiliated, be abused, threatened and finally be killed?

There was Oskar Schindler: These are not my people, what happens to them is none of my business, maybe they are evil people and that is why they are being punished, I have a family to consider, I cannot put them in danger or these are innocent human beings, they don't deserve such a fate, I will do whatever I can to stop this from happening?

There was Nelson Mandela, who had the same choices as Martin Luther King: to shut up and make the best of a bad situation, or speak up, be sent to jail, lose years of his life, lose the companionship and love of his loved ones?

There was the Buddha: Stay, listen to his father, become emperor, rule over a vast empire, enjoy the good life, or listen to his conscience, go in search of Truth?

These are the famous people, but there are millions of good, honest unknowns going out of their way to make this a better world. Who better than Pat Tillman walking away from a lucrative NFL contract to go serve his country? Libyans, Egyptians and now Syrians are shedding blood fighting dictators. A young American girl loses her life to an Israeli bulldozer leveling Palestinian homes. A young man in India risks his life trying to rescue children chained and made to work as slaves. Good, honest cops and ordinary people lose their lives in Mexico standing up to drug lords.

Do you see what these people did? They did the exact *opposite* of what almost every religion encourages one to do: run away from pain and suffering. Run away from your obligations and responsibilities. What values!

I am sure every one of these good people were asked, "Are you crazy? Don't you want to be happy?"

Why did these people not want to be happy? Why not just shut their mouths, ears and eyes like the famous three monkeys statue and get on with their lives?

Aristotle said that the end or aim of a human life is happiness. I guess the individuals referenced above did not get the memo. For some strange reason, they walked right into the arms of pain and suffering.

Why?

Because these people reached for something greater than themselves, they reached for the hand of God. Their hearts beat for others and they felt the pain of others. They didn't care about their own needs or wants. They put their needs and desires aside and tried to make the world a better place.

Here is the epiphany: the day you feel other people's pain, stop thinking only of yourself, what benefits you, stop thinking of "I", then, then, that particular day, that particular moment, you will find God!

This then is the essence of Hindu ideas. Does your heart beat for others? Do you consider yourself an empathetic person? Someone who cares about others? If so, God has plenty of work for you.

God puts a choice in front of you: you can either give up or keep trying. You can see an insurmountable obstacle in front of you—too much pain, too much suffering—and opt to check out.

Most people magnify their own problems and tend to downplay the problems others encounter—the same way most of us think we have it hard today—but, believe me, we have it easy compared to our ancestors. We have survived and progressed. A while ago some scientists were warning against the coming starvation because of too much population. Well, that did not happen. It did not happen, not because of some magic or miracle, but because we found a solution, a cure!

We have a great opportunity in front of us. One day man or woman will walk on Mars! One day we will travel to the stars! One day we will conquer hunger, poverty, inequality! One day we will conquer all diseases!

But not right now. Unfortunately we are not there yet. Right now there is much work to be done. The other day, waiting in the Chicago cold, a young teenage lady approached me asking for a few bucks. I couldn't help but wonder—was this young lady always like this? Maybe at one point she had a loving mother and father, a loving home, a future to look forward to. Then her father died, a new man entered into her mother's life, a man who took advantage and who abused her while her mother looked the other way. She had to run away and take to the streets. A promising life now lies shattered.

There is the old begging couple that I see back in India. Were they always so poor? There is no pension or social security in India. Maybe at one point this couple was doing okay while bringing up their children with what little they had, working hard to make their future. One day retirement comes, but maybe none of their children could help or wanted to. With no income coming in, begging on the streets might have been the only option.

These are just a few of so many sad tales in life. So much pain, so much suffering. I pledge to stay! I want to stay to help make the world better in any small way I can. Gandhiji couldn't care less about Moksha or Heaven. He wanted neither of them. He wanted to stay and help turn his India into a great nation. I am confident that he is doing just that right now. I am confident that he has been reborn. It is not for Gandhiji to be sitting in Heaven, wasting away.

I am reminded of the small squirrel that helped God Sri Rama build his bridge to Lanka. The story goes that God Sri Rama had to travel across the ocean to reach his captured wife, Sita. So he decides to build a bridge and his army starts doing that using big boulders. There was a squirrel who wanted to help God Sri Rama, but he was so little! What could he do? He rolled around on the ground, letting the sand and dirt stick to his body, picked up some more dirt with his teeny-weeny hands and ran out to the boulders and started shaking the dirt onto and in between the boulders to help them bind. God Sri Rama was so touched by this little squirrel's indomitable spirit that he took him in his arms and stroked his back; and to this day, people say that the squirrel has two white lines on his back because of God Sri Rama's finger strokes.

The opportunity is in front of us to create a paradise with our own hands using hard work, sacrifice and persistence. To make God proud of us, that's the goal.

Please do not disappoint God and do not pass up this opportunity. I know times will be tough. Hinduism is not going to sugar coat things. We offer pain and suffering, but we promise that at the end of the rainbow there is a pot of gold. That pot of gold is called God. That pot of gold must be worked for, sacrificed for and it must be earned.

Make no mistake, the worthless things in life can be begged for. Ever heard of a beggar becoming a millionaire or an industry titan? The good things in life, the great things in life, all have to be worked for. Stop being a baby, a child, a weakling. Be strong, grow a backbone and get to work.

Earlier I wrote about the Gift of Pain and Suffering – let us revisit those ideas. We now see that the nadir for pain & suffering is Death. In Death you will find "peace" – no more pain or suffering. Hinduism has declared that the soul will go thru life stages starting from a microscopic bug to the apex – human life! We now see that as we move up, pain and suffering increases as does joy and happiness. At the lowest stage – a microscopic bug – there is no pain or suffering, life is easy, joyful, and as we move on up to a bigger animal, we find pain and suffering increases and the apex of this pain and suffering is reached once we reach human life. Not only do humans feel physical pain, they also feel mental pain so intensely, some choose to die to escape such pain. *And then there are those who walk towards such pain and suffering, as we have seen a few paragraphs above. We call such people great souls, those who are with God! Did you get it? If you want to find God, do you now see which way you must proceed?*

I fear those who seek heaven are headed the wrong way, they reject God, human life, and are headed towards the microscopic world!

That's the realization that we need to make. Being with God does not mean a life of ease. It is, in fact, the exact opposite. Being with God means facing pain and suffering, hard work, sacrifice, self-reliance and strength.

ONE GOD

When you hear the words *one God*, you might automatically think of the popular Christian and Muslim beliefs that only Jesus or only Allah can save you. Unfortunately this "one" idea of God has led to hate, infighting, threats, abuses, and mass killings.

Hatred has led to fragmentation—one Christian writer has lamented that we are all together from Monday to Saturday but on Sunday, we go our separate ways, to separate places of worship! Hinduism has stood apart. Whether it is 1,000 or 100,000 Hindus getting together, they all go to the same temple. Ironically, this religion—which is mocked for having millions of Gods—is the one that does not kill or abuse others in the name of religion. It is the one in which believers do not go their separate ways to worship.

It is not correct to say that Hindus pray to millions of Gods. We pray to billions! Trillions! *All Gods in all religions, from all times and from all people—not only from this earth, but from this universe and beyond—are Hindu Gods.* We respect other faiths because we are all one. We are all praying to one and the same God. Hinduism is a mono-polytheistic religion, which means that all these millions of Gods are one and the same.

The names are many but it is the one and the same person.

Gandhiji's favorite religious hymn starts with the words *Ishwar, Allah Tere Naam* ("God, your names are Ishwar and Allah"). Can you imagine a Muslim invoking the name of God Rama or a Christian invoking the name of God Krishna? Only a Hindu would do such a thing.

God Sri Rama is Krishna is Jesus is Buddha is Allah is Durga is Mahavira…

Eyes cannot see God; prayer is not done with words;
Only the heart can see God; prayer is done with action.

As you can see, the Hindu view is a not typical. First of all, a being capable of creating this vast universe, with millions of galaxies and planets, could not be so petty as to align herself with a small religion. God is for ALL—ALL good souls are dear to God Sri Rama—by they may be atheist or theist. Whether they are Christian, Muslim, Hindu, Buddhist, Jain, Sikh, Atheist or Klingon—it does not matter—and in the present situation it must be said—yes, gays also are God's children—no exceptions!

There is no your God or my God in Hinduism, there is only one God, OUR God!

The notion that God runs a segregated Heaven—that he favors only one religion—came from primitive times when the world was little understood, when people thought the earth was the center of the universe and humans were the most important beings.

However, humans are nothing special. Animals and other life forms are all God's creation. Hindus pray before all sorts of life forms, including cows and rats, because we see God in all life forms. God is all around us. What we see before us is Her creation, so we bow to it. Like a man who sees his lover in everything, even when he closes his eyes, Hindu devotees see God everywhere.

We are happy to see the children of a loved one, because they remind us of that person. For Hindus, the whole world is a reminder of God. God is everywhere; we see God in all things.

In the ancient Hindu texts, the human being is compared to a chariot: The body is the chariot, the horses are the senses, the reins are the mind, the intellect is the charioteer, and the soul is the rider. If the senses control the chariot, a person could end up destroying his or her life. Those who indulge in drugs, alcohol, sex, or food—those who let their senses control their bodies and let their desires take over—end up regretting having wasted their lives. However, there is something else inside of you, something that warns you not to do such things. It is the soul, your conscience. It is the soul that tries to steer you on the right path.

There are evil people in this world—people who have done terrible things. We point to these people and say, "They have no soul, no conscience." Not only Hindus feel this way. Deep down, we all "get it".

This is what Christianity meant by saying humanity has fallen: Once we were all pure souls, and then we discovered our body and felt shame when we saw its nakedness. The goal is to lose this outer shell, this body, and become one with God again. It is the soul, once freed from the body by death that goes to meet God. The soul becomes one with the one God—the supreme self, the supreme soul—the one without a body!

Exactly how are we to accomplish this? Is it a simple matter of dying, at which point we go back to God's abode? Hinduism does not believe it is that simple. The soul has been corrupted, and it is here on earth that the soul can become purified. How do we do that? It is not by chanting God's name innumerable times, by singing his praises, by aggressively proselytizing, or by building elaborate temples in Her honor. The opportunity to be with God is available to all, atheists included. Purifying the soul is not easy. The Hindu way is to not look for pity from God. Being with God is *earned.*

Can you make such a sacrifice? Even today many good people—journalists, policemen, etc.—are threatened with dire consequences if they speak out or do the right thing. Incredibly some have chosen to embrace Truth and, sadly, have paid with their lives. There may be no payoff for embracing Truth, honesty, and compassion. Will you still do it? God does not provide enticements.

Being with God will not be easy.

I am sorry if my words are not so pleasing. Quite a few religions out there, promising the easy life for eternity, Hinduism is not one of them.

21. Karma and Rebirth Means That the One True Heaven Is One That is *Built* by Us! Let's Build-A-Heaven

Heaven = some guy will make good things happen.
Reincarnation = good things are the result of our own efforts, hard work and sacrifice.

A tourist strolling in a section of a city where a large building was being constructed asked the three masons what they were doing. The first replied, "I'm laying bricks." The second said, "I'm building a wall." But the third answered, "I'm building a cathedral!"(From the book "An Argument for Mind" by Jerome Kagan.)

Let us build temples, cathedrals and mosques: temples of knowledge, cathedrals of learning, and mosques of enlightenment.

Heaven is not a place waiting for you to crawl into. It must be BUILT!

Do you think you can simply escape to a better life, or are you a person who battles, sacrifices, and works hard for a better life?

To paraphrase a famous movie line: "A sword in the hands of a coward is not a good sight." Some people want no part of this fight, no part of life—they want to turn back, and they choose death. The coward is happy underneath the bed.

A Heaven built for us is a false Heaven. It is a test from

God. How low are we ready to sink in order to experience the pleasures of the flesh? How low can we go? How quick are we to drop our cherished principles and values?

Is the sky green? *Yes, master, it is.*

How is a person who is down on his knees able to hang on to her principles and values? It is wrong to be down on your knees and begging for mercy. You have sold your soul when you are ready to abandon your principles, ethics, and values.

Do you think abortion is a woman's right? Assume that God disagrees. Are you ready to stand up and stick to your values? You are down on your knees, with the threat of eternal torture hanging over your head. Will you abandon your cherished values and give in?

Do you think gays should have equal rights? Assume that God disagrees. Are you ready to stand up and stick to your values? You are down on your knees, with the threat of eternal torture hanging over your head. Will you abandon your cherished values and give in?

Heaven on earth doesn't just mean a rich, prosperous earth. It also means an earth where good people stick to the Truth, hold their values and morals dear, are kind and generous to a fault, and welcome strangers.

Great men like Socrates chose to be put to death rather than give up their principles and values. It is such great men and women that are on the path to Moksha; it is such great men and women who are touched by the hand of God. Such are the people who make Heaven on earth possible!

You must earn your way; that is the only way. Let us build Heaven right here on earth. It will not be easy: there are plenty of weak people who will want nothing to do with hard work. It will take hard work, sacrifice, sweat, toil, and tears—and some blood spilled, too!

Heaven built by your own sweat and your own muscle is the real Heaven. It can never be taken away from you. Think of earning those high marks or grades: they are yours. You earned them. No one can take them away from you.

Anything unearned is worthless.

An instantaneous Heaven is a false Heaven. Let us assume Heaven is like Hawaii. Would you like to visit Hawaii? Who wouldn't? But you don't have to wait. You can do it right now as you are reading these words: simply close your eyes and imagine that you are in Hawaii. Let the cool ocean breeze wash over you, hear the peaceful sounds of the waves lapping on the shore, and take in the pleasant smells. You might say, "I would love it, except for this cold winter wind that keeps spoiling things!" You are back to reality.

You can imagine any number of wonderful things happening to you: winning an Oscar, winning an Olympic gold medal, getting the winning hit in the World Series, winning the Nobel Prize, or doing what you love as a career—any number of things can be imagined and dreamed of. However, these are just dreams. Anything that is instantaneous is unreal. Sorry, you just don't walk into a ready-made paradise. Sorry, there is no tooth fairy coming to magically create a paradise for you.

A Heaven that you crawl into down on your knees is a fake Heaven, as real as the Hawaii above. Real Heaven, just like real life, must be worked for, must be built!

In the real world, wonderful things have to be worked for and sacrificed for. It takes a lot of time and effort, but it is worth it because now these things are yours. No one can take them away from you; they are real, solid.

Of course, people love to be given things for free. Why work hard when you can just have it all? For this reason, Hinduism will not appeal to everyone. All Hinduism can do is to appeal to your sense of right and wrong and remind you of the old adage that nothing is free—neither in this world nor in the afterlife. God is not a genie or a servant.

Karma and Reincarnation ask us to live in the real world. Let's not waste our lives away dreaming and hoping. It is good to have dreams, but we must work hard to make them a reality. So let's build a Heaven, right here. Make God beam with pride!

Are you a person who is always wishing for things? Do you play the lottery frequently? Do you hope for a miracle? Then maybe Hinduism is not for you. A Hindu does not wish for good things to happen—she will make them happen! As I mentioned before, Hinduism is difficult, but you will be the better for it. When you follow Hindu principles, the goal is to make a better you—a better person.

The goal is to bring you to God, not to religion.

Hinduism will make you a stronger, tougher person. Do you want a better life? Is life on earth is too harsh? Well, stop dreaming of something "up there" or "out there". Stop building castles in the air.

Let's get to work.

In the past, life was very harsh. Thankfully we live in better times today, but it is not because a tooth fairy waved her magic wand. It took tremendous sacrifices by millions of good people striving to make this a better world, not only for themselves, but for others as well.

A Parent working two or three jobs comes home late at night every day and her children are asleep by that time. She wakes up to go to work and the kids are still asleep. So this hardworking good Parent does not get to see her kids all week. But millions of such Parents soldier on, making sacrifices for the good of the next generation. The world is better today because of such people.

As Martin Luther King, Jr. said, "Philanthropy is commendable, but it must not cause the philanthropist to overlook the circumstances of economic injustice which make philanthropy necessary."

We don't always acknowledge the contribution of the dreamer, the entrepreneur, or the businessman. We think all these people are just out to get money any way they can. Sometimes this is true and their reputation is well deserved, but quite a few of them have an admirable dream and are pursuing it. When they succeed, as a J.R.D. Tata in India or a Bill Gates in the United States did, their efforts help millions. Thanks to such people, millions go to bed with their bellies full. They are able to start a family, buy a home, and spend money, which in turn creates more jobs. The world becomes a better place because of such people.

However, their work is unfinished. Do we have paradise on earth? Not at all. For millions the earthly life is a living Hell. Much needs to be done.

How can a religion like Hinduism compete when it says God's praise must be earned, might take hundreds or thousands of lives to make God proud, versus a religion that promises a God who will reward you in a few minutes, all you have to do is beg and cry?

Today many people ask—"Why do they hate us?"—fact is, as I have mentioned before, the world has changed, many have been left behind. In today's world and in the future, education will dominate—those that are educated will be the winners and the losers will be the uneducated. And it is these people who brood and resent, unlike in the past, they can see on TV how the rest of the world lives, especially the rich. How can they have what the rich countries have? They forget and refuse to believe that these societies were BUILT! The riches were not given, people worked hard, made good decisions and built a successful society. Good things take time to fruition, do they not?

A terrorist recently killed himself while killing innocents—later they found his writings, he had hoped to be rewarded in heaven, get away from all the hardship of life.

Here we see the total lack of willingness to work hard and build a life for himself, wanting instantaneous rewards and this is where some religions take advantage.

Just as Heaven is a metaphor for childhood and Reincarnation for adulthood, these may also be metaphors for the way we view life. When you envision a rich and successful life for yourself, do you see yourself winning a lottery and having your dreams come true (Heaven) or by working hard, becoming an entrepreneur, taking risks and working your way up (Reincarnation)? Are you the person who is constantly in the lookout for a sugar daddy or mommy (Heaven) or are you the person who will accept nothing but the results of your untiring efforts (Reincarnation)?

Take a good look around—how many people do you see being successful using the former method vs the latter. Which person do you admire and which do you despise? And in which camp do you find yourself in?

But you see for a long time in the past, power and wealth were handed down—the king's son became the new king, the no-good brainless son of a wealthy man was the new boss and religions born in those days reflect those same old primitive ideas. It is only today do we see a person born in poverty yet make himself or herself a successful and wealthy person by sheer will and hard work—that's the idea of Moksha!

The difference with a king religion is clear-cut—those that dream of a ready-made Heaven want to part of all the hard work, sacrifice, sweat and toil that go with making such a world happen. By forcing you to come back, by making it clear that there is no heaven to run away to, Hinduism is making it clear that it is up to you to make that dream a reality.

That is why your only choice must be Karma and Reincarnation. You die and you come right back. You come back and work alongside God for a better earth. This is a fight that we must win. God supports us; but this is our fight—our work—and we must finish it.

Hindus choose to come back and work some more. Hindus are not ready to retire; we choose to work. The harshness of life on earth is not a problem but an opportunity—an opportunity to show God what we can do. It is an opportunity to earn praise *from* God! What a golden opportunity. Do not pass it up!

Of course, this Heaven will be vastly different from the ones that are popular. Yes, there will be pain and suffering here, because this is a Heaven that will have to be built and earned. There will be dreamers here: hard workers, good people ready to help total strangers, tellers of Truth, honest people, and God-loving people. The pleasures you get here are the pleasures of the heart and soul. This Heaven will be different—it is a Heaven that God Herself will find warm and welcoming!

Retire, Sit, and Do Nothing (Heaven) or Keep Working (Karma and Reincarnation)

"The life of Socrates dissatisfied is better than that of a fool satisfied"—JS Mill

Would you rather live the life of a Socrates dissatisfied or a pig satisfied? Would you rather live for 200 years as a "nobody" or for 30-odd years as a Mozart? Mill asks us to aim higher: knowledge, honor, and achievement. Many religions offer you the easy life of a pig, but Hinduism offers you the life of a Mozart or a Tyagaraja. But it must be earned!

Surely there is a better goal than living the lazy life at someone else's expense. Is there nothing to do in Heaven but sit, eat, drink, and watch time go by? What kind of a life is that, and how is it that religions have duped millions by presenting the lazy life as something desirable? In the past, life was sheer Hell for many—they grasped at religions offering the free and easy life. But in today's times, should we not aspire to something higher and better?

This is why you come back and keep working. There are rich and powerful men and women, rich beyond their dreams, who could quit today and live a luxurious life until they die. But they keep working! Why? Why are so many good people willing to risk their lives, face danger, and embrace pain and suffering to save total strangers? Has anyone achieved greatness by being lazy?

There is a Hindi word, *chamcha*, which means one who dislikes work and instead befriends a rich man, praising him and living off his dole—a hanger-on, a moocher, a parasite. He sits at the rich man's feet and is ready to abuse and lash out at anyone who does not like the rich man. The chamcha praises the rich man sky-high, boosts his ego, all in the hope that some money is thrown his way, get the easy life the easy way. Does that sounds like any religions you know?

Karma and Reincarnation offer you something different: honest work, an honest living, and respectable dreams. Karma and Reincarnation encourage you to achieve greatness.

22. Karma and Reincarnation Mean Hindus Are the Participants, Not the Spectators

"And as in the Olympic Games it is not the most beautiful and the strongest that are crowned but those who compete (for it is some of these that are victorious), so those who act win, and rightly win, the noble and good things in life."
—Aristotle

Others are just passing through. The earth belongs to Hindus! Say it out loud!

The above quote from Aristotle seems pretty obvious. However, you cannot participate if you are not here. Being a spectator may be comfortable if you are at a football game watching modern-day gladiators run into each other at top speed for your enjoyment. You get to "enjoy" the hit without feeling any of the consequences.

We are all spectators—all of us have favorite teams for which we cheer, either sitting in the stands or watching in front of the TV. Who would you rather be, the cheering spectator or one of the team members?

When a team wins, no one recognizes the cheering fans. It is the team that is congratulated and featured on TV. It is the team that gets the big money, the shiny rings, or the big cup. The team gets its name recorded in the record books, not the fans.

Admittedly, team members are the ones who will have to bear crushing losses and the ire and abuse of disappointed fans. Some players have even been killed by fans.

Still, knowing that, which would you rather be—a cheering fan or a member of the team? I think we all know the answer: It is much better to be part of the team.

That is what Karma and Reincarnation offers you—being part of the team. The team that will lead humanity forward!

The book of humanity has only just begun to be written. If it were a 1,000-page book, we would only have made it to the second page! The future is ours to write.

Will you help write it?

Imagine being a spectator watching from afar while a celebration is going on—a wedding perhaps—and you are not there. Your loved ones remember you and cry for you, but all you can do is watch from afar and choke back tears. Weddings, birthdays, graduations, first jobs, soldiers coming home, home team victories—all these little joys make life worthwhile. Life is here on earth and only on earth; life is not in Heaven.

It is not the joys of life that this book is about: it is the struggles.

Into every life a little rain must fall, as the saying goes. Every one of us must go through life struggling against the odds. What would hurt us most would be the knowledge that our loved ones are going through tough times without us. We want to share life with them; we want to be right here fighting alongside them.

Nothing hurts more than realizing we are totally helpless: we can't reach out and embrace our loved ones; we can't hold them or wipe away their tears.

Heaven turns into Hell.

But why limit ourselves to our loved ones?

Are you a person who spends his or her time at an animal

shelter? The dogs, cats, and other animals learn to recognize you; they miss you when you don't come, and they are happy to see you when you do. All they want is a little love.

How many of you devote your time and effort to helping others? Some of you may work at a homeless shelter. Others may walk to raise money for your favorite causes—to build a library, perhaps, or fight a disease, or help the unfortunate. You might buy toys for poor kids: imagine the delight in the eyes of those kids when they wake up in the morning and see those delightful toys!

It is wonderful to see people helping total strangers. Every year many communities are threatened by floods, and every year total strangers line up to help protect those communities by piling up sandbags. Every year thousands of young kids turn up missing, and without fail, total strangers spend incredible amounts of time and money to help out.

Imagine a child who is lost in the forest. He is hungry, disoriented, tired, and crying for his mother. He lies down in the shade of a tree and cries himself to sleep. Who is with him at this time? God, of course. But God is looking for you to come help.

As a Hindu, the responsibility for the health of the planet rests on your tiny shoulders. Are you up to it? Unfortunately we seem to be practically alone in this endeavor—most others are building fancy castles in the air and running away to live in them.

Do you see the difference? Heaven is for those who look to God for help. Hinduism, Karma and Reincarnation are for those who choose to help God.

But really, you don't have to be a hero to make a difference. Just pulling your weight, living your life, and earning your paycheck is contribution enough.

Most religions offer you a nice getaway place where you can live in comfort, forget your loved ones, and forget those who are in need. You can be selfish, thinking only of what makes you happy. Such religions make you but a guest here on this earth, for a limited amount of time. The majority of time—eternity—will be spent elsewhere. Then why do anything, why commit to a healthy planet? Why not let God and the succeeding generations worry about that?

Can you be that callous, that insensitive?

Hinduism offers you a chance to come back to earth to continue your work. The pain has not gone away. Embrace the suffering—embrace those who are going through difficult times—and you will stand with God.

They say that you find out who your friends are not when times are good, but when times are hard. How true.

Life is harsh and cruel. We cannot blame our ancestors for wishing for a nice way out. Life was much harsher in the old days. Death is frightening; it is natural to wish for a way out. Amazingly it is Hinduism—which is much older than many religions— that asks you to turn back to earth, to stand your ground and fight back.

Hinduism is not for everyone. Karma and Reincarnation are not for everyone. There are those who, when someone yells *fire*, will knock down their own grandmother as they rush out. Then there are those who rush in to help. Which one are you?

Reincarnation is for those who want to stay with God—stay and work for a better earth, stand and fight for a better future. The cowards have created a nice fantasyland for themselves "up there" and are running away. Let them go.

Hindus have decided to stay.

Stay with God, stand by God.

Stand tall with God, face the pain and suffering, make life better for all of us.

Hinduism asks: Who is willing to be a hero? Who wants to be the firefighter running into the burning building?

Who wants to jump into a roaring river to save a child? That is what being a Hindu or a Buddhist means. That is what Reincarnation means: a willingness to stand with God and face danger head-on.

You are needed here; the pain is here, the suffering is here. The world is crying out for good people to help. There is much evil in this world. We need all the help that we can get. God needs your help. What is your answer?

I feel sad for those who have chosen to remain mute spectators. They are unable to help or participate. All they can do is watch from afar and wring their hands. Most will turn away because the pain will be too much for them. They will choose to forget their former life, forget their loved ones, and forget that they were ever once human. For them life on earth will be reduced to a bad dream. The memories of their loved ones—father, mother, grandma, grandpa, kids, friends—will slowly fade over time. They have made their choice. They have rejected life and chosen death. They have chosen "life" in a coma.

We all wish for uninterrupted joy and limitless fun and happiness, but that is a dreamland. It is not real life. We can't live in our dreams. We have to wake up and work to overcome problems.

If Heaven is the dream, fake life, Karma and rebirth is the harsh but real life.

Stop dreaming, stop thinking of running away. Stand and fight. Stand with God and realize that the world's problems are not insurmountable. Find the strength within you. Work, learn, and work some more. Slowly but surely, evil will be overcome.

Problems don't have a chance against those who stand united and are willing to work. Problems don't have a chance against those who are willing to make the tough choices and the sacrifices necessary to get the job done. Hinduism says that if you want a life of ease—if you want paradise—you have to work for it.

Researchers say that it takes about ten thousand hours of work before you become good at any particular thing. Ten thousand hours! If you want to be good at something, put in that much time. The results will speak for themselves. Want to be a great musician? Put in those 10,000 hours of practice. Want to be a physician healing the sick? Put in those 10,000 hours of study. Want to be a ballplayer? Put in those 10,000 hours of practice!

Nothing is going to come easily. The more you put in, the more you will get out.

This is what we should be teaching our kids: If they work hard and put in the time, results will follow.

Let us participate in the making of a golden future. Let us make God proud of us.

God Sri Rama

Who is this Rama? And why is he considered a God? You may already have heard or read his story in the Ramayana, the story of Sri Rama.

Briefly, the story goes that God Rama was born a prince. To keep his father's promise to his wife, he dutifully went to the forest accompanied by his wife Sita, and younger brother Laxmana. While in the forest, his wife Sita was abducted by an evil King, Ravana, and Rama went to war with him, ultimately succeeding in killing him and rescuing his wife. The story ends with Rama triumphantly returning to his kingdom and being crowned king.

As you can see I have been quite brief with His story. Why is that? Because my focus is not on Rama's accomplishments but on how he reacted to certain situations. The story of

Rama is a story of strength, valor and bravery, but it is also a story of a man—yes, just a man, just a human being striving to do the right thing whatever may be the cost. In my mind's eye I see him as a young man standing tall, unafraid, while a tsunami of trouble is rushing towards him. In much of this book, I talk about values, principles and ethics, and Rama embodies these ideals. No wonder he has been called "Parama Purusha", the perfect man.

Although he has been called the perfect man, Rama made his share of mistakes. When looked through the prism of history, one can find fault with many things that happened in the past. We fail to realize that life was different in previous times. But it has to be said: Rama was not perfect, but then which human being is perfect? That's the great lesson here. We are human but we can aspire to be great, to do great things, things that even Gods would hesitate to do. This is what it means to pursue Moksha.

The story of Rama is devoid of magic and miracles. There are exaggerations here and there (storywriters can't help but try to inject some magical situations), but the story of Rama is about a God who came down to earth and lived the life of a normal human being, a human being who did extraordinary things! But he did not need magic or miracles to do so.

And nowhere in the Ramayana does Sri Rama say that He is God! Nowhere!

This may disappoint a lot of people, but most people are looking for that magic man, the man who says he is God and does magical things. Sri Rama showed that you could be a puny human and yet aspire to do great things—things great Gods could not accomplish. Ravana could not be killed by any of the Gods; but a human, Sri Rama, defeated and killed him!

Let us be clear—why is Sri Rama considered a God? Not

because our holy texts say so but because of his actions. This is why we say the Buddha is a God, based on his actions. Great people like Gandhiji, Schindler—are these people close to God? Can you answer why? Let our actions bring us close to God.

Many see God as a savior, the knight in shining armor coming to rescue the damsel in distress, please realize that God Rama should not be seen this way. The former view is for the weak, the coward, not for the strong, the warrior. Remember, we talked about reaching for the stars, aspiring to higher things? The story of Sri Rama embodies those values. When the going gets tough, the tough get going, and that is exactly what Sri Rama did.

That is also our story, the story of humanity. Religions keep telling tall tales of magic men, with miracles aplenty, but the story of humanity has been one long struggle against incredible odds, if you believe in evolution, that is, as I do—no room for creationism here. Any number of times humanity could have been wiped off the face of earth, but we kept battling, persevering, when all hope seemed lost. Some wounds were self-inflicted: humanity has indulged in an astounding number of wars over the years. Diseases ravaged humanity, and primitive medicine could do nothing to stop them.

This is not a God who runs around doing magic and miracles. That kind of God would have an ego and like people boosting his ego, hmm, like a king! If God were like that, then why limit these miracles to a select few? Why not wave that magic wand and make this world a happy paradise? There'd be no more work for the Schindlers, Confuciuses and Gandhijis.

The story of Rama is the story of us, ordinary folks, without magic. The future story of humanity also will also depend on hardworking people making incredible sacrifices, doing the right thing. This is what a faith should be doing—talking about values, ethics, fighting the good fight, building a wonderful future. It seems only Hinduism is doing this these days.

23. Karma and Reincarnation Mean "We" and Not "I"

True happiness is found when we make others happy.

The vast majority of our problems can be traced to people selfishly thinking of themselves. We have had dictators looting their countries and holding onto power even as their countries sink into utter hopelessness—Kim Jong-Il and Mugabe come to mind. Do they not see what is happening in their countries? Do they not see their own people living in utter poverty, suffering? These dictators have stopped caring; they only think of themselves. It is all about "I".

There is so much pain, so much suffering in this world—the warlords, drug lords, dictators, terrorists, greedy bankers, Ponzi schemers: *all* only thinking of what benefits them, the rest of the world be damned!

During normal times, while waiting to board a bus or a train, we are happy to stand aside and let others board before us or wait our turn in a queue. Sadly we forget these lessons in times of stress, and that selfish "I" comes back to bite us.

None of this will make sense as long as we remain selfish, thinking only of ourselves: *I get to go to the fantasyland, I get to enjoy, lead a life of pleasure, a life full of happiness and joy! Yay for me!*

As I mentioned before, life on earth is very taxing. Unable to deal with the harshness of life, people have invented religions that tell them what they want to hear: *Beyond that nice, "smooth" mountain, waa-aay over there, awaits a nice, wonderland full of bounties. Life will be smooth and easy.*

This is what people are after, this is why they are ready to drop their values, principles and ethics and beg before any being that promises them that ease of life. They do not want God. They want what religion offers them.

Hinduism promises the opposite. We offer work—hard work. We offer an opportunity to make a difference, to earn praise from God, to make God proud of you.

We offer God!

We offer an opportunity to finish what you started, to dive into a raging river to save a drowning child. Many good people have done that, only to lose their own life.

We offer an opportunity to teach eager children and adults deprived of the chance for an education.

We offer an opportunity to help out any way you can when you see others in need, and many, many ways to impress God. Think of the difference you can make by choosing to stay, choosing to come back.

But this life is not for everyone. This is a difficult choice to make. As I wrote earlier, Hinduism will find few takers. Our path to God is dark and strewn with rocks and sharp objects. Who would choose to walk with God?

How is the Hindu way any different from the way of those who are committing their lives to helping others? The difference is that you are now committing to help until the job gets done, no matter how long it takes, no matter how many lifetimes it takes. This is not just a weekend job, not just summer work, but the project of several lifetimes!

Just stop and think about this: many claim they want to

serve God, but *"with term limits, please—just for this one life-time, and after that, it is time to claim our reward. It is time for God to serve us! For eternity!"*

These religions serve religion—theirs. They do not serve God.

The day you think of God and equate Her with Truth, ethics, values and principles, is the day you have found God, the day you have found faith and spirituality, the day you have found Hinduism.

When you stop thinking of yourself and your selfish needs, and start thinking of others, you have found God. But this God is unlike others. She will not pamper you or give you an easy life. She demands that you strive to be good, to choose the side of Truth, to work hard, pull your weight, pay for whatever you take, be honest, compassionate, and put others first.

She will put you to good, hard work.

Recently a woman in Mexico was killed by the drug lords for speaking out against them in an online forum. Her work must not be halted. Someone has to step in and carry it forward. If she had been Hindu or believed in Reincarnation, I am sure she would not have hesitated to come back and carry on the fight.

Earth faces innumerable problems. Life throws so many challenges at us. God is not going to blow them away magically. That work is up to us.

We all have our passions. At this point I ask each reader to reflect on his or her passion. What do you care about?

Then ask yourself, "If I were gone, would the problem, the pain, go away?" Not at all. The problem would still be here, the pain would still be here, the need would still be here. God is still here, awaiting a solution.

Do not leave work unfinished.

Come, let us work with God and get the job done.

Hinduism, Karma and Reincarnation will not make sense unless and until you stop focusing on yourself and start thinking about others. You are wanted and needed here.

Please do not misunderstand the "we" and "I" that I talk about here; I am not against capitalism nor am I advocating socialism or communism. It is my opinion that a mix of the two is what a society needs. True communism has failed, and the true capitalism of a dictator such as the one in North Korea or a Mugabe also fails society. What we need is the middle path.

Just because I ask you to think of "we" does not mean there is no place for "I"—Gandhiji saw his people suffering and said "I" am going to do something about it and he did! Schindler saw crimes being committed and said let *me* do something about it. Lincoln, Confucius, Sankaracharya and many a nameless, faceless person saw a need and jumped right into troubled waters to calm them. They saw the "I" making a difference.

Remember, there is no need for a hero in Heaven.

No need for a Buddha in Heaven.

No need for a Parent in Heaven.

No need for an innovator in Heaven.

No need for a warrior in Heaven.

No need for a volunteer in Heaven.

No need for a firefighter in Heaven.

No need for a soldier in Heaven.

No need for a Schindler in Heaven.

No need for a dreamer in Heaven.

No need for a journalist in Heaven.

No need for a healer in Heaven.

No need for an achiever in Heaven.

No need for an Olympian in Heaven.

No need for a Teacher in Heaven.

No need for a leader in Heaven.

They are *all* needed here. God needs you down here!

A beautiful earth will be the result. One day humankind will travel the stars. Poverty, hunger, disease, natural disasters—*all* will be conquered and will be things of the past. But the path to that glorious future will be hard. Now you can see why so many desert the ship. Will you pull a Lord Jim? Or are you made of stronger stuff? Only those who have spent their lives working for the benefit of others, those who put others first, have found God. I repeat: death is not a qualification to meet God. God is not simply waiting for you to die so that you may see Her.

Is God worthwhile? Is making a difference in the lives of others worthwhile? Is going down in history as a great person worthwhile?

None of this is guaranteed to happen—now *that* should drive some people away.

Come to God because you want to. We offer no mouthwatering incentives or fear-inducing threats. Do good because you want to. Choose Karma and Reincarnation because you want to. Come to God because you want to.

Why Hinduism is Unique

Of course, every religion says the same thing, right? There are always some differences in all religions that make them unique, and Sanatana Dharma(Hinduism) is no exception. As we have talked about, Hinduism is a Teacher faith as opposed to a King religion. A person may serve only one King, hence the threats against respecting other religious ideas or Gods, but one can have many Teachers. This is a fact of life isn't it? Starting first with our mother, as we grow up, we meet many a Teacher. Some inspire us, some wake us up, some disappoint us – I have to say that I have learned a lot from people who have disagreed with me – it made me think and reflect more on my ideas, made me better – so not all Teachers are saintly, some can be real nasty. But that is not what this topic is all about – it is about realizing what Hinduism is trying to teach us – to not shackle ourselves to just one Teacher – to realize that Teachers are many and we must be open to all ideas

Again, to repeat – God Sri Rama is Krishna is Jesus is Durga is the Buddha is Allah is….

In this regard Hinduism seems unique when we see that fellow Teacher faiths like Buddhism and Sikhism seems to have let King like aspects seep into their faiths. Buddhists follow only the teachings of the Buddha or his followers, Sikhs only follow the teaching of Sikh Gurus and none other. A True Teacher faith does not shut out other teachings of other religions – it is not surprising to see a Hindu wearing the icons of other religions – as we know Gandhiji's favorite hymn contained the word Allah – a lot of Hindus will pray at Islamic shrines. Not just God Krishna or Durga but the Buddha, Mahavira, Jesus and Mohammed are also our Teachers, let us learn from them all! These are the ideas that set Hinduism apart, which makes it so unique.

24. Karma and Reincarnation Mean It Is Better to Give Than to Receive

Heaven is for takers; Karma and Reincarnation is for givers.

In one humorous Charlie Brown cartoon, a little girl comes running towards Charlie Brown and excitedly shows him her list of all the nice things that she is going to get from Santa. Charlie Brown asks, "But where is your give list?" And the little girl replies, "My *what?*"

Many people believe that serving God here on earth is sufficient; but once they pass on, it is now God's turn to take care of them. *Nice God will now take care of me.*

In return for part of a lifetime of serving God, they must now be rewarded for eternity! It is payback time. God now owes them a happy, contended retirement for eternity!

God is stuck with these selfish folks. The poor man has even signed an agreement with them. He is forced to nurse-maid billions through eternity!

Take, take, take!

Everyone begging for a hand-out: *God, make me happy.*

Hinduism begs to differ. Hindus think it is better to give than to receive.

We aim to make God happy.

In Heaven, you spend eternity as a taker, dependent on God for all your daily needs, You are a parasite, a free-loader.

How did this happen? There are plenty of good, honest,

highly intelligent, educated and yes, *OMG highly-educated* people at that, all around the world. Yet, they have been seduced by the ease of living.

There is no such thing as a life without any pain or suffering. A drug addict feels no pain or suffering while he is under the influence. Life is bliss, full of joy. This is why he becomes addicted to the drug. Is this what Heaven is like? You enter a drug-induced state and never come out? You go to sleep and enter a nice dream world? Is that the state you want to be in for eternity?

Why do people slap drug-addicted people and shout, "Snap out of it! You need to get a *Life*!" There's a similarity here: Being in Heaven is like being under the influence—a place without life.

When all you can think of is taking, when all you can think of is how you can be happy, when you are a selfish, uncaring person, nothing good can come from you.

Those who choose to come back should have no illusions. You are not guaranteed a rich, easy life. Nothing is guaranteed. Maybe you will live in one of the poorest nations on earth or find yourself in the middle of a brutal war. These possibilities are enough to scare off anyone.

But here on earth, you get to stay with God!

People have the wrong idea about God. Who would associate God with pain and suffering? Not that God *causes* pain and suffering, but that God is *with those* who are in pain. God is with those who need Her desperately.

Turn on the TV and you will see images of innocent children undergoing chemotherapy—their Parents sit beside them with haggard faces, putting on a brave front, praying for a cure. The children remain calm and are so brave. Yes, God is with these children. God is with these families.

God has a job for you. Stay, fight for a cure!

Give.

Here and only here on earth, you give back to God!

In Heaven, you spend eternity as a taker. Only here, only here on Mother Earth, can you give back.

You can become a giver. You can be with God.

As I mentioned before, in Hinduism there is no Heaven or Hell. Once you wish Hell upon someone, you let hate enter your heart. Hating someone only hurts you in the end.

A giver does not hate.

As a child, you may not see the value of an education. You may not see the purpose of endless days and years spent studying, when you could be out playing. Many quit school early. It may seem to those who are still in school that those who quit have it made, that these guys get to enjoy themselves (Heaven) while you suffer (Karma and Reincarnation). But once you are an adult—perhaps around middle age or maybe even younger—you see the value of an education. You are thankful that you stayed in school.

Coming back to earth may not seem like a great idea. The idea that you are coming back to a harsh life may not sit well with you. But when you choose to stay with God, when you choose to make a difference, you can never go wrong.

Each life is like spending a year in class. Each life can teach you something new. In each life you learn, you become a better person. Each life is an opportunity for you to change the lives of the people around you, in your society, maybe even the lives of people you have never met!

You sit in *God's* class. You are on the path to Moksha.

Again, let the reader make a choice—giver or taker? *When we wonder how do we get close to God, how do we become a God? The answer is simple – Be a Giver! That's it!*

Religions for the Weak

I am not the first person to say this (Nietzsche has beaten

me to it): Most of today's religions cater to the weak, just as they have done in the past. I feel it is time that we finally grow up, stop being children, stop being weak, and embrace a faith that is for the strong.

One thing you notice about the weak is their lack of a will to work, their lack of willingness to make the necessary sacrifices. They are either blaming others, looking around for a savior, or running away from responsibilities.

I have said this before, and I will say it again: Hinduism simply cannot compete with these easy-life religions. Can a leader who says, "We must tighten our belts, work harder during these tough times," compete against a wily politician who promises easy times to all people? "I will lower taxes, strengthen the military, create millions of jobs, etc. etc." How can an honest leader compete with that?

I've made this analogy before: a flood is about to hit your town. How can you convince a coward to stay, work to strengthen the defenses, move people to safety, risk his life when all he has to do is to get in his truck and keep driving until he reaches safety?

How? How can I convince you to stay with God and do the right thing?

But values and principles don't change once this life is over—or do they? That's a question you must ask yourself.

There is no free lunch—you know that. You have worked hard all your life, built your life by sheer hard work and sacrifices. So many people have sacrificed so much so that today we might have a better life. Have their sacrifices been for naught?

That is why I keep insisting that Hinduism is a Teacher faith. Unfortunately, many Hindus hope that God is like a king. Some of the temples that are being built nowadays remind me of palaces fit for a king—or even an emperor. It makes me sad to see that.

Living as a subject in a kingdom is simple. The king takes take care of everything. In the old days, if trouble were to strike, what would the subject of the kingdom do? Why, he'd go to the king, of course, and ask the king to fix the problem. And the king might say, "I will take care of it. You can now stop worrying and go home." Nice.

But what if you did the same thing in a Teacher faith? The Teacher might say, "Well, here's what you can do about this problem." I emphasize the "you" here. The onus is on you. The problem is your responsibility. It is up to you to take care of the problem.

I get sick when I hear a kid say, "Sports is my ticket out of poverty." The sports magazines and sports television channels play up these kids. He faced long odds but he persevered, did not let the naysayers stop him, worked hard and finally made it to the big leagues!

Kids hate to study. Which kid doesn't love to play? Parents are under incredible pressure when a scout shows up and says their kid is gifted and he could be in the big leagues in the near future. Sports are a quick fix. The kid wants to play, but the Parent has to be strong and tell the child that his future lies in getting an education. Education is not a quick fix. It takes years and years. Does this remind you of one of the complaints about Karma and Reincarnation? That one is born again and again, to face life's troubles over and over? It's the same thing here: a kid sees going to school as a burden, something that has to be done year after long year, starting as a little kid and extending sometimes well beyond one's 30s or 40s or even later. What is the alternative? People want the quick fix: 18-year-old instant millionaire kids. One day he's without a buck in his pocket, and the next day he's driving a Lexus.

This is what a Parent is up against. This is what Hinduism is up against. Religions are promising the instant fix. All one has to do is either get away from life or have a magic man come to fix up things.

Parents have to fight against this mindset. They have to make their kids realize the value of a good education, the value of earning things. Quick fixes don't last. When you work hard for things, sweat, sacrifice, build up things with your own hands, the satisfaction you get is sweet. I don't understand how people would want to live as dependents on some being for eternity, twiddling their thumbs with nothing to do, time stretching towards eternity, day after day, night after night... sit and do nothing? What kind of a life is that?

But then this is the mindset of the strong, the adult, the brave.

It is time for a new faith—to discard the old, tired medieval ideas—to embrace democracy and freedom and dump those kings and queens on the roadside.

25. Karma and Reincarnation Mean a Commitment to Doing God's Work for Eternity!

God is work, work is God.

Plato's question: is something good because God commends it, or is it intrinsically good and therefore God commends it?

I am asking for a change in paradigm. Most religions ask you to believe and tell you that this belief is very important. It is important for you to believe, they say, for without firm belief nothing will happen—God will not shower blessings on you.

Well, let's discuss some Truths that are not so pleasing to your ears.

I am going to change the paradigm: I don't ask for belief, I ask for commitment—a commitment to what will definitely please God: Truth, honesty, and doing the right thing for this earth and all its living creatures.

Commit yourself to dharma. Dharma encompasses Truth, honesty, compassion, a desire to help others, work, righteousness and your place in society. Prince Sri Rama embodies dharma. Read the book on his life, *The Ramayana*.

When you commit yourself to being honest, to telling the Truth, doing your best to help others in need, leading your life on the straight and narrow, you commit to earth, you commit to God! Religion does not matter; you can be an atheist for all God cares, you are still with God!

Let Hindus show their belief in God by telling the Truth, being honest, compassionate, loving, kind, practicing their dharma, ahimsa—this is how we show we are the true children of God. You are committing yourself to things that you are very well familiar with. Hinduism asks you to change the paradigm. Can you commit to standing strong instead of looking for a handout from above?

Think of the day Mumbai was attacked by gunmen indiscriminately killing anyone in sight, or the day when the Norwegian gunner started shooting down young innocent teenagers. Most people on these days ran away to safety, away from the burning buildings, away from the marauding gunmen. But a few ran towards the trouble, towards the burning buildings, towards the gunmen. The police, the firefighters, ran towards the scene of the trouble, and some paid for it with their lives: this is Hindu-like. Hinduism urges you to come back. Want a fancy, trouble-free life? Work for it! Make it happen right here. With hard work, enough sacrifices and tough choices, we can make a paradise happen right here. Let us start by committing ourselves to doing good, to dharma. Let us commit ourselves to Truth, to compassion for our fellow beings on this planet, and to the right principles and values.

To commit to doing God's work for eternity—now, that's some commitment, isn't it?

Let us not forget that God's work can only be done down here, only here! Can you make that kind of a commitment to do God's work not for just a few years of one adult life but for each and every life, again and again?

Can you commit to helping others, raising funds to help those injured in a terrorist bombing, raising funds to fight diseases by walking, by speaking up against drug lords, telling the Truth, taking nothing for free (there goes Heaven!), being a productive member of society?

Those who commit to doing God's work choose to be with God.

Let us forget about Heaven. Let us discover faith, spirituality.

Let us forget about God.

Yes, I said it: let us forget about this God who is seen as nothing but a Santa, a giver of gifts. It seems we think of God only because we want something from Her. We have a selfish need, a need to escape the troubles of human life, so we look for our sugar daddy to bail us out of this harsh life.

We can do better, but we need to be strong. Instead of worrying about how to get to a cushy afterlife, let us ask ourselves, "What would please God? What conduct would God find admirable?"

That means worrying less about ourselves and worrying more about the state of our country, this earth.

Here, we should mention the story of Sati Anasuya. Anasuya was a devout Hindu—good, honest, kind and pleasant to everyone, always helping others. No one had anything bad to say about her. But some people hated her for her kindness and gentleness, so they went to the Gods, the Trimurthi—Brahma, Vishnu and Siva—and implored them to destroy Anasuya (these stories are allegorical—there is always an underlying message to these stories, so let us grasp that Truth). Well, the Gods decided to teach these people a lesson. They went to Anasuya and told her that they came to destroy her. She promptly turned them into little babies! The entire universe was turned into turmoil; here were the great Gods turned into little children, no longer able to take care of the universe and all the people within. Of course the evil people learned their lesson. They rushed to Anasuya and begged her to return the Gods to the way they were before, and she did so.

Did you understand the Truth within this story? The message here is that when you walk the path of the righteous, *NO ONE* can harm you, not even the Gods. God is Truth, so how can God harm a person who tells the Truth? God is good, so how can God destroy a good person?

People constantly ask, "How do I find God?" Easy! Tell the Truth, be honest, compassionate, make a difference in the lives of others, help the unfortunate, be somebody, lead the life of a Rama, and then truly God will be with you.

Easy? But it is not so easy to tell the Truth, to be honest, is it? And where is the payoff in it? Join religion X or Y and they promise that their God will bestow his blessing on you. Now that is something! That is what everyone wants to hear.

Commit to Truth? What will that get us?

Let us remember the good people who risked everything for *Truth*—not for God (by that I mean a being in the sky) and not for a personal reward either here or in the hereafter.

The great ones did not set out to do the great things that they did with God in mind. Instead, Truth was their guiding light. They came across situations in life and they each asked themselves, "What should I do? What is the right thing to do?"

Let Truth inspire you, Let Truth be your guide.

In front of God, *this* is where it all matters, *this* is where you tell the Truth, *this* is where you hold onto your cherished beliefs! This is where you stand tall and face the music, if any!

When you choose religion over Truth, you choose evil over God! And yes, evil is to be feared. And yes, evil will tempt you with the easy life.

Hinduism emphasizes commitment to Truth.

Karma and Reincarnation emphasize dharma.

We are responsible for the state of our society, our country. Indians are responsible for the state that India is in; the

Chinese are responsible for the health of the Chinese society, Africans for Africa, Russians for Russia, Americans for America, etc. All of us are responsible for the health of this planet.

Heaven is here, Hell is here. They are not somewhere "up there". They are both right here, and it is up to us to make this world a Heaven or a Hell.

That's the job before us: to make this earth a living Heaven. Who will step forward? Will you? Karma and Reincarnation make this point clear. We need to live moral, ethical lives. That is the essential lesson of Karma and Reincarnation. Do not come to God empty-handed.

Hinduism is a Teacher faith. Remember going to the Teacher, proud of your accomplishments, eager to show her what great things you have done?

Tell me, are you proud of your life? Are you proud of how you have led your life, how you have achieved everything that you have achieved? Was it done morally, ethically? Are people afraid of you? Do people feel pain when they think of you?

If so, once you die, turn around and come right back! You do not want to show your face to your Teacher. There is much work for you to do, many changes yet to be made.

Well, obviously, this won't be easy. If this was so easy, everyone would follow it, would they not? Would we have such crime in our societies? No. There would be no need for the police or crime fighters if everyone were dharmic. The fact remains that following a dharmic life is difficult. It is easier to break the rules. It is easier to commit a crime and enrich ourselves, to tell a lie to get out of a jam, to only think of ourselves, to be selfish.

But the sad fact remains that those countries where the people followed the rules and were honest and Truthful are the more successful societies. Countries where people cut corners, took to crime, or took the easy way out, remain backward and poor.

Sadly, this essential lesson remains forgotten, common sense seemingly opaque.

Rich nations are not necessarily the happiest places. The happiest place is where you feel you are loved. Longtime marriages break apart when love moves out. Love comes from a calm, dharmic mind. When you decide to follow dharma and be Truthful, honest and compassionate in your dealings with others, you set the tone for others to follow. A society made up of people like you will be a delight to live in.

Such a place is a place where God will come and decide to stay.

That then, remains our goal: to invite God to the house that we will build, to the Heaven that we will build right here on earth. We will build a society of Truth-seekers, dharmic people—compassionate, helping, loving people.

But today we remain weak. We look for answers from above. We desperately hope for something elsewhere. We don't like what we see before us because what we see needs fixing—and this means hard work, sacrifices and difficult choices. Unable and unwilling to make such choices, we believe in the magic tooth fairy who will come to save us.

In the Hindu way, it is important that we measure up to God's standards. One of the nice things Christians do is that they dress up to go to church. We also need to "dress up"— to make our hearts clean, to lead a clean life, help others, and work towards a better society.

There is much that is wrong with the world today; who is the culprit? Look in the mirror. Every animal on this planet fears us. I say that if human beings were to magically disappear from this planet, every creature on this planet would stop and cheer our departure. Sadly, that is our legacy so far. It does not have to be. We can change, we can do better.

Life is a great gift from God. Once we become better, stronger people, reshape our societies, banish the harshness from our lives, make living a joy, we will finally stop saying life is a sin and that life on earth is a prison sentence. We will stop looking for answers elsewhere, "up there". We will rediscover the gift of life from God. We will finally realize the value of this great gift.

I am confident that the good days will come when each and every living creature on this planet will love life and will enjoy this gift from God.

The strong shall inherit the earth.

The Hindus shall inherit the earth.

Then, and *only* then, the great day will come. God will come down to earth to take a look at our handiwork and She will be proud of us!

Let me end this section by posing a question: what if you decided that there is no God, no afterlife, no reward in the afterlife, no fancy Heaven waiting, no Moksha, no Reincarnation, nothing; you just go poof after you die. Would you still stay committed? If you say yes, you have truly understood the point I am trying to make.

To answer Plato's question, God is not separate from good, from Truth. Truths are self-evident; they do not have to be sanctioned as such by a super being. We do not have to read from an ancient book to realize the difference between right and wrong. Let our conscience guide us. Let us break away from getting our Truths from moth-eaten books. Blindly following what is written by ancients will get us into trouble. The terrorism that is stalking this world and insisting that evolution is false is an example of this wrong mindset.

Can Hinduism Compete?

Let's make one thing clear: the difference between some religions and Hinduism is simple. They reduce you to a groveling slave/servant intent on getting to the good easy life and God is seen as that Santa—the giver of gifts. Hinduism says you are a child/student of God, your place is not on the ground on your knees, but in God's lap. They seek forgiveness, so that they can put their earthly life behind them and get to the good life; we seek enlightenment, we reach for the hand of God. They seek a life of ease, we seek a life of doing God's work, reaching for the stars, reaching for greatness. Their goal: the pleasures of the flesh, our goal: pleasures of the heart, mind and soul. Their ultimate goal—the easy life stretching for eternity, our ultimate goal—to make God proud of Her children!

Here, once you become an adult, you have to work for a living, you may not be able to make much money, and you might be forced to lead a dreary, dull life of hardship working long hours, seven days a week. How can we compete against a sugar daddy who will let you sit and do nothing and lead the life of the lazy bum, where you can sit, eat, drink, have sex, sleep and enjoy? How do we compete against that?

I do get a little depressed while writing this book. I wonder if this book will resonate. I keep saying Hinduism is tougher, harder. There is no easy afterlife, no Heaven, no easy sugar daddy to take good care of you, no easy God who will gladly forgive you and send you off to play, no "Am Phat" way of doing things.

Here is a faith that will hold you accountable, will ask you to stand tall before God, to be an Atlas, to take the responsibility for the future of humanity, this earth, on your tiny shoulders, to stand for Truth, honesty and doing things the right way, to forge a great future for all living things on this planet, to make God proud!

Will you step up?

Time and again I have described how easy it is to fall for the easy promises of a comfortable afterlife and a nice forgiving God, to dump your responsibilities on the coming generation, to run away from debts, cheat your victims or worse, your loved ones, to take the easy way out.

How can Hinduism compete with that?

How can Hinduism fight the "Am Phat", "Abracadabra" easy life?

It is the same problem that science faces today. Our lives have become incredibly comfortable and better when compared to the harshness of life that our ancestors faced—look around, reader—everything around you is thanks to science. When you get sick you don't rely on prayer, do you? You rely on science! So then why do people desperately cling to a primitive and backward notion of the earth being 5,000 years old despite the mountain of evidence? Because accepting what science says means there may not be a God, there may not be an easy, comfortable afterlife! Because evolution is a bit too much like REAL LIFE—things happen over an incredibly long period of time. In real life getting the good things in life is not only a matter of a lot of hard work, sacrifice but also being patient and not giving up, because these will take time! That is not very appealing to the weak—they seek the "Am Phat" way—close my eyes, snap my boots and presto—magic land! And so they desperately cling to, as Obama so eloquently put it, guns and religion! But we can see how scary these ideas can be when we look at the areas currently being ruled by the Taliban.

You can see the problem here: one way is to sacrifice, be disciplined, then go back to school for years and years and learn so as to make yourself more employable and finally to build that prosperous society that we all want.

or

Turn to the magic genie who will give you the easy life in an instant: a magic land that waits for you after death. But wait, it gets better: a magic, tranquil land will come down *to you* any day now!

Now you see the attraction for the Taliban, the attraction of Heaven and religions that dangle that carrot in front of you. But as they saying goes, the empty pot makes a lot of noise: "You *must* believe!" they say. The reason "Magic Man" has not shown up is because you have not believed enough! Or wait, those atheists, those people of other religions, yes, *they* are the problem! (Enter hate.)

Science, Hinduism cannot compete with these easy-breezy religions. I truly fear things will get worse in the future.

So, the weak will take the easy way out promised by their religions. God is their trump card: simply cut our hair this way, grow our beard that much, confine women to the kitchen, ban this, ban that, pray X times a day, and God will be so pleased, She will rush to make our dreams come true! When this does not happen, they resort to killing scape-goats. The final result is mass murder.

Is this the future we want?

We *have* to be strong. We *must* accept science. If it were up to me, I would ban all religious teachings in ALL schools. Religion belongs in our homes, our places of worship. Religion does not belong in schools.

Hinduism says God is Truth, Truth is God. That is enough for me. Is that enough for you? Can you accept a faith that asks you not to focus on what God can do for you, but asks you to focus on what you can do for God? The responsibility is shifted here. We move from a society ruled by a king to a democracy where citizens have the opportunity to build their own country.

Can you accept not just one but several lifetimes helping others, working to make this world a greater place and deriving satisfaction and contentment from the process?

Do you love to help God? Do you love to help others? Then embrace Karma and Reincarnation. Stand by God! Stand with God!

Let's build a Heaven right here! Then God will come down to live with *us*! Let's make God proud of our accomplishments!

26. Karma and Reincarnation Mean Hindus Pray for a Hand Up, Not for a Handout

Heaven is a handout.

Arjuna's Choice: In the Mahabharata, before the war is about to take place, Arjuna travels to the kingdom of God Sri Krishna to request his help in the upcoming war. God Krishna gives him two options:

1. *His army:* Fit men armed to the teeth ready to fight for those who choose them. Let's be clear about this choice. This is a king who, upon hearing that there is a problem in his kingdom, tells his subjects that he will personally deal with the problem. God is seen as a king here.

2. *Himself:* But he will not fight. He will not lift a weapon. He will not slay anyone. All he will do is advise and instruct. In this instance, God is a Teacher. You go to Her for help, She will advise and instruct you on what *you* should do (emphasis on the YOU), how *you* should take care of the problem.

Arjuna does not hesitate. He chooses God, the Teacher. Much has been written about Arjuna's choosing God because Sri Krishna is God, but little has been written about the fact that Arjuna made this choice because he was strong.

God Krishna asks Arjuna, "Why did you choose me? I

have told you that I will not fight. I will only advise, instruct and encourage, that is all. Still you chose me?" To this Arjuna replies, "But Sir, if you had decided to fight, then what would have been the need for us to do the fighting? We could have all stayed home, all our men, our entire army. We could have put our weapons aside and simply watched. You alone could take on all of Duryodhana's army, and they would not stand a chance. What is the use of our weapons, our training? Let us have this glory."

Arjuna conducted himself as a hero should, the way a strong man should. And Arjuna paid a terrible price for his choice: he lost his son in the war! After the war, the Pandavas lost more of their sons. That is what it means to be strong, it is very, very tempting to let others handle things and run away. But that is not what the strong do. That is not the Hindu way.

But isn't it so tempting? Leave everything to God and just sit and enjoy (Heaven)? Leave the troubles of life, of the earth, to future generations, to others, while we just go to Heaven to enjoy ourselves? All we have to do is pray for God to come down and wave that magic wand and give us paradise through magic!

This kind of thinking makes us weak, keeps us weak. Why work hard and earn a living? Maybe there are easier ways. Why not find a rich sugar daddy, and praise him sky-high: "You are so great, Sir. You have such a beautiful voice, Sir. Were you a singer at one time? You have such a fine mind, Sir. You grasp everything so quickly, Sir. It is amazing!" Pleased, maybe the rich man will throw down some coins. Why not boot-lick your way to an easy life?

But if Arjuna had taken the easy way out, then we would not have the Mahabharata today, would we? We would not have known about Arjuna and the Pandavas.

The Bhagavat Gita would have been lost to us. If there was no war, there would not be a Sri Krishna who gave us the Gita on the battlefield!

The name of Arjuna would have been lost in the annals of time. We would not have known him today. It is such courageous men and women who live for eternity. They live the *real* eternal life!

We must do the same, follow in Arjuna's footsteps. The problems life throws at us are *our* problems to solve. *We* must do the fighting. It is our struggle.

If one idea encapsulates this book, it is this: the eternal fight between the weak coward and the strong hero, where the coward sees blood, pain and suffering, and the hero sees glory and a chance make God proud!

Do not ask God to do your job for you. In life we will face problems. This is where we separate the child from the adult. This is where we separate the weak from the strong.

Remember, at one time people thought that the world was flat and if you sailed far enough, you would fall right off the planet into the void. People thought that there were monstrous creatures lurking in the depths waiting to gobble up ships whole!

America would never have been discovered if these cowards and worrywarts had had their day.

Even today we see these cowards using fear as a tool, warning that the end of the world is near. Yes, the signs are all there (just as they have been every year). Any calamity gives them an opening to instill fear, make us weak and turn us into cowards. It is strange to think that a calamity that causes great pain and suffering is the sign of the coming of God. Then what does peace and prosperity mean? — the coming of Satan?

The attempt to denigrate evolution is the same. The same

tactic is being used. Knowledge is power, power leads to strength. They want to keep us ignorant, fearful. The more you know, the more you question, the less you believe in this fairy-tale God.

When mommy and daddy do everything for you, you become weak.

You are down on your luck, without a job, down to your last rupee. As you walk along the street, you see to your left a soup kitchen, a little hot meal for the down-and-out, handed out lovingly by generous, good people. To your right, a person is standing, shouting, "Jobs! Jobs!" He is a hard-nosed businessman, out to make a profit. He has hard labor in store for you; he will pay you little for the hard work.

Which way will you turn? The strong will turn to the right.

A job gives you dignity, self-respect. They say the most important thing for a woman is love. Not to sound sexist, but to a man, it is self-respect. Without it, without a job, a man will fall apart.

With a good, permanent job, one can have a life, find a soul mate, buy a home, start a family—but all this starts with a job.

The soup kitchen offers a handout; the businessman, a hand up.

But we as a society tend to look down upon businessmen; we elevate people like Mother Teresa to a higher status. Not that she was not a good person, nor that she was not doing great things, but as an Indian, I have always resented her presence. Her presence in India meant that we were poor, we needed help, we needed handouts.

When Mother Teresa found her calling, she did not head west, she did not head for England or Germany; she headed to India, a broken-down country, looted, picked clean to the bone by her colonial powers.

A person like JRD Tata or Bill Gates does not engender

the same good feelings in us as Mother Teresa. We think they are hard-nosed businessmen out to make a buck at our expense, which is probably true. But what is also true is that these gentlemen, and other men and women like them, offer a hand up! They want something from you, but in return they give you something: a barter, a business, an exchange. You keep your dignity, you keep your self-respect!

Let us pray to a God who lets us keep this self-respect; let us pray for a hand up, not a handout.

There are a lot of interfaith prayer groups lately. I caution Hindus: do not pray with the weak—the weak pray for handouts. A Hindu does not beg, a Hindu does not grovel, a Hindu does not get down on his knees. Go to any temple and watch the devotees; most of them are either sitting down or on their feet, which is the right position to be in.

Let us pray, let us worship God by working hard.

Let us pray, let us worship God by making an honest living.

Let us pray, let us worship God by doing the right thing.

Let us pray, let us worship God by practicing ahimsa, dharma.

Let us pray, let us worship God by helping others.

Let us pray, let us worship God by making this world a better place.

Pray to God the right way. When you are overwhelmed with difficulties, certainly seek God's help, but in the right way. As a Hindu you do not have the right to ask God to wipe away your tears, to destroy your difficulties, to annihilate your enemies. All you may ask God for is strength, encouragement and advice, just as God Krishna promised Arjuna he would do.

Be Arjuna. Do not ask God for more than that. This is your war, your fight; you win, you get the glory. You move one step closer to God. Make God proud of you.

Blame God

"Did you hurt your hand beating me, Master?"

Recently a tornado ripped through Oklahoma causing immense devastation, entire neighborhoods disappeared, people killed including about 20 children. And then I read a story about people talking about a miracle that so-and-so survived, thanking God for sparing their lives! What? So, who sent the tornado? Who killed those innocent children? Was it not the same agent that spared your life? And you are thanking a murderer who spared yours?

So, a woman who is raped but her life spared should thank her rapist? A gunman runs through a school killing people at random. He could have shot one child but spares him, so the child's Parents should express their gratitude in sparing their loved one's life?

"Thank you for not beating me to death Master"?

Let us suppose you know this guy who is stockpiling guns and weapons. You know that he is angry at his alma mater, his professors and his fellow students. He tells you that he plans to shoot and kill them all and heads off! You pick up the phone and call a friend of yours at this university to tell him to get out? You make no effort to call the authorities, the university, to prevent this horrible tragedy from happening—all you are concerned with is your friend? And after the devastation, after innocents are brutally murdered, do you think everyone will praise you for saving your friend? In what bizarro world?

But no, not in a bizarro world—it is actually happening right before our eyes, it has happened before, it will happen again! People thanking God for saving a few, totally ignoring all the hundreds dead, the thousands rendered homeless! Ah, the amazing power of religion, the brainwashing it is capable of, no wonder people in the past and some today are so ready to kill and commit mass murder of innocents.

The amazing way people rush to give credit to God when good things happen but stand silent when evil happens. A tsunami or a flood hits a town, causes total devastation, hundreds are killed but a baby is saved! A miracle! Get down on our knees and thank the Lord!

If a person is dying from cancer and is suddenly cured, praise the Lord! He has performed a miracle! And if this person dies, well, he is in a better place now. Happy, no more pain! You see, with a slave mind, God cannot lose, the religions have an answer either way.

Slave mentality begets slave religions and vice versa. Yes, in the 21st century, with all the progress we were supposed to have made, with all our education and yet it is so easy for religions to brainwash intelligent, educated people to become groveling slaves. Amazing power, and we see it happening right before our eyes!

It just does not make sense—why does a so-called loving God allow such horror to happen? Ah, the "Grand Plan", which ends with us in comfortable retirement for eternity.

The only answer that makes sense is that God is a Teacher—a Teacher who treats us humans like adults. This is our home, let us shape it whichever way we want it to be. It can be a paradise if we want it to be, but we have to work at it.

One day the earth will be a paradise—but that's our job to make it happen.

Disasters will happen, life will be hard but the solution is not to run away. It is to make a stand and work to make things better—Karma and Reincarnation. God is with us in this great journey, it is okay to give credit to God when good things happen but it is also all right to give ourselves a pat on the back, we also had something to do with this.

And when bad things happen let us realize that such is life on this planet; but more than any other life form on this planet we have been given the muscle and most important the *brains* to deal with the problems that life throws at us.

Let us succeed at this great endeavor, let us show what we can do, what stuff we are made of, make God proud of us.

Even if we fail, stand tall and take the responsibility for our failure. Do not blame God for it nor expect Her help when things go bad. We are strong, we will overcome!

Your Work, not God's Work

We have talked extensively about doing God's work. Where there is God's work being done, there is God. Sounds nice, I am sure it gives a lot of people a lot of comfort, but we are missing the point here.

Hinduism asks you to come to God because you want to, not because of some threats of being abused and tortured. Do it for the right reasons. Finding God is finding Truth, finding honesty, compassion, kindness that has resided deep in your heart. You become a better person, make this world a better place.

Find God through your work.

Any good thing you do in life should be done because you want to do it, because you love doing it, because it is your life's calling. Please do not do good works in an effort to curry favor with God.

Help people in need because you love doing it, because your heart tells you to do it. Help animals in need because you love working with animals, because you love spending time with them.

Listen to your heart, not to your religious leader.

Make God's work your work.

27. Karma and Reincarnation Mean Human History Is Not a Lie

I have heard from most religions that this life doesn't matter. It is the afterlife that matters, even some Hindus seem to think that life is a big burden, let's get it over with as soon as possible... next stop, paradise!

Does this mean that all of human history is a big lie? Did thousands of men and women who sacrificed their lives for the betterment of humanity die in vain? Was there no point in their sacrifice? And if there was no point, then one could ask, "Why do *anything* if the span of human life counts for just a blip when compared to the life of the universe, this earth?

Millions spend good money contribute their time and effort to noble causes such as trying to find cures for diseases like cancer. Why not just wait for the Tooth Fairy to come and wave his magic wand and make life easier for all? Why make the effort? Why do anything at all?

After all, if I am merely going to be a guest in a town or country for only a day, is it really any of my concern if there is a problem in that town or country? How about if I am only passing through? If, while waiting in the airport for a connecting flight, I see a disturbance, is it not just a curiosity for me, something to snap pictures of and tell my friends about? Is it any of my business? Not really.

But for Hindus, our history is not a lie. We are not guests here, but permanent residents. This is our home! We die, then we come right back. We can't wait to see our loved ones again and be with God once more!

I believe it is because of this one fact—that God is here—that people do not wish to die. They are scared of death, because evil represents death! To leave the God that is here and go with evil—no wonder people are scared of death—and they *should* be. But evil is clever, he will offer nice inducements, an easy life, a life of pleasure, with 72 virgins, with all the sex, food and drink that you could ever want, with all your desires fulfilled, all joy and happiness, with nary a dark cloud in sight. Weak people will fall prey to such inducements.

There is no need to lose our souls to evil. That is why our conscience desperately tries to tell us to stay! "Stay with God!" it says. That is why we fear death. That is why we beseech the doctor to find a way to keep us alive.

Our life here on earth has taught us that nothing comes easy, that there is no free lunch, that everything that we cherish has to be fought for and we have fought for these things! There is a reason why some countries are successful, why they enjoy a high standard of living, while others struggle with poverty and hopelessness. You have to make the right choices, be disciplined, be prepared to work hard and sacrifice.

Along the way we encounter problems sometimes of our own making. We are our own worst enemies. So then we fight, and we discover heroes in our midst—heroes who risk everything, sometimes getting nothing in return for themselves, leaving behind the fruits of their labor for everyone else to enjoy.

Thanks to all these brave and good people, we are able to live better lives. Their sacrifices must not go in vain, their work must be continued, carried forward. There is much left to do, with so many problems confronting the world today.

These problems have to be faced, conquered. They demand strength. This is not a job for the weak. This is not a job for the cowardly. Let them have their happy fantasies, let them run to their imaginary Heavens, let them run and hide underneath their beds.

Climate change may yet prove to be a reality. If so, the earth will be deluged. There will be much pain, much suffering. Some crazy dictator or terrorist might let loose nuclear weapons on innocent people, causing massive deaths and destruction! Greedy bankers or politicians might cause another massive financial meltdown, dragging not only their country down, but pulling others down also.

A scary future might await us.

Am I doing a good job? Am I scaring you away from Hinduism? This is no carrot-and-stick faith—there is no stick, and the carrots have to be earned!

Life is not a jail sentence, life is not like going to a dreary job, putting in our eight hours or doing our time and being happy to get out. Life is worth living, life is a great gift from God. Life is about counting our blessings, showing thanks for being alive, and making sure that others less fortunate than us can do the same.

This is what the heroes who have gone before us have done. They recognized this great gift from God, recognized the God within themselves, and so left us with a legacy that must be carried forward!

What will be your choice? Will you choose to stay with God and work for a better earth?

Only One Way to Pray

"Prayer, chanting is like chanting the name of a medicine

when sick. It does you no good."
—Adi Sankaracharya in Vivekachudamani

Well, there goes prayer. I paraphrased the words of Adi Sankaracharya, the man who saved Hinduism in India a long
time ago. According to him, it does us no good to chant and
pray without cleansing our hearts of malice and hate. This is
why I urge people to dump the very concept of a Hell. Torturing our enemies does us no good—it is but vengeance,
not justice—we get consumed by hate.

Just as you would take medicine instead of chanting
its name, Sankaracharya urges us to invite God into our
hearts. God lives in our hearts, but our hearts need to be
pure, unsullied, clean, gentle; the reason why everyone says
children are dear to God becomes clear when we recall the
famous image of God Hanuman tearing apart his chest and
showing God Sri Rama within.

Most people pray to God with selfish intentions: "God,
do this for me, give me this, give me that, save me." This
God is the Santa for adults.

Pray with your actions and conduct. "Helping hands are
better than praying lips," said Mother Teresa.

The prayer that we are all familiar with is the one where
we sit in a place of "worship", chant, sing, recite holy words.
I call for a change in paradigm—that is not prayer, these
words are tinged with selfishness: "if I do this, God will be
pleased and reward me". Let us change the definition—let
us start calling this praise, instead of prayer. And if you feel
God is a Teacher, then we know a Teacher has no use nor
patience for praises sung in Her honor, in fact, a Teacher
would be insulted by such false encomiums.

*Let your actions be your prayer. Go do something to make
this world a better place—go help someone, raise funds for char-*

ity (Bhakti Yoga), read, enlighten yourself, teach (Gnana Yoga), diligently work at your place of employment (Karma Yoga).

The devotee who sits and chants is the one who is taking the cheap, easy way. Who doesn't like to sit in a comfortable place and chant and sing? But the true devotee is out of this place of worship, the true devotee is outside helping people or animals, the true devotee is outside making a difference.

So, the only reason you go to a temple should be to offer God thanks for all that She has done for us. Let us be strong, let us stop bothering God with our petty problems and thank God for the joys in our lives. Many of us live comfortable lives today, let us not take for granted the good fortunes in our lives.

Pray the right way—first cleanse your heart of all malice and hate, then go out and DO something, something that would make this world a better place. Remember the old saying, "Through work may we find God". Let your actions, work be your prayer to God!

28. Karma and Reincarnation Mean Following a Path to Moksha—Karma Yoga, Gnana Yoga and Bhakti Yoga

The Vedas and the Gita teach us the path to Moksha. Please bear in mind that Moksha is not a place, but a state of mind. It is also not static. Knowledge is as vast as this universe, and never-ending, so Moksha is simply being on a path that is never-ending, forever moving forward—a path where one is forever on an exhilarating journey.

It is relevant here once again to talk about the difference between Heaven and Moksha. Heaven is a dream (and as real as one) whereas Moksha is real, something to be achieved.

As you grow up, you see so many things that you like and would like to possess, to acquire. You see a bright toy and your heart yearns for it. You see a delicious food like "ice-scream" and you scream for it. As you grow older, your tastes change, your heart now yearns for different things: clothes, electronics, a wonderful vacation, a brand-new hot car, a big house, sex, jewelry, gourmet food and drink—the desires are never-ending.

And then there are other desires—a desire to become somebody, to have a successful career—maybe as a physician, surgeon, lawyer, actor, musician, engineer, writer. You see someone playing some beautiful music and you think, "I wish I could play like that." You see a great actor and wish that that could be you. You read a wonderful book or read some wonderful poetry and you hug that book to your heart and wish that could be you writing those lines!

And then it happens—a rich relative leaves you millions or you hit the big lottery! Now you are worth millions! Now you can enjoy everything that you dreamed about! Now you can buy everything that you ever wanted!

Or can you?

You find quickly that this is not the case. Yes, you can buy cars, clothes, vacations, houses, jewelry—all those things listed above in the first category, but not those listed in the second. Sorry, you cannot buy a law degree, or a medical degree. No matter how much money you have, you cannot sing like M. S. Subbulakshmi or play the cello like Yo-Yo Ma. Millions won't buy you writing ability—you still cannot write a poem to save your life.

You then realize that some things in life cannot be bought—they have to be worked for, sacrificed for. If you put in the sweat and toil, you may one day be successful. Let us remember the 10,000 hours rule. Put in those 10,000 hours going to school and getting that medical or law degree and then you can confidently and proudly hang that degree on your wall and start practicing.

Here is the difference between Heaven and Moksha: Heaven is a place to indulge in the pleasures of the flesh, while Moksha is an awakening of the heart, mind and soul!

Heaven is a dream. Here also you can see the difference between a dream and a goal. A goal is something you work to attain. Let's say you dream of becoming a physician or a lawyer. At some point in your life, unless that dream changes into a goal, you will forever regret not changing it.

Once you change that dream to a goal, you begin to ask yourself some questions, such as, "How long will it take to become a physician? What courses do I need to take in school? How much will it cost? Can we afford it? If I cannot, would I be able to get a scholarship, a loan or a second job, to help pay for the costs?"

It is not wrong to dream of having a nice life, to dream about having the good things in life—but it is wrong to expect them to appear before us like magic.

God is not a sugar daddy.

The only way is to earn our way! Earn your way to Moksha!

The Vedas say that there are three ways to Moksha: Karma Yoga, Gnana Yoga and Bhakti Yoga.

Karma Yoga: This is the simplest, easiest way—something that you do once you are an adult, earn your way through life, get a job, work hard at it, *do not cheat your employer, do not cheat your customers, earn your paycheck.* And while you are doing it, do what you can to help others less fortunate than you are. Get involved in the issues that affect you and your family, your society, issues that are important to you. What could be simpler, right?

Unfortunately, that is not always the case. A lot of people cheat their employers and a whole lot of people are rude to their customers. A great number of people would rather take advantage of generous government benefits than work for a living. I was once talking to someone in Europe who wrote about how generous the European benefits were for unemployment; since he had few needs, he could remain unemployed for the rest of his life and enjoy a nice "retired" life, all paid for by his government. But what he did not realize was that the taxes being paid by his hard-working fellow citizens were footing the bill for his "retired" style of life. I was able persuade him to go back to work, to go back to being a productive member of society.

When a few people sit on a cart and the cart is being pulled or pushed by others, then the cart will move swiftly. If more people got off the cart and pushed, then the cart would move even more swiftly. And, of course, if more people jumped into the cart and took it easy, the cart would move at a slower pace. This, in a nutshell, is how the economy of a country moves.

Karma Yoga, to be put simply, is about realizing the value of work. Let us go back to the point about giving a hand up vs a handout. Mother Teresa, bless her heart, did a lot of good; but all she was doing was giving a handout! She was helping people who were poor and hungry, but her efforts did little to help stamp out or get at the root of these problems!

Enter Karma Yoga. A consequence of the hungry American consumer's demands for goods and products is that millions of Chinese and Indians were lifted out of poverty. China's voracious appetite for raw materials is making a huge difference in the lives of Africans and Australians.

Billions in aid were poured into Africa over time without making much of a difference in the level of poverty—all those handouts made people feel good about their giving, but in the end the problems remained unsolved.

But now we see a change. What people need is work— Karma! Give people jobs and you see a sea of change in their attitude toward life. There is an old saying, "Give the man a fish, you feed him for a day. Teach the man to fish and you feed him his entire life."

You have changed his life!

Do not take the power of Karma Yoga lightly. Realize its power and realize why God Krishna extolled it.

Gnana Yoga: Read! Read, read and read some more. Improve your mind. Then teach others. Share your joy of reading and learning. Bring that joy to others. It is no wonder that Hinduism says God Herself is a Teacher! There is no other profession that is more highly esteemed than a Teacher's profession. First, starting with your mother, you go through life meeting so many Teachers who help you expand your mind. You delight in this newfound learning.

A new desire is born within you to pursue this new delight.

In addition to reading, learn something new, learn something that excites you. When you read, you pleasure your mind; and when you learn, you challenge your brain. Learning something new keeps you young. Learn a new language, a new skill like learning to swim, learn to play a musical instrument. Do something offbeat, there is a car commercial on TV where this couple driving around with their new car, doing things they have never tried before—like skydiving or scuba diving or visiting strange places.

As we get older most of us compile a "bucket list" of things to do. Well, let your "bucket list" be one big, huge, humongous, *long* list.

While young we are experiencing everything for the first time, we are fascinated with everything, our minds grow and develop to take in all this new information. But as we get older, we settle into a routine. Every day we take the same route to work and the same route back, watch the same TV shows, hit the bed at the same time every day. Not much changes from day to day, our brains atrophy just as muscles do when they are not exercised.

We need to change that: find that child that we once were, find that Teacher that inspired us to explore new pathways.

It is a fact that as a child we were inspired to become what we are as adults by a Teacher—a Teacher who delighted us with something that we had never experienced before, and we wanted more of it. Some of us are lucky—we pursued that passion that was lit in us by that Teacher.

This should be our mission in life. There are so many bright young men and women who never get the chance to experience these delights that we sometimes take for granted. A desire to learn, to experience the joy of learning, is heart-breakingly far out of reach of most people on this earth. As they say, "A mind is a terrible thing to waste," and it is deplorable how minds are wasted all over the world.

If there is one thing that you want to do, let this be it: help others read and learn. Contribute as much as you can, monetarily or physically. Do your best to help others delight in the joys of reading and learning.

If you love reading, pass on this love by giving the gift of being able to read, being able to study. Use this gift to help people make a living for themselves.

Time was when brawn power ruled the world. Education was not considered important or necessary. Men ruled and dominated the world because they had the strength. But now the times have changed. It is brain power that rules; and it will only get better for those who can reason better than others. But you need education to do it—education levels the playing field.

I celebrate every time when India does poorly in Olympics—it tells me that Indian Parents are stressing the right thing—Education. Olympic or athletic glory is nothing but brawn power, it is a thing of the past. Take the fastest runner in the world and have him race against a horse or a dog and suddenly you realize how poor we are, but would anyone want to be a horse or a dog? The strongest man in the world is easily pushed around by a common cow! Let us delight in the amazing feats of education! Let India light the way!

Education is what makes a living-wage job possible. Those who depend on their brawn power, those who have little education, find themselves trapped in jobs that barely give them a living—they eke out a bare living, if you can call it that. Education opens up a world of possibilities, not to mention that reading gives you an unmatched delight in your later years.

Moksha is nothing but an awakening of the mind, heart

and soul; and it is education that is the key to this awakening.

I feel that we Hindus are building the wrong kind of temples. The real Hindu temples are schools, colleges, libraries and universities. Instead, we are building palaces more fit for kings than Teachers. *Every time you open a book, you are in a Hindu temple! Every time you enter a school or a library, you are entering a Hindu temple!*

After all, the vast majority who go to temples are Hindus, Jews also have their own temples, the vast majority of people who visit churches are Christians, the vast majority of visitors to mosques are Muslims—but a library is open to all! A college, a university is open to *all!*

Blessed are those who have funded education, schools, colleges and universities.

Bhakti Yoga: My view of Bhakti Yoga may be different from the view of some Hindus. Most view it as going to the temple, doing Puja, chanting the God's name, reading the Puranas, chanting, "Hamsa, Hamsa," a million times, or writing God Rama's name a crore times. I feel all this is well and good, but isn't it a bit selfish? Are you doing all that because you want God to take care of you? In the end, who will benefit if God is pleased with your efforts? You, and only you.

How is this any different from praising the man in power, the king, the powerful minister or politician? He will be pleased by your praises—Mukha Stuthi—and will reward you? God is so easily fooled?

Let your chants and songs put you in a good mood and then go out and do something to help your fellow man— that is real Bhakti Yoga. Did Gandhiji have spare time to go to temples, pray to God and read our ancient texts? No, he was too busy trying to deal with the issues of the day, planning his next strategy as events unfolded. The Second World War had just been declared—what should Indians have done? Support the British or use our support as a bargaining chip to hurt them? Gandhiji felt that it was wrong to support Hitler, that, "the enemy of my enemy is not necessarily my friend." He urged all Indians to support the British fully while he was sitting in jail (courtesy of the British, imagine that!).

Gandhiji's whole life was spent in the service of humanity. Not once did he think of himself, not once did he think of an easy, cushy life for himself. If he had, maybe he never would have plunged into the independence movement. He was a lawyer based in England. He could have simply devoted himself to his practice, led the pleasant life that was open to him in a first-world country. Instead, he moved to a poor country, spent the majority of his life in jail, fasted several times (almost to the death), and in the end was denied a comfortable and happy retirement.

Whom would God embrace? Gandhiji or someone who sits in a corner of a temple chanting, enjoying himself? *Remember, if you want to be with God, you must be open to pain and suffering.* There are millions of others who are doing yeoman service to humanity, contributing their time and money to help others in need. That is the real Bhakti Yoga.

The Teachers of Hinduism have consistently emphasized that we should not focus on the "I". Many Hindus have misinterpreted this to mean that we should not focus on the body (that is, on bodily pleasures or pleasures of the flesh); but I believe the message of Hinduism is actually saying to us, "Look outward to the world around you. Please think of "we", concentrate on the "we", and realize that what is important is the health of the society around you. If there are poor people, if there is pain and suffering around you, then it is not a good situation. You cannot say that is not my problem, no, it is your problem. You must do something."

In Hinduism it is said, "Manava seva is Madhava seva."

("Service to man is service to God.")

Work to build true Hindu temples. Donate to a library or a school. Put poor children through school. Buy school supplies for the needy. Raise funds for animal welfare, to find a cure for cancer or other diseases. There are a million things you can do to help others. Billions of people and animals need your help.

Did you notice a couple of "strange" things about the 3 ways listed above? For one, *not one of them involves entering a place of worship* and second, all 3 are action-based. A king may be satisfied and made happy with praise, even a false one, but you cannot satisfy a Teacher with empty or even real praises. The Teacher demands action. I urge all Hindus as well as other Teacher God followers to stop wasting your time in places of "worship" and start doing one or all three of the above—that would be the real prayer. Let us stop with the false prayers and for once stop thinking of our selfish needs and start helping those who are less fortunate than us.

I wish to note here that service to the less fortunate has nothing to do with religion. I have already stated that it is character that is important, not religion. It stands to reason that if a person involves himself in the betterment of his society, of the world around him, whether he believes in God or not is *irrelevant*!

An "atheist" who does not believe in God but spends his free time making the lives of others better is with God. There is no better way to gain praise *from* God than by making the less fortunate happy. Put a smile on a child's face and you will see God smiling back at you.

Let us remember that Hinduism is a Teacher faith. It's not with empty praise that you please your Teacher. It is not by pleading unfailing loyalty that you please God.

Let your conduct speak for you. It is not with words but by your actions that you impress God.

Ask yourself, have you made a positive difference in the lives of others? Is the world, your society, your country, better off with you in it? Do you put a smile on others' faces?

Learn to distinguish the true Bhakta from the false one. The true Bhakta is not worried about himself or herself. It is not about how you can get Moksha for yourself. Listen to your conscience, listen to the God within you, and act accordingly.

Read the story of Raja Harischandra and follow in his footsteps. Practice true Bhakti Yoga.

Heaven is a Ponzi scheme

Heaven is supposed to be so wonderful, full of joy, happiness, then why the threats? We are going to a land of happiness and joy, so why isn't that enough? Why the dire threats against those who don't share the same beliefs?

Why the threats?

Because it is just a Ponzi scheme? Ponzi schemes are without substance, we know that, the same way the talkers of dreamy Heavens have no real facts to back them up—it's in this old book, so-and-so said so and it must be true—quite a lot of "you *must* believe"; you *must* because they have no facts to show you.

Listen, if a person has real facts, real evidence to show you, would he resort to threats? Of course not—he would let the facts speak for themselves. The very fact that threats of Hell are being hurled at non-followers is the elephant in the room that tell you that such religions are using Ponzi schemes!

The very same people who are telling you of the joys of Heaven today, tomorrow you find them in the hospital fighting tooth and nail to stay away from all those same joys!

Tomorrow if you are able to discover a pill that would double or triple our present lifespan, will you hesitate to announce it to the whole world? By living longer, aren't people staying away from God? From Heaven? Yet, if one such pill were available tomorrow, would anyone be surprised if not one individual refuses to take it?

The more people use common sense or logic, the less the appeal of a Heaven and so the threats—the drive to recruit more and more people to join. Today, we deal with verbal threats, but in the olden days people had to deal with real threats to their lives, so many people were killed because they spoke up, did not believe in what was being sold to them.

Just as the guy who runs a Ponzi scheme who is forever running after new victims, these power-hungry men needed new converts while existing members must be kept in line.

You will have easy access to Heaven *only* if you go through us! If you dare leave, beware! The greed for the good life after death is behind the success of this religious Ponzi scheme.

Rather than emphasis on character, the emphasis is on *religion*! Why? Because emphasizing character means anyone can do that: tell the Truth, be honest, compassionate, help others, do the right thing. What is the need for religion? If all good people are close to God, without the label of religion, then religion may no longer be needed. There goes power, there goes the wealth!

29. Karma and Reincarnation Mean We Hindus Are the Future

Heaven represents the past, going backward, the womb, child-hood, the weak, the dependent.

Karma and Reincarnation represent the future, the way forward, adulthood, self-reliance, strength and leadership.

Make your choice—either choose to live in the past (Heaven) or be part of a glorious future, play a part in shaping the future of humanity (Karma and Reincarnation)!

Think about this: We are the ones coming back. Almost everyone else is building pretty fantasy castles in the air "up there" and running away to them. Well, at least that is what they are happy to tell you. Fantasies aside, Hinduism wants you to commit to the future of this planet, commit yourself to God. This means not becoming a parasite (to mooch off of God, to become a burden on God), but to commit to the values and principles that will make God proud of you.

Their goal is to sit on their collective butts and doze off till eternity!

Our goal is to make God proud of us!

Which goal is higher? Slam-dunk! Ours!

A strong person will not run away. A strong person will stay and finish the job. A good person puts others first. A good person will do the right thing.

There is much to do here and now. So many people and other living beings on this planet need our help. There are so many beautiful people all around the world risking their lives, setting aside their own selfish needs, helping others.

What is a heart if it is not moved by the plight of the unfortunate in need?

And so the strong person will join others, pick up a rock and take on a brutal dictator's well-staffed army. The strong person will stand before the bulldozers of an occupying force intent on destroying the homes of the occupied. The strong person will write an exposé on the doings of the drug lords and the powerful corrupt stealing from his country at great risk to himself.

I could go on and on. There are so many stories of the good and the strong.

But the vast majority do not have to go that far to make a contribution. If they can just practice Karma Yoga, earn their own paycheck, pull their own weight.

Will you choose to sit, to do nothing and sit in the cart (Heaven), or will you choose to get to work and pull the cart (Karma and Reincarnation)?

Hindus, more than any other people of faith, must realize that since we are the future, we are the owners. We are not guests here, staying for only a limited time. We are permanent residents; it is up to us to make this earth a paradise to live in.

Thomas Friedman in his best-selling book, *The World is Flat* writes, "When memories exceed dreams, the end is near." Choosing Heaven is to put an end to dreams, to be choosing memories for eternity, you will have to live with those memories, no more dreams for you.

You are left reliving the past, stuck living in the past.

Heaven is where dreams go to die.

But if you choose Karma and Reincarnation, Hinduism will give you the power to dream, again and again, over and over and then use those dreams to create and shape the future world! For dreams are made here, dreams are achieved here, and yes, sometimes dreams are broken here! But in Heaven, there are no dreams, only memories.

Imagine for a moment for argument's sake that this fantasy exists. Some man dies back in the year 1700. He meets up with a guy who has died just recently. The old timer asks, "What did you do on earth?" and the newcomer says, "I was a programmer." The old timer has no clue, no idea what a programmer is or what he does, he has no knowledge of computers, cars, planes, bullet trains, the internet, mega-cities, cellphones! He is stuck in the past, the primitive past, the horse-drawn carriage past.

We Hindus won't live in the past, we move on to the future, we will forge that future, we will build that glorious future. The health and vitality of the earth is in our hands—God has entrusted us with this planet.

One day man will land on Mars and will walk on it; who will make that possible? Hindus!

One day man will find a cure for cancer; who will make that possible? Those who choose to stay!

One day poverty and hunger will become a distant memory; who will make that possible? Hindus!

One day a despot or a strong man taking over his country and exploiting it will become a thing of the past; who will make that possible? Those who choose to come back!

One day man will travel to the stars and beyond; who will make that possible? Hindus!

One day the animals on this planet will cease to be exploited and abused by us humans; who will make that possible? Those who chose Karma and Reincarnation!

One day a man or woman will be born who will be the next Michelangelo, the next Tyagaraja or the next Darwin; and who will that be? A Hindu!

One day Tibet will be a free country; who will be here to see that and help make it happen? That could be *you*!

One day all over the world women will gain equality with men; a woman will get to lead this world, and we will be right here to make sure that happens.

The future will be full of new inventions, new exciting discoveries; but you have to be here to enjoy them—to help create them! Let's imagine that future for a second. Perhaps one day aliens will land on earth. Is the galaxy populated by beings just like us? Will mankind one day be able to travel back in time, faster than light? Are there other universes? Will we one day build a wormhole and travel to another universe? Will we be replaced by robots one day? What amazing inventions await us in the future? We see glimpses of that in today's futuristic movies.

And you want to miss all that and just sit on your big "behind" and do nothing for eternity? That's God's "Grand Plan" for you?

The future is in our hands. The future of humankind is in our hands.

We get to shape the future. But one has to be here to do all that. One must want to be here!

You are playing a basketball game, your team is down 20 points with a few minutes to go. What is your mindset at this time? Are you resigned to a defeat or do you see in front of you a glorious opportunity, an opportunity to make history or do something that no one, no one before you had ever done?

Life on earth is your opportunity! An opportunity to earn praise *from* God!

The bottom line—do you want to help create the future world of unlimited possibilities or seek happiness for yourself?

Imagine the world back in the year 1812 or thereabouts. Imagine living in those times, then suddenly as in some movie, you are suddenly transported to the present day; you see cars, airplanes, highways, tall huge buildings, flashing billboards, laptops, cell-phones, tablets, the Internet. Oh my! So many new inventions, even just in the last few decades, so many new inventions have sprung up and grabbed our attention! So many new things to absorb, it will make that person's head spin!

Can you imagine what the world will look like in the year 2200? Even more new inventions, dazzling us, dizzying us! And we can proudly say that we were here, we made it happen!

But the future may not be as rosy as we think it will be. The world could fall victim to another terrorist attack, maybe much worse this time. A kooky dictator might get his hands on nuclear weapons and cause untold damage. A natural disaster might strike the earth, killing and harming millions. As I write this, many still remain skeptical about climate change—but if it does come about, it will harm not just millions but billions of people!

Who will be here to dig us out of this mess? Hindus will!

Let us recall the dog in Japan that stayed with his friend. The dog was offered food, warmth, shelter, yet chose to stay close to his injured friend!

The choice is yours: You can listen to the primitive and backward religions' promises of a nice, easy, cushy, idle life; or you can choose to stay where you are desperately needed.

There are two kinds of people in this world—the hero and the coward. Which one are you? The coward or the hero? The leader, the self-reliant or the meek follower, the obedient, the slave?

Are the Rules different in Heaven?

The very same person who works hard all her life, refuses to take charity or anything being given away for free, pays for whatever she takes even if the store employee is missing, is then is reduced to begging and pleading her way into Heaven?

Are the rules different up there?

Religious discrimination actively practiced? It is a crime to discriminate on the basis of religion here on earth? But these religions say "God" sets people apart by religion, discriminates and tortures. And everyone condones it. So on earth, God would be held for committing a terrible crime?

Is God is committing a crime right now? He is committing a crime every second of every 24-hour day?

Gandhiji wrote that in his day in South Africa, some parks were deemed off-limits of colored people, for whites only. Yes millions of people are familiar with those words—whites only. Some religions say Heaven is for their members only—off limits to the vast majority. Heavens that are *segregated*, open to members of Religion X only? Does God run a "pure" Heaven? Do we really want to revisit those dark days?

Are we to be tortured for our beliefs? Here on Earth, you have the freedom to practice your faith without fear. There, are we to be tortured for our beliefs?

Muslims, living in western countries, upset and angry when they are targeted because of their religion. Christians in Egypt, Muslims in Myanmar targeted for their religion. Evil, right? Yet the very same people happy to tell the atheist, the Hindu that their "God" will target them, separate people by religion and will send us off to gas chambers?

Let us use the same words but let us apply them to a

Stalin or Hitler and see where that takes us. Let us say a Stalin or a Hitler guy rides into your small village with his gun-men, separates people by religion and starts to kill certain members of a religion. Young, old, women, children, and even babies are not spared. Would you not call that evil? And yet, change the guy's name to God and millions are happy to look the other way, in fact, find ways to support such evil? How can religion turn good people into such callous, heart-less people?

Where are we, in the dark ages? Are you sure we are with God? I think not. As long as we remain weak, looking to God to come give us the easy life that we crave, we will be open to religious exploitation and much suffering will be the result.

Take something without paying for it? Gain something unearned? Beg, grovel, crawl your way into a place that you are not invited in?

You apply for a job but another person gets it because of his religion—wrong, right? Yet millions are happy to believe that their chosen religion will get them into Heaven?

Are the rules different up in Heaven?

Before you can be admitted to a prestigious institution like Harvard or Yale, the authorities insist that you have to be qualified. Before! Also, they insist on you entering their halls through the *front* door, and not through the back door.

Tell me, are the rules different up in Heaven?

The rules must be different up there, why are they worse? Shouldn't God mean Truth, honesty, values? I guess not, God must mean the good life, a sugar daddy. Once you see God as nothing but a sugar daddy, the giver of the good life, morals and ethics go out the window.

If you take on a debt, society expects you to pay it back, no matter how long it takes. You are expected not to cry, beg, and sneak your way out the back door with the help of a "forgiving" judge.

313

Whatever happened to ethics and values? Whatever happened to giving your word? Whatever happened to standing up for your principles?

If your child makes a mistake, would you not be proud if he stands tall in front of you, acknowledges his mistake and promises to make the proper restitution?

Do we not laud the ballplayers who stands tall and accepts responsibility after making a mistake that cost their team the ball game, patiently answering every stinging and stupid question thrown at them?

Then why do religions encourage you to get down on your knees, cry, and sneak out the back door? What happened to encouraging one to do the right thing? Where is the—stand tall in front of God, calmly accept your mistakes, vow and ask for a second chance, to make things right, *to ask forgiveness from the victim?*

The rules must be different in Heaven.

Such ideas being taught to our children in schools, being written in books, shown on TV, conveyed in the mass media without anyone challenging them—in the 21st century!

Where oh where are the educated?

Is democracy too recent? Today millions live in democracies where freedom of action and thought is celebrated, but why are the same millions following an undemocratic religion that says, "Our way is the only way, you disagree, you get hell!"?

I can't believe it! The only explanation to me is a mass brainwashing. Amazing, it is happening before our very own eyes!

30. Karma and Reincarnation Mean We Are Last

I am going to make this last section simple and short.

When I was young, I wanted to come in first at everything. This included silly things such as jumping on the first car when taking the train. Somehow this seemed important to me at that time.

But as I have gotten older, I have come to appreciate the joys of letting others go in front of me.

While Stalin let Ukrainians starve, or when Churchill let three million Indians starve to death, in contrast hungry starving mothers lovingly watched their starving kids eat the last morsel of food, the last grain of rice.

If you are a grandma or a mother who made sweets for her grandchildren and their friends, and lovingly watched them eat, laughing and joking, then you know what it means to come in last.

I pray that before God showers any favors upon me, let them fall on someone else—someone who needs God's beneficence more than I. Let all those who choose Reincarnation make a promise to themselves and to God—as long as there is even on little child suffering and crying, I will not leave! Let me give you two heart-breaking stories:

The first is of a little girl whose young single-mother died suddenly while at home. There was no one else in the home except the mother and her little girl. This brave little girl survived for several days eating whatever she could find around the house while waiting for her mommy to "wake up"!

Second is that of another little child who was the last of her family of 7 or 8 who starved to death in Ukraine under Stalin's rule. Imagine the torture that this little girl went through, seeing her entire family die right in front of her eyes!

I ask the reader—how can you even think of leaving such pain and suffering? You know the magic man coming to save the day is just a myth—this pain and suffering is ours to face and face it we will!

Sometimes I hope that the wishes of every religious person would come true—that would mean all those hoping to get to the easy life promised by their religions would leave from earth chasing after their dreams and the earth would be left to those who chose real life, those who chose Reincarnation. That would be just, that would be wonderful for everyone.

What is your goal? How much are you willing to work for it, to sacrifice for it?

There is so much pain, so much suffering in this world. Hindus have already cast their lot with God. We have chosen to stay and work for a better world. But this work may be never ending; there may never come a time when the world is free from cruelty, prejudice, crime, racism and bigotry. There may never be a time when all people and all life on earth is free and happy.

So, if you choose to be Hindu, choose wisely. Realize what you are getting into.

Karma and Reincarnation, Hinduism, asks you to create a Heaven right here on earth! To make God proud! To dream of achieving that high goal is wonderful but in the way will stand many a pitfall—so much pain and suffering to bear.

You may already be following in the footsteps of Gandhiji; you are the one donating to the needy, you are the one raising money for a good cause, you are the one working to find a cure for a dreaded disease, you are the one fighting for the welfare of innocent animals, you are the one rushing toward the burning buildings on 9/11 and pursuing the killers of 26/11, you are the one rushing to help your neighboring village battle the floods, you are the one teaching a young child or a senior citizen a new language, you are the one delivering medicines and dinner to the elderly, you are the one writing about drug gangs in your neighborhood at a great risk to yourself. Ask yourself, is the work done? Obviously, not done yet.

Then you must not stop, you must continue to keep going, keep working, until the last hungry child is fed, until the last dreaded disease is wiped out, until there is no more crime, racism or sexism. Until there is no more pain or suffering in this world, and then, then, we look up and God will smile down upon us and say, "Good job, I am proud of you"—*Wow!*

Will there be a time when you run into a terrible situation, perhaps in a war zone or in a burning building? Will you walk away while there are people still trapped inside? Not you! Your conscience (God) won't let you run away. You run back (Karma and Reincarnation) to help, to do the right thing.

In his seminal book *Intelligence and How to Get It*, author Richard E. Nisbett cites an interesting experiment conducted on little children. Kids were taken into a room and given a treat, but were told to wait until the researcher returned from running an errand. Most kids couldn't wait that long, but a few kids exhibited excellent self-control and delayed their gratification until the researcher came back. Well, the researcher waited ten long years and then looked up the kids who were tested. He found that a majority of the kids that exhibited good self-control did better than most in life.

This example has been cited not just in this one book but others also. Apparently a lot of experts have found that self-control is a strong indicator of good character, discipline and intelligence—all assets that help a person do well in life.

This is what Karma and Reincarnation asks you to do— delay your gratification. Set your goal higher. Reach for the hand of God. Reach down and touch the hand of God. Moksha is that higher goal. But it must be earned! It will take a lot of lives, a lot of time. Are you willing to put in the time and effort? Are you ready to make God proud of you?

Show God what you're made of. Show God your heart. Do not disappoint God.

Blessed are the Hindus. We will be the last ones out of the war zone, we will be the last ones out of a burning building. Join me in making a promise: "I will not leave until all the pain and suffering is gone from this world! I will not leave until I have made God proud of me, I will not leave until this world is a paradise for all living creatures."

If ever the blessed day will come and God Sri Rama will show himself to us, let others go see him before we do. Let the aged, young, the disabled go before us. Let all others go before us. If someone is unable to see, let us give our eyes to him so that he can see.

Let us be last.

4 Religions—2 Opposite Ways

As we saw before, the 4 dominant religions can be divided into two camps—not only in the way they view God and what it takes to please Her, but we are also headed in different and opposite directions. They are headed to live in the past, as a servant/slave for eternity, down on the ground on their knees, as a dependant living off someone else's hand-outs.

WE are to be Gods! Yes, Gods! That is what Moksha is all about—to reach for the hand of God—to follow in God's footsteps! We choose life, the future, to be an adult and stand on our two feet, to dream, to aspire, to be the hero and do great things that will make our Parent proud!

I have always maintained that with all these concepts there is a down-to-earth, rational explanation—the concept of Heaven represents quitting school, sitting at home watching TV all day or playing games, living off one's Parents or society at large, aspiring for nothing, amounting to nothing. Moksha and Reincarnation represent aspiring for the higher things in life, to dream, whether one wants to become a physician, engineer, artist etc. or the bigger dreams for our society, our country, the world we live in, we know that there is a price to pay, nothing will be handed down to us, hard work and sacrifices are required and it is through these that we shall find God.

AHAM BRAHMASMI

We need to put the religious ideas of the old in context—go back a few thousands of years, when kids were not asked what they were going to be when they grew up—life was harsh enough, it was tough enough just to eke out a living, forget about having a dream of becoming something. That was true for the vast majority of people then and it is in this context one can see why the prospect of a Heaven, a life of ease and little work held such appeal. God made in the image of the local king, the dispenser of favors, democracy not yet born, and so a God who acts like a brutal dictator—religions made a killing making easy promises of an easy life just by becoming a member.

But life has changed—today we have democracy, today

kids get asked what they want to be when they grew up—they get to dream, aspire, reach for the stars! There is more to life than just pleasures of the flesh—yes there are pleasures of the heart, mind and soul! Moksha! Or Aham Brahmasmi—literally it means I am God, I am Brahman, God is within me.

There are 3 steps to attaining Moksha:

1. To be a God, to become a God—not very difficult to do, easy to accomplish
2. To walk with God, to be with God—extremely difficult
3. Finally, to be one with God—Moksha!

Please, let us not settle for the pleasures of the flesh—what a disappointment to God! Our goals must be higher, our reach must be higher! Why choose to be utterly useless doing nothing, contributing nothing in Heaven, when you can be a God?

I am asking for a change in paradigm, well, a few in fact—God seen no longer as a master or a king, but as a Teacher or Parent. We need to see ourselves as no longer weak slaves/servants desperately looking for a way out but as strong children/students of God ready to take on the world! Life was seen as a sin because of the pain and suffering that accompanies it, religions of the past creating magic lands and sugar daddy Gods so that we may run away from our troubles. The faith of the future, Sanatana Dharma is asking us to see life as a great gift from God, face and fight pain and suffering, let us overcome and defeat it! Build the Heaven of our dreams right here on earth! Why settle to be a servant when you can be a God?

Let us make God look down upon our handiwork and beam with pride! God will say, "That's my boy! That's my girl!" WOW!

I end this book with a question. Hopefully if you have imbibed what I have written in this book, you will answer this question correctly:

What is Greater Than God?

CPSIA information can be obtained
at www.ICGtesting.com
Printed in the USA
FFOW05n1547020515

9 781909 477636